PHILOSOPHY OF BUDDHISM

PHILOSOPHY OF BUDDHISM

Manohar Bhardwaj

CYBER TECH PUBLICATIONS
4264/3, Ansari Road, Daryaganj, New Delhi-110002 (India)
Ph.: 011-23244078, 011-43559448 Fax: 011-23280028
E-Mail: cyberpublicationsdelhi@yahoo.com
Website: www.cybertechpublications.com

PHILOSOPHY OF BUDDHISM

Manohar Bhardwaj

First Edition 2010

Published by . Asian Offset Printers

G.S. Rawat for **Cyber Tech Publications**
4264/3, Ansari Road, Daryaganj, New Delhi-110002 (India)
Ph.: 011-23244078, 011-43559448 Fax: 011-23280028
E-Mail: cyberpublicationsdelhi@yahoo.com
Website: www.cybertechpublications.com

Preface

The purpose of this book is, as the title suggests, to examine Buddhism as philosophy. Before we actually start doing that though, it might be good to first get a bit clearer about what each of these two things – Buddhism and philosophy – is. That will help us see what might be distinctive about studying Buddhism as a form of philosophy.And it is important to be clear about this, since there are some preconceptions about these matters that might get in the way of fully grasping how the philosophical study of Buddhism works.

Buddhist philosophy deals extensively with problems in metaphysics, phenomenology, ethics, and epistemology. The Buddha rejected certain precepts of Indian philosophy that were prominent during his lifetime. His general outlook has been described as empirical, as opposed to ontological or metaphysical. The Buddha taught dependent origination as the correct paradigm for analyzing causality; Buddhists view it as avoiding the two extremes of reification and nihilism. Particular points of Buddhist philosophy have often been the subject of disputes between different schools of Buddhism. While theory for its own sake is not valued in Buddhism, theory pursued in the interest of enlightenment is consistent with Buddhist values and ethics.

Proponents of the view that Buddhism is a philosophy argue (a) that Buddhism is non-theistic, having no particular use for the existence or non-existence of a god or gods; and (b) that religion entails theism. However, both prongs of this argument are contested by proponents of the alternative view, that Buddhism is a religion. Another argument for Buddhism qua philosophy is that Buddhism does not have doctrines in the same sense as other religions; instead, Buddhism offers specific methods for applying its philosophical principles.

— *Author*

CONTENTS

1

INTRODUCTION

NIRVANA

The Buddha describes the abiding in Nirvna as "deathlessness" (Pali: amata or amaravati) or "the unconditioned" and as the highest spiritual attainment, the natural result that accrues to one who lives a life of virtuous conduct in accordance with *dharma*.

Such a life (called Brahmacarya in India) dissolves the causes for future becoming (Skt, *karma*; Pali, *kamma*) that otherwise keep beings forever wandering through the impermanent and suffering-generating realms of desire, form, and formlessness, termed *samsara*.

OVERVIEW

The Buddha agrees that though Nibbana should the ultimate goal for all samsaric existences, the attainment of it is difficult to comprehemd as it is beyond that outlined in any human experience. In Aggi-Vacchagotta Sutta he likens it to the cessation and extinguishing of a fire where the materials for sustenance has been removed:

> *"Of course you are befuddled, Vaccha. Of course you qre confused. Profound, Vaccha, is this phenomenon, hard to see, hard to realize, tranquil, refined, beyond the scope of conjecture, subtle, to-be-experienced by the wise."*

> *"'the liberated mind (citta) that no longer clings' means Nibbana" (Majjhima Nikaya 2-Att. 4.68).*

"There is that dimension where there is neither earth, nor water, nor fire, nor wind; neither dimension of the infinitude of space, nor dimension of the infinitude of consciousness, nor dimension of nothingness, nor dimension of neither perception nor non-perception; neither this world, nor the next world, nor sun, nor moon. And there, I say, there is neither coming, nor going, nor stasis; neither passing away nor arising: without stance, without foundation, without support [mental object]. This, just this, is the end of stress."

When a person who has realized Nirvna dies, his death is referred as his pariNirvna, his *fully passing away*, as his life was his last link to the cycle of death and rebirth (samsara), and he will not be reborn again. Buddhism holds that the ultimate goal and end of samsaric existence (of ever "becoming" and "dying" and never truly being) is realization of Nirvna; what happens to a person after his pariNirvna cannot be explained adequately, as it is outside of all conceivable experience of this world.

NIRVNA AND SAMSARA

In Mahayana Buddhism, calling Nirvna the "opposite" of Samsara or implying that it is apart from Samsara is doctrinally problematic. According to early Mahayana Buddhism, they can be considered to be two aspects of the same perceived reality. By the time of Nagarjuna, there are teachings of the identity of Nirvna and Samsara. However, even here it is assumed that the natural man suffers from at the very least a confusion regarding the nature of Samsara.

The Theravada school makes the antithesis of Samsara and Nibbana the starting point of the entire quest for deliverance. Even more, it treats this antithesis as determinative of the final goal, which is precisely the transcendence of Samsara and the attainment of liberation in Nibbana.

Where Theravada differs significantly from the Mahayana schools, which also start with the duality of Samsara and Nirvna, is in not regarding this polarity as a mere preparatory lesson tailored for those with blunt faculties, to be eventually superseded by some higher realization of non-duality. From the standpoint of the Pali Suttas, even for the Buddha and the Arahants suffering and its cessation, Samsara and Nibbana, remain distinct.

In the experience of all, Nirvna is a state which all six bases (Eye, Ear, Nose, Tongue, Body and Mind) cannot feel.

It is probably best to understand the relationship between Nirvna and Samsara in terms of the Buddha while on earth. Buddha was both in Samsara while having attained to Nirvna so that he was seen by all, and simultaneously free from Samsara.

Nirvna in Buddhist Commentaries

Sarvastivadin commentary, Abhidharma-mahavibhasa-sastra, gives the complete context of the possible meanings from its Sanskrit roots:

- Vana, implying the path of rebirth, + nir, meaning leaving off' or "being away from the path of rebirth."
- Vana, meaning 'stench', + nir, meaning "freedom": "freedom from the stench of distressing kamma."
- Vana, meaning "dense forests", + nir, meaning "to get rid of" = "to be permanently rid of the dense forest of the five aggregates" (panca skandha), or the "three roots of greed, hate and delusion" (lobha, dosa, moha) or "three characteristics of existence" (impermanence, anitya; unsatisfactoriness, dukkha, soullessness, anàtma).
- Vana, meaning "weaving", + nir, meaning "knot" = "freedom from the knot of the distressful thread of kamma."

NIRVNA IN THE MAHPARINIRVNA SUTRA

The nature of Nirvna assumes a differently aspected Mahayana focus in what alleges to be the final of all Mahayana sutras, allegedly delivered by the Buddha on his last day of life on earth-the *MahapariNirvna Sutra* or *Nirvna Sutra*. Here, as well as in a number of linked "tathagatagarbha" sutras, in which the Tathagatagarbha is equated with the Buddha's eternal Self or eternal nature, Nirvna is spoken of by the Mahayana Buddha in very "cataphatic", positive terms. Nirvna, or "Great Nirvna", is indicated to be the sphere or domain (vishaya) of the True Self. It is seen as the state which constitutes the attainment of what is "Eternal, the Self, Bliss, and the Pure". *Mah-Nirvna* ("Great Nirvna") thus becomes equivalent to the ineffable, unshakeable, blissful, all-pervading and deathless Selfhood of the Buddha himself-a mystery which no words can adequately reach and which, according to the *Nirvna Sutra*, can only be fully known by an Awakened Being-a perfect Buddha-directly.

Strikingly, the Buddha of the *Mahaparinirvna Sutra* gives the following definition of the attributes of Nirvna, which includes the ultimate reality of the Self (not to be confused with the "worldly ego" of the five skandhas):

> "The attributes of Nirvna are eightfold. What are these eight? Cessation (*nirodha*), loveliness/ wholesomeness (*subha*), Truth (*satya*), Reality (*tattva*), eternity (*nitya*), bliss (*sukha*), the Self (*atman*), and complete purity (*parisuddhi*): that is Nirvna."

He further states: "Non-Self is Samsara (the cycle of rebirth); the Self (atman) is Great Nirvna."

An important facet of Nirvna in general is that it is not something that comes about from a concatenation of causes, that springs into existence as a result of an act of creation or an agglomeration of causative factors: it was never created; it always was, is and will be. But due to the moral and mental darkness of ordinary, samsarically benighted sentient beings, it remains hidden from unawakened perception. The Buddha of the Mahparinirvna sutra insists on its eternal nature and affirms its identity with the enduring, blissful Self, saying:

> *It is not the case that the inherent nature of Nirvna did not primordially exist but now exists. If the inherent nature of Nirvna did not primordially exist*

but does now exist, then it would not be free from taints (asravas) nor would it be eternally (nitya) present in nature. Regardless of whether there are Buddhas or not, its intrinsic nature and attributes are eternally present... Because of the obscuring darkness of the mental afflictions (kileshas), beings do not see it. The Tathagata, endowed with omniscient awareness (sarvajna-jnana), lights the lamp of insight with his skill-in-means (upaya-kauualya) and causes Bodhisattvas to perceive the Eternal, Bliss, the Self, and the Pure of Nirvna.

Vitally, according to these Mahayana teachings, any being who has reached Nirvna is not blotted out or extinguished: there is the extinction of the impermanent and suffering-prone "worldly self" or ego, comprised of the five changeful skandhas, but not of the immortal "supramundane" Self of the indwelling Buddha Principle [*Buddha-dhatu*].

Spiritual death for such a Nirvna-ed being becomes an utter impossibility. The Buddha states in the "Mahyna Mahparinirvna Sutra" (Tibetan version): "Nirvna is deathless... Those who have passed into Nirvna are deathless. I say that anybody who is endowed with careful assiduity is not compounded and, even though they involve themselves in compounded things, they do not age, they do not die, they do not perish."

Paths to Nirvna in the Pali Canon

In the Visuddhimagga, Ch. I, v. 6 (Buddhaghosa & NGamoli, 1999, pp. 6-7), Buddhaghosa identifies various options within the Pali canon for pursuing a path to Nirvna, including:

1. by insight (*vipassana*) alone.
2. by jhana and understanding.
3. by deeds, vision and righteousness.
4. by virtue, consciousness and understanding.
5. by virtue, understanding, concentration and effort.
6. by the four foundations of mindfulness.

Depending on one's analysis, each of these options could be seen as a reframing of the Buddha's Threefold Training of virtue, mental development and wisdom.

Quotations

- Gautama Buddha:
  - o "Nirvna is the highest happiness."
  - o "Where there is nothing; where naught is grasped, there is the Isle of No-Beyond. Nirvna do I call it—the utter extinction of aging and dying."
  - o "There is, monks, an unborn—unbecome—unmade—unfabricated. If there were not that unborn—unbecome—unmade—unfabricated, there would not be the case that emancipation from the born—become—made—fabricated would be discerned. But precisely because there is an unborn—unbecome—unmade—unfabricated, emancipation from the born—become—made fabricated is discerned."
  - o This said: 'the liberated mind/will (citta) which does not cling' means Nibbana."
  - o "'The subjugation of becoming means Nirvna'; this means the subjugation of the five aggregates means Nirvna."
  - o "Parinibbuto thitatto"-"PariNirvna is to be fixed in the Soul."
- Said immediately after the physical death of Gautama Buddha wherein his mind (citta) is =pariNirvna=the essence of liberation:
  - o "No longer with (subsists by) in-breath nor out-breath, so is him (Gautama) who is steadfast in mind (citta), inherently quelled from all desires the mighty sage has passed beyond. With mind (citta) limitless (Brahman) he no longer bears sensations; illumined and unbound (nibbana), his mind (citta) is definitely (ahu) liberated."

- o "The mind (citta) being so liberated and arisen from defilements, one is fixed in the Soul as liberation, one is quelled in fixation upon the Soul. Quelled in the Soul one is unshakable. So being unshakable, the very Soul is thoroughly unbound (parinirvna)."

- Sutta Nipata, tr. Rune Johansson:
  - o acc+ yath vtavegena khitto

    atthaA paleti na upeti sankhaa

    evaA muni namakaya kimutto

    atthaA paleti na upeti sankhaa
  - o atthan gatassa na pamGam atthi

    ynea naA vajju taA tassan atthi

    sabbesu dhammesu samkhatesu

    samkhat vdapathpi sabbe
  - o Like a flame that has been blown out by a strong wind goes to rest and cannot be defined, just so the sage who is freed from name and body goes to rest and cannot be defined.

    For him who has gone to rest there is no measure by means of which one could describe him; that is not for him. When all (dharmas) have gone, all signs of recognition have also gone.

- Venerable Sariputta:
  - o The destruction of greed, hatred and delusion is Nirvna.

MIDDLE WAY

In general, the Middle Way or Middle Path (Skt.: madhyama-pratipad; Pali: majjhima patipada) is the Buddhist practice of non-extremism. More specifically, in Theravada Buddhism, the Middle Way crystallizes the Buddha's Nirvana-bound path of moderation away from the extremes of sensual indulgence and self-mortification and toward the practice of wisdom, morality and mental cultivation. In Mahayana and Vajrayana Buddhism, the Middle Way refers to transcendental ways of approaching seemingly antithetical claims about reality.

Theravada Contexts

In Theravada Buddhism's Pali canon, the Middle Way was articulated by the Buddha in his first discourse, the Dhammacakkappavattana Sutta:

> *"Monks, these two extremes ought not to be practiced by one who has gone forth from the household life. (What are the two?) There is addiction to indulgence of sense-pleasures, which is low, coarse, the way of ordinary people, unworthy, and unprofitable; and there is addiction to self-mortification, which is painful, unworthy, and unprofitable.*
>
> *"Avoiding both these extremes, the Tathagata (the Perfect One) has realized the Middle Path; it gives vision, gives knowledge, and leads to calm, to insight, to enlightenment and to Nibbana. And what is that Middle Path realized by the Tathagata...? It is the Noble Eightfold path, and nothing else, namely: right understanding, right thought, right speech, right action, right livelihood, right effort, right mindfulness and right concentration."*

Thus, for the attainment of Nibbana, the Middle Way involves:

- Abstaining from addictive sense-pleasures and self-mortification
- Nurturing the set of "right" actions that are known as the Noble Eightfold Path.

In this discourse (Pali: *sutta*), the Buddha identifies the Middle Way as a path for "one who has gone forth from the household life" (Pali: *pabbajitena*) although lay Buddhists may centre their lives on this path as well. In regards to the Buddha's admonition against the "indulgence of sense-pleasures" (Pali: *kamesu kama-sukha-allika*), Ven. Dr. Rewata Dhamma has written:

"...This kind of practice is the concern of so-called 'urban civilization,' which condones sensuous pleasues as the highest attributes of bliss; the greater the pleasures, the greater the happiness....

"The Buddha taught that indulgence in sensuous pleasures is not the practice of enlightened, noble ones (*ariyas*). Noble ones who live the worldly life do not have attachment to sense objects. For example, in the first stage of an enlightened noble life, the sotapanna, or stream winner, has not yet overcome lust and passions. Incipient perceptions of the agreeableness of carnal pleasures (*sukhasanna*) still linger. Nevertheless, the stream-winner will not feel the need to indulge in worldly pleasures."

When the Buddha delivered the Dhammacakkappavattana Sutta, he was addressing five ascetics with whom he had previously practiced severe austerities. Thus, it is this personal context as well as the broader context of Indian shramanic practices that gives particular relevancy to the caveat against the extreme (Pali: *anta*) of self-mortification (Pali: *atta-kilamatha*).

Mahayana Contexts

In Mahayana Buddhism, the Madhyamaka ("Middle Way") school posits a "middle way" position between metaphysical claims that things ultimately either exist or do not exist.

In the Tendai school, the "middle way" refers to the synthesis of the thesis that all things are "empty" and the antithesis that all things have phenomenal existence.

NOBLE EIGHT FOLD PATH

The Noble Eightfold Path (Pali: *Ariyo ammhaegiko maggo*; Sanskrit: *Arya 'cmaega marga*; Chinese: *Bazhengdao*; Japanese: Hasshodo; Thai: *Ariya Mugg Paad*; Mongolian *qutuctan-u naiman gesigun-u mor*) is, in the teachings of the Buddha, declared to be the way that leads to the end of *dukkha*, or suffering.

Essentially a practical guide of bringing about ethical and meditative discipline, the Noble Eightfold Path forms the fourth part of the Four Noble Truths, which have informed and driven much of the Buddhist tradition.

As the name indicates, there are eight elements in the Noble Eightfold Path, and these are divided into three basic categories as follows:

- Wisdom (Sanskrit: *prajna*, Pali: *panna*)
  1. Right view
  2. Right intention
- Ethical conduct (Sanskrit: *uila*, Pali: *sila*)
  3. Right speech
  4. Right action
  5. Right livelihood
- Mental discipline (Sanskrit and Pali: *samadhi*)
  6. Right effort
  7. Right mindfulness
  8. Right concentration

In all of the elements of the Noble Eightfold Path, the word "right" is a translation of the word *samyanc* (Sanskrit) or *samma* (Pali), which denotes completion, togetherness, and coherence, and which can also carry the sense of "perfect" or "ideal".

Though the path is numbered one through eight, it is generally not considered to be a series of linear steps through which one must progress; rather, as the Buddhist monk and scholar Walpola Rahula points out, the eight elements of the Noble Eightfold Path "are to be developed more or less simultaneously, as far as possible according to the capacity of each individual. They are all linked together and each helps the cultivation of the others".

In Buddhist symbolism, the Noble Eightfold Path is often represented by means of the Dharma wheel (Sanskrit: *dharmacakra*, Pali: *dhammacakka*), whose eight spokes represent the eight elements of the path.

Wisdom (Prajna-Panna)

The "wisdom" subdivision of the Noble Eightfold Path is constituted by those elements that refer primarily to the mental or cognitive aspect of a Buddhist practitioner's practice.

Right View

Right view (*samyag-dicmi-samm-dimmhi*) can also be translated as "right perspective" or "right understanding". This element of the Noble Eightfold Path refers explicitly to the Four Noble Truths of Buddhism, stating that these must be fully understood by the Buddhist practitioner. In the *Mahasatipahana Sutta*, one of the Buddha Uakyamuni's discourses, right understanding is explained directly in terms of the Four Noble Truths:

> *And what, O bhikkhus, is right understanding? To understand suffering, to understand the origination of suffering, to understand extinction of suffering, to understand the path leading to the extinction of suffering; this is called right understanding.*

Additionally, right understanding is sometimes considered to encompass an understanding of the Buddhist idea of the non-permanence, or even non-existence, of the self, an idea known as *anatman* in Sanskrit and *anatta* in Pali. There are two stages for every stage of the eightfold path, a preliminary stage and the higher stages gradually obtained through the journey towards enlightenment. The preliminary stage of Right Views or right understanding is the knowledge of the Four Noble Truths. The higher stage requires more than the comprehension of the Four Noble Truths, it also includes the knowledge and understanding of the not-self doctrine, impermanence, dependent origination, the five aggregates, "karma", rebirth, and so on.

Right Intention

Right intention (*samyak-sackalpa-samm-saekappa*) can also be translated as "right thought", "right resolve", or "right aspiration" or the exertion of our own will to change. This element of the Noble Eightfold Path deals, fundamentally, with the Buddhist practitioner's reasons for practicing Buddhism, and with his or her outlook towards the world. It enjoins renunciation of worldly things and an accordant greater commitment to spiritual matters; good will; and a commitment to non-violence, or *ahias*, towards other living beings. In the *Magga-vibhanga Sutta*, it is simply explained as follows:

> *And what is right thought? Being resolved on renunciation, on freedom from ill will, on harmlessness: This is called right thought.*

Ethical Conduct (*Uila-Sila*)

The "ethical conduct" (Uila) subdivision of the Noble Eightfold Path is considered the cornerstone or foundation upon which unwholesome thoughts and practices end and higher meditative states begin.

In AN 11.2 Cetana Sutta (An Act of Will) Buddha states it is virtue (without clinging to virtue) which gives freedom from remorse, which leads to joy, serenity and subsequent rapturous states of meditation. It is in the nature of things that freedom from remorse arises in a person endowed with virtue, consummate in virtue.

In Buddhism, this is also one of the Ten Recollections along with the Triple Gem.

> *"There is the case where the disciple of the noble ones recollects his own virtues, thus: '[They are] untorn, unbroken, unspotted, unsplattered, liberating, praised by the wise, untarnished, conducive to concentration.'*

This aspect of the Noble Eightfold Path is the most outward-oriented aspect of the Noble Eightfold Path insofar as it deals directly with a Buddhist practitioner's relationship with other members of his or her society.

Right Speech

Right speech (*samyag-vac-samma-vaca*), as the name implies, deals with the way in which a Buddhist practitioner would best make use of his or her words. In the Pali Canon, this aspect of the Noble Eightfold Path is explained as follows:

And what is right speech? Abstaining from lying, abstaining from divisive speech, abstaining from abusive speech, abstaining from idle chatter: This, monks, is called right speech.

Other discourses in the Canon elaborate:

"Abandoning false speech, he abstains from false speech. He speaks the truth, holds to the truth, is firm, reliable, no deceiver of the world...."

"Abandoning divisive speech he abstains from divisive speech. What he has heard here he does not tell there to break those people apart from these people here. What he has heard there he does not tell here to break these people apart from those people there. Thus reconciling those who have broken apart or cementing those who are united, he loves concord, delights in concord, enjoys concord, speaks things that create concord...."

"Abandoning abusive speech, he abstains from abusive speech. He speaks words that are soothing to the ear, that are affectionate, that go to the heart, that are polite, appealing and pleasing to people at large....

"Abandoning idle chatter, he abstains from idle chatter. He speaks in season, speaks what is factual, what is in accordance with the goal, the Dhamma, and the Vinaya. He speaks words worth treasuring, seasonable, reasonable, circumscribed, connected with the goal...."

Regarding telling the truth about mundane knowledge, the *Cunda Kammaraputta Sutta* ascribes to the Buddha the following elaboration:

"There is the case where a certain person, abandoning false speech, abstains from false speech. When he has been called to a town meeting, a group meeting, a gathering of his relatives, his guild, or of the royalty,

if he is asked as a witness, 'Come & tell, good man, what you know': If he doesn't know, he says, 'I don't know.' If he does know, he says, 'I know.' If he hasn't seen, he says, 'I haven't seen.' If he has seen, he says, 'I have seen.' Thus he doesn't consciously tell a lie for his own sake, for the sake of another, or for the sake of any reward. Abandoning false speech, he abstains from false speech."

Regarding telling the truth about spiritual knowledge, the *Canki Sutta* ascribes to the Buddha the following cautionary statements:

"If a person has conviction, his statement, 'This is my conviction,' safeguards the truth. But he doesn't yet come to the definite conclusion that 'Only this is true; anything else is worthless.'..."

"If a person likes something... holds an unbroken tradition... has something reasoned through analogy... has something he agrees to, having pondered views, his statement, 'This is what I agree to, having pondered views,' safeguards the truth. But he doesn't yet come to the definite conclusion that 'Only this is true; anything else is worthless.'..."

Walpola Rahula glosses this path factor by stating that not engaging in such "forms of wrong and harmful speech" ultimately means that "one naturally has to speak the truth, has to use words that are friendly and benevolent, pleasant and gentle, meaningful and useful".

Right Action

Right action (*samyak-karmanta-samma-kammanta*) can also be translated as "right conduct" and, as the name implies, deals with the proper way in which a Buddhist practitioner would act in his or her daily life. In the *Magga-vibhanga Sutta*, this aspect of the Noble Eightfold Path is explained as follows:

And what is right action? Abstaining from taking life, from stealing, & from illicit sex. This is called right action.

The Cunda Kammaraputta Sutta *expands:*

"And how is one made pure in three ways by bodily action?

"There is the case where a certain person, abandoning the taking of life, abstains from the taking of life. He dwells with his rod laid down, his knife laid down, scrupulous, merciful, compassionate for the welfare of all living beings."

"Abandoning the taking of what is not given, he abstains from taking what is not given. He does not take, in the manner of a thief, things in a village or a wilderness that belong to others and have not been given by them."

"Abandoning sensual misconduct, he abstains from sensual misconduct. He does not get sexually involved with those who are protected by their mothers, their fathers, their brothers, their sisters, their relatives, or their Dhamma; those with husbands, those who entail punishments, or even those crowned with flowers by another man."

Together with the idea of *ahias* and right speech, right action constitutes the Five Precepts (Sanskrit: *pancauila*, Pali: *pancasila*), which form the fundamental ethical code undertaken by lay followers of Buddhism, and which are as follows:

1. To refrain from destroying living beings.
2. To refrain from stealing.
3. To refrain from sexual misconduct (adultery, rape, etc.).
4. To refrain from false speech (lying).
5. To refrain from intoxicants, which lead to heedlessness.

Right Livelihood

Right livelihood (*samyag-ajiva-samma-ajiva*) is based around the concept of *ahias*, or harmlessness, and essentially states that Buddhist practitioners ought not to engage in trades or occupations which, either directly or indirectly, result in harm to other living beings or systems. Such occupations include "trading in arms and lethal weapons, intoxicating drinks, poisons, killing animals, [and] cheating", among others. "Business in human beings"—such as slave trading and prostitution—is also forbidden, as are several other dishonest means of gaining wealth, such as "scheming, persuading, hinting, belittling, [and] pursuing gain with gain".

Mental Discipline (*Samadhi*)

The "mental discipline" subdivision of the Noble Eightfold Path is constituted by those elements that deal with how a Buddhist practitioner can best go about shaping his or her outlook towards the world.

Right Effort

Right effort (*samyag-vyayama-samma-vayama*) can also be translated as "right endeavour", and involves the Buddhist practitioner's continuous effort to, essentially, keep his or her mind free of thoughts that might impair his or her ability to realize or put into practice the other elements of the Noble Eightfold Path; for example, wishing ill towards another living being would contradict the injunction—contained in the "Right thought" element—to have good will towards others, and the "Right effort" element refers to the process of attempting to root out such an ill wish and replace it with a good wish.

And what, monks, is right effort?

(i) There is the case where a monk generates desire, endeavours, activates persistence, upholds & exerts his intent for the sake of the non-arising of evil, unskilful qualities that have not yet arisen.

(ii) He generates desire, endeavours, activates persistence, upholds & exerts his intent for the sake of the abandonment of evil, unskilful qualities that have arisen.

(iii) He generates desire, endeavours, activates persistence, upholds & exerts his intent for the sake of the arising of skillful qualities that have not yet arisen.

(iv) He generates desire, endeavours, activates persistence, upholds & exerts his intent for the maintenance, non-confusion, increase, plenitude, development, & culmination of skillful qualities that have arisen: This, monks, is called right effort."

By making right effort, a Buddhist practitioner is considered to be engaging in an effort that is wholesome in terms of *karma*; that is, in terms of that effort's ultimate consequences to the practitioner. The four phases of Right Effort: (in simple English)

(1) make effort to prevent the evil that has not yet come.

(2) make effort to destroy the evil that has come.

(3) make effort to produce the good that has not yet come.

(4) make effort to cultivate the good that has come.

Right Mindfulness

Right mindfulness (*samyak-sm[ti-samma-sati*), also translated as "right memory", together with right concentration, is concerned broadly with the practice of Buddhist meditation. Roughly speaking, "mindfulness" refers to the practice of keeping the mind alert to phenomena as they are affecting the body and mind. In the *Magga-vibhanga Sutta,* this aspect of the Noble Eightfold Path is explained as follows: And what, monks, is right mindfulness?

(i) There is the case where a monk remains focused on (his/her) *body* in and of itself... ardent, aware, and mindful... having already put aside worldly desire and aversion.

(ii) (He/she) remains focused on *feelings* in and of themselves... ardent, aware, and mindful... having already put aside worldly desire and aversion.

(iii) (He/she) remains focused on *the mind* in and of itself... ardent, aware, and mindful... having already put aside worldly desire and aversion.

(iv) (He/she) remains focused on *mental qualities* in and of themselves... ardent, aware, and mindful... having already put aside worldly desire and aversion.

This, monks, is called right mindfulness. This is also an important aspect of what constitutes the concept of "self" or Buddhist concept of Atman:

> *"And how, Ananda, is a bhikkhu an island unto himself, a refuge unto himself, seeking no external refuge; with the Dhamma as his island, the Dhamma as his refuge, seeking no other refuge?*
>
> *"When he dwells contemplating the body in the body, earnestly, clearly comprehending, and mindfully, after having overcome desire and sorrow in regard to the world; when he dwells contemplating feelings in feelings, the mind in the mind, and mental objects in mental objects, earnestly, clearly comprehending, and mindfully, after having overcome desire and sorrow in regard to the world, then, truly, he is an island unto himself, a refuge unto himself, seeking no external refuge; having the Dhamma as his island, the Dhamma as his refuge, seeking no other refuge. (DN 16 Maha-parinibbana Sutta)*

Bhikkhu Bodhi, a monk of the Theravadin tradition, further glosses the concept of mindfulness as follows:

> *The mind is deliberately kept at the level of* bare attention, *a detached observation of what is happening within us and around us in the present moment. In the practice of right mindfulness the mind is trained to remain in the present, open, quiet, and alert, contemplating the present event. All judgments and interpretations have to be suspended, or if they occur, just registered and dropped.*

Right Concentration

Right concentration (*samyak-samadhi-samma-samadhi*), together with right mindfulness, is concerned broadly with the practice of Buddhist meditation.

And what, monks, is right concentration?

(i) Quite withdrawn from sensuality, withdrawn from unwholesome states, a monk enters in the first jhana:

rapture and pleasure born from detachment, accompanied by movement of the mind onto the object and retention of the mind on the object.

(ii) With the stilling of directed thought and evaluation, (he/she) enters and remains in the second jhana: rapture and pleasure born of concentration; fixed single-pointed awareness free from movement of the mind onto the object and retention of the mind on the object; assurance.

(iii) With the fading of rapture, (he/she) remains in equanimity, mindful and fully aware, and physically sensitive of pleasure. (He/She) enters and remains in the third jhana which the Noble Ones declare to be "Equanimous and mindful, (he/she) has a pleasurable abiding."

(iv) With the abandoning of pleasure and pain...as with the earlier disappearance of elation and distress...(he/she) enters and remains in the fourth jhana: purity of equanimity and mindfulness, neither in pleasure nor in pain.

This, monks, is called right concentration.

Ninth and Tenth Elements

In the *Great Forty Sutra* (Mahacattarisaka Sutta), which appears in the Pali Canon, the Buddha explains that cultivation of the Eightfold Path leads to the development of two further stages once enlightenment has been reached.

These also fall under the category of panna and are *Right Knowledge* (sammnga) and *Right Liberation* (or *Right Release*; sammavimutti). Some consider *Right Association* as an implicit ninth aspect of the Path.

To further the foregoing, Bucknell & Martin (1986: p.6) state:

The Eightfold Path as described gives an impression of orderliness and completeness. However, closer study of the texts indicates that it is not after all a complete account of Gautama's course of practice. A number of suttas describe a Tenfold Path. This differs from the

Eightfold Path in having two further stages following right concentration, namely right insight or knowledge or wisdom (sammnga) and right liberation (samma vimutti). These two extra stages are nowhere described, nor is any explanation given for their frequent omission. The tenth state, right liberation, is presumably to be equated with the final goal, nirvgna. However, the ninth stage, right insight, which appears from its position in the list to be of crucial importance, remains unaccounted for.

2

THE EIGHT-FOLD PATH

From the standpoint of modern cognitive psychology, the Noble Eightfold Path can be seen as rooted in what is called cognitive dissonance, which is the perception of incompatibility between two cognitions. In the essay "Buddhism Meets Western Science", Gay Watson explains this dissonance as it relates to Buddhist teaching:

Buddhism has always been concerned with feelings, emotions, sensations, and cognition. The Buddha points both to cognitive and emotional causes of suffering. The emotional cause is desire and its negative opposite, aversion. The cognitive cause is ignorance of the way things truly occur, or of three marks of existence: that all things are unsatisfactory, impermanent, and without essential self.

The Noble Eightfold Path is, from this psychological viewpoint, an attempt to resolve this dissonance by changing patterns of thought and behaviour. It is for this reason that the first element of the path is right understanding (*samm-dimmhi*), which is how one's mind views the world. Under the wisdom (*panna*) subdivision of the Noble Eightfold Path, this worldview is intimately connected with the second element, right thought (*samm-saekappa*), which concerns the patterns of thought and intention that controls one's actions. These elements can be seen at work, for example, in the opening verses of the *Dhammapada*:

Preceded by perception are mental states,

For them is perception supreme,

From perception have they sprung.
If, with perception polluted, one speaks or acts,
Thence suffering follows
As a wheel the draught ox's foot.
Preceded by perception are mental states,
For them is perception supreme,
From perception have they sprung.
If, with tranquil perception, one speaks or acts,
Thence ease follows
As a shadow that never departs.

Thus, by altering one's distorted worldview, bringing out "tranquil perception" in the place of "perception polluted", one is able to ease suffering. Watson points this out from a psychological standpoint:

Research has shown that repeated action, learning, and memory can actually change the nervous system physically, altering both synaptic strength and connections. Such changes may be brought about by cultivated change in emotion and action; they will, in turn, change subsequent experience.

FOUR STAGES OF ENLIGHTENMENT

The four stages of enlightenment in Buddhism are the four degrees of approach to full enlightenment as an Arahant which a person can attain in this life. The four stages are Sotapanna, Sakadagami, Anagami and Arahant.

The teaching of the four stages of enlightenment is a central element of the early Buddhist schools, including the surviving Theravada school of Buddhism (current in Sri Lanka, Thailand and Myanmar).

The Ordinary Person

An ordinary person, or puthujjana (Pali; Sanskrit: prthagjana) is trapped in the endless changes of Samsara. Doing good or evil as influenced by his desires and aversions, he is born in higher or lower states of being (heavens or hells) according to his actions. As he has little control over his mind and behaviour, his destiny is haphazard and subject to great suffering. The ordinary person has never seen (experienced) the ultimate truth of Dhamma, and therefore has no way of finding an end to his predicament.

The Noble Persons

One who begins sincere training on the Buddhist path (known as Sekhas in Pali or those in training) and experiences the truth to the extent of cutting of a number of the ten mental fetters (Pali: saCyojana), becomes an ariyapuggala (Sanskrit: ryapudgala); a "noble person" who is sure of enlightenment as an Arahant in the near future (within seven lives).

Their specific destiny is governed by the degree of attainment reached.

The Sangha of the Tathagata's disciples (Arya Sangha), *i.e.* the four [groups of noble disciples] when taken as pairs, the eight when taken as persons. The four groups of noble disciples (Buddhist Sekhas) when taken as pairs are those who have attained:

- I

(1) the path to stream-entry;

(2) the fruition of stream-entry;

- II

(3) the path to once-returning ;

(4) the fruition of once-returning;

- III

(5) the path to non-returning ;

(3) the fruition of non-returning;

- IV

(7) the path to arahantship ;

(8) the fruition of arahantship.

Taking each attainment singly gives eight "individuals."

Stream-enterer

The first stage is that of Sotpanna (Pali; Sanskrit: Srotapanna), literally meaning "one who enters (padyate) the stream (srotas), with the stream being the Noble Eightfold Path regarded as the highest Dharma. The stream-enterer is also said to have "opened the eye of the Dharma" (dharmacakcus, Pli: dhammacakkhu). A stream-enterer is guaranteed enlightenment after no more than seven successive rebirths, and possibly in fewer. The stream-enterer can also be sure that he or she will not be reborn in any of the unhappy states or rebirths (that is, as an animal, a preta, or a being in hell). He can only be reborn as a human being, or in a heaven. The stream-enterer has attained an intuitive grasp of Buddhist doctrine has complete confidence in the Three Jewels of Buddha, Dhamma, and Sangha, and has good moral behaviour (Sila).

Once-returner

The second stage is that of the Sakadgm+ (Sanskrit: Sakrdagamin), literally meaning "one who once ever (sakrt) comes (gacchati)". The once-returner will only be born one more time in the human world, where he will attain enlightenment as an Arahant.

Non-returner

The third stage is that of the Angm+ (Sanskrit: Angmin), literally meaning "one who does not (an-) come (gacchati)". The non-returner does not come back into human existence, or any lower world, after death. Instead, he is reborn in one of the worlds of the Rupadhatu called the Zuddhvsa worlds, or "Pure Abodes", where he will attain Nirvna; some of them are reborn a second time in a higher world of the Pure Abodes, but in no case are born into a lower state. An Angm+ has abandoned the five lower fetters that bind the mind to the cycle of rebirth. An Angm+ is thus partially enlightened, and on the way to perfect and complete Enlightenment.

Arhat

The fourth stage is that of Arahant, a fully enlightened human being who has abandoned all fetters, and who upon decease (Sanskrit: PariNirvna, Pali: Parinibbna) will not be reborn in any world, having wholly abandoned Samsara.

SAKADAGAMI

In Buddhism, the Sakadagami is a partially-enlightened person, who has cut off the first three chains with which the ordinary mind is bound, and significantly weakened the 4th and 5th. Sakadagamiship is the second stage of the four stages of enlightenment.

The Sakadagami will be reborn into the human world once more. If, however, he attains the next stage of enlightenment (Anagamiship) in this life, he will not come back to the human world.

The three specific chains or fetters (Pali: saCyojana) of which the Sakadagami is free are:

1. Sakkya-dimmhi (Pali)-Belief in self
2. Vicikiccha (Pali)-Skeptical doubt
3. Silabbata-paramasa (Pali)-Attachment to rites and rituals

   The Sakadagami also significantly weakened the chains of:

4. Kama-raga (Pali)-Sensuous craving
5. Byapada (Pali)-Ill-will

Thus, the Sakadagami is an intermediate stage between the Sotapanna, who still has comparatively strong sensuous desire and ill-will, and the Anagami, who is completely free from sensuous desire and ill-will.

ANAGAMI

In Buddhism, an *anagami* (Pali) is a partially-enlightened person who has cut off the first five chains that bind the ordinary mind. Anagami-ship is the third of the four stages of enlightenment.

Anagamis are not reborn into the human world after death, but into the heaven of the Pure Abodes, where only anagamis live. There they attain full enlightenment (arahantship). The Pali terms for the specific chains or fetters (Pali: sacyojana) of which an anagami is free are:

1. Sakkya-dimmhi-Belief in self
2. Vicikiccha-Skeptical doubt
3. Silabbata-paramasa-Attachment to rites and rituals
4. Kama-raga-Sensuous craving
5. Byapada-Ill-will

The fetters from which an anagami is not yet free are:

6. Rupa-raga-Craving for fine-material existence (the first 4 jhanas)
7. Arupa-raga-Craving for immaterial existence (the last 4 jhanas)
8. Mana-Conceit
9. Uddhacca-Restlessness
10. Avijja-Ignorance

Anagamis are at an intermediate stage between sakadagamis and arahants. Arahants enjoy complete freedom from the ten fetters.

ARHAT

In the sramanic traditions of ancient India (most notably those of Mahavira and Gautama Buddha) Arhat (Sanskrit) or Arahant (Pali) signified a spiritual practitioner who had—to use an expression common in the tipitaka—"laid down the burden"—and realised the goal of Nibbana, the culmination of the spiritual life (brahmacarya). Such a person, having removed all causes for future becoming, is not reborn after biological death into any samsaric realm.

The word literally means "worthy one" (an alternative etymology is "foe-destroyer") and constitutes the highest grade of noble person—*ariya-puggala*—described by the Buddha as recorded in the Pali canon. The word was used (as it is today in the liturgy of Theravada Buddhism) as an epithet of the

Buddha himself as well as of his enlightened disciples. The most widely recited liturgical reference is perhaps the homage: *Namo Tassa Bhagavato, Arahato, Samma-sammbuddhassa—Homage to him, the Blessed One, the Worthy One, the perfectly enlightened Buddha.*

Origin

The word *"Arahan"* literally means "worthy one" (an alternative etymology is "foe-destroyer") and constitutes the highest grade of noble person—*ariya-puggala*—described by the Buddha as recorded in the Pali canon. The word was used (as it is today in the liturgy of Theravada Buddhism) as an epithet of the Buddha himself as well as of his enlightened disciples. The most widely recited liturgical reference is perhaps the homage: *Namo Tassa Bhagavato, Arahato, Samma-sammbuddhassa.—Homage to him, the Blessed One, the Worthy One, the perfectly enlightened Buddha.*

Variations

- Chinese: aluohan, luohan; rarer terms: yinggong, yingzhen, zhenren, normally refers to a respected Taoist, and the term comes from the book Huangdi Neijing.
- Hindi: arhant
- Japanese: arakan, rakan
- Korean: nahan
- Tibetan: dgra bcom pa
- Vietnamese: la han

Jainism

In Jainism, the term "arhat" or "arihant" is a synonym for jina or tirthankara. The Jain Navakar Mantra starts with "Namo Arhantanam". An arihant has destroyed the karmas ("ari" means "enemy", "hant" means "destroyer") and is thus approaching nirvana.

Theravada Buddhism

In Theravada Buddhism the Buddha himself is first named as an Arahat, as were his enlightened followers, since he is free from all defilements, without greed, hatred, and delusion, rid of ignorance and craving, having no "assets" that will lead to a future birth, knowing and seeing the real here and now. This virtue shows stainless purity, true worth, and the accomplishment of the end, Nibbana.

In the Pali canon, Ven. Ananda states that he has known monastics to achieve Nibbana in one of four ways:

- one develops insight preceded by serenity (Pali: *samatha-pubbaggamac vipassanac*);
- one develops serenity preceded by insight (*vipassan-pubbaggamac samathac*);
- one develops serenity and insight in a stepwise fashion (*samatha-vipassanac yuganaddhac*);
- one's mind becomes seized by excitation about the Dhamma and, as a consequence, develops serenity and abandons the fetters (*dhamma-uddhacca-viggahitaC manasaC hoti*).

Mahayana Buddhism

Mahayana Buddhists see the Buddha himself as the ideal towards which one should aim in one's spiritual aspirations. Hence the arhat as enlightened disciple of the Buddha is not regarded as the goal as much as is the Bodhisattva. Bodhisattva carries a different meaning in Mahayana Buddhism to Theravada Buddhism.

In the Pali scriptures the Tathagata when relating his own experiences of self-development uses a stock phrase "when I was an unenlightened Bodhisattva". Bodhisattva thus connotes here the absence of enlightenment (Bodhi) of a person working towards that goal. In Mahayana Buddhism, on the other hand a Bodhisattva is someone who seeks to put the welfare of others before their own, forfeiting their own enlightenment until all beings are saved.

THREE JEWELS

The Three Jewels, also rendered as Three Treasures, Three Refuges or Triple Gem are the three things that Buddhists give themselves to, and in return look toward for guidance, in the process known as *taking refuge*. The Three Jewels are:

- Buddha (*The Enlightened* or *Awakened One*; Chn: *FO*, Jpn: *Butsu*, Tib: *sangs-rgyas*, Mong: *burqan*), who, depending on one's interpretation, can mean the Historical Buddha, Shakyamuni, or the Buddha nature or ideal within all beings;
- Dharma (*The Teaching*; Chn: *FI*, Jpn: *Ho*, Tib: *chos*, Mong: *nom*), which is the Teachings of the Buddha.
- Sangha (*The Community*; Chn: *Scng*, Jpn: *So*, Tib: *dge-'dun*, Mong: *quvarac*), The Community of those great people who have attained Enlightenment. So that those people(Sangha) will help you to attain Enlightenment.

Gachchamis

Also the Three Jewels are known as the Gachchamis. The first is *Buddham, sharanam, gachchami*, I go to the feet of the Awaken One. The second is *Sangam sharanam gachchami*, I go to the feet of the Sangha, the Awaken One's community. And the third is *Dhammam sharanam gachchami*, I go to the feet of the Dharma, the Eternal law.

The Three Jewels and "Taking Refuge"

Taking refuge in the Three Jewels is central to Buddhist lay and monastic ordination ceremonies, as originated by Gautama Buddha. Taking refuge in the Triple Gem is generally considered to make one officially a Buddhist. Thus, in many Theravada Buddhist communities, the following Pali chant, the *Vandana Ti-sarana* is often recited by both monks and lay people:

Importance of the Triple Gem

The Triple Gem is in the centre of one of the major practices of mental "reflection" in Buddhism; the reflection on the true qualities of the Buddha, Dharma and Sangha. These qualities are called the Mirror of the Dharma in the Mahaparinibbana Sutta and help the practitioner attain the true "mind like a mirror".

In the Apannaka Jataka Buddha declares:

"Disciples, nowhere between the lowest of hells below and the highest heaven above, nowhere in all the infinite worlds that stretch right and left, is there the equal, much less the superior, of a Buddha. Incalculable is the excellence which springs from obeying the Precepts and from other virtuous conduct."

"By taking refuge in the Triple Gem, one escapes from rebirth in states of suffering. In forsaking such a refuge as this, you have certainly erred. In the past, too, men who foolishly mistook what was no refuge for a real refuge, met disaster."

Discussions of the Three Jewels

The qualities of the Buddha, Dharma, and Sangha are frequently repeated in the ancient texts.

- *The Buddha:* "The Blessed One is an Arahant, perfectly enlightened, accomplished in true knowledge and conduct, fortunate, knower of the world, unsurpassed leader of persons to be tamed, teacher of devas and humans, the Enlightened One, the Blessed One."

In some traditions *the Buddha as refuge* is taken to refer to the historical Buddha and also 'the full development of mind', in other words, the full development of one's highest potential, *i.e.* recognition of mind and the completion or full development of one's inherent qualities and activities.

- *The Dharma:* "The Dhamma is well expounded by the Blessed One, directly visible, immediate (eternal or not subject to time), inviting one to come and see, applicable, to be personally experienced by the wise."

Refuge in the Dharma, in the Vajrayana, tradition includes reference not only to the words of the Buddha, but to the living experience of realization and teachings of fully realized practitioners.

In Tibetan Buddhism, it includes both the Kangyur (the teaching of the Buddha) and the Tengyur (the commentaries by realized practioners) and in an intangible way also includes the living transmission of those masters, which can also be very inspiring.

- *The Sangha:* "The Sangha of the Blessed One's disciples is practising the good way, practising the straight way, practising the true way, practising the proper way; that is, the four pairs of persons, the eight types of individuals-This Sangha of the Blessed One's disciples is worthy of gifts, worthy of hospitality, worthy of offerings, worthy of reverential salutation, the unsurpassed field of merit for the world."

In the Vajrayana, a more liberal definition of Sangha can include all practitioners who are actively using the Buddha's teachings to benefit themselves and/or others. It can be more strictly defined as the 'Realized Sangha' or 'Arya-Sangha', in other words, practitioners and historical students of the Buddha who have fully realized the nature of their mind, also known as realized Boddhisatvas; and 'Ordinary Sangha', which can loosely mean practitioners and students of the Buddha who are using the same methods and working towards the same goal.

The Three Jewels and the Three Roots

In Vajrayana traditions, a second formulation of refuge called the Three Roots is added to the three jewels. They are

- the guru, considered the "Root of Blessing"
- the Ishtadevata, which is the "Root of Methods"
- Dakini or Dharmapalas, considered the "Root of Protection"

These are seen as forms of the Body (Sangha), Speech (Dharma) and Mind (Buddha) of the Buddha. Of these, the guru has the most prominent place in the Vajrayana, as without his personal assitance and guidance, a practitioner cannot achieve proper spiritual progress.

History of the Triple Gem Metaphor

The three gems are so called because of their treasured value to Buddhists as well as their indestructible and unchanging nature. The *Three Gems* when used in the process of taking refuge, become the *Three Refuges*. In this form, the metaphors occur very frequently in the ancient Buddhist Texts, and here the Sangha is used more broadly to refer to either the Sangha of Bhikkhus, or the Sangha of Bhikkhunis.

> *"I go to Master Gautama for refuge and to the Dhamma, and to the Sangha of Bhikkhus."*

"Diamond Mind"

Buddha's mind in his earth body or sambhogakaya is frequently associated with the greatest gem of all, the diamond, the hardest natural substance. In the Anguttara Nikaya(3:25), Buddha talks about the diamond mind which can cut through all delusion.

"Gems" in the Ratana-sutta

The expression *Three Gems* are found in the earliest Buddhist literature of the Pali Canon, besides other works there is one sutta in the Sutta-nipata, called the Ratana-sutta which contains a series of verses on the Jewels in the Buddha, Dharma, and Sangha.

In the *Ratana-sutta*, all the qualities of the Sangha mentioned are attributes of the Buddha's enlightened disciples:

- One who is irascible and very irritable, displaying anger, hatred and sulkiness; such a one is said to be a person with a mind like an open sore.
- One who understands the Four Noble Truths correctly is said to have a mind like a flash of lightning.
- One who has destroyed the mind-intoxicating defilements and realized the liberation of mind and the liberation by knowledge is said to have a mind like a diamond.

Shared Metaphor with Jainism and Taoism

When Buddhism was introduced into China, *ratnatraya* was translated as *sanbao* (Pinyin: *sanbao*; Wade-Giles: *san-pao*; literally "three jewels/treasures"), a word that first occurs in the *Tao Te Ching*.

In his analysis of the *Tao Te Ching*, Victor H. Mair notes that the jewel metaphor was already widely used in Indian religious metaphor before the *Tao Te Ching* was written. The notion of Three Jewels used by both Buddhist and Jain literature. For the Jains, the Three Jewels signified

- *samyag-darshana* (correct perception or insight)
- *samyag-jnana* (correct knowledge)
- *samyag-caritra* (correct conduct).

Symbolism in Art

The *Three Jewels* are also symbolized by the *triratna*, composed of (from bottom to top):

- A lotus flower within a circle.
- A diamond rod, or vajra.
- A Gankyil.
- A trident, or trisula, with three branches, representing the threefold jewels of Buddhism: Buddha, the Dharma and the Sangha.

On representations of the footprint of the Buddha, the Triratna is usually also surmounted by the Dharma wheel.

The Triratna can be found on frieze sculptures at Sanchi as the symbol crowning a flag standard (2nd century BCE), as a symbol of the Buddha installed on the Buddha's throne (2nd century BCE), as the crowning decorative symbol on the later gates at the stupa in Sanchi (2nd century CE), or, very often on the Buddha footprint (starting from the 1st century CE).

The Triratna is also on the 1st century BCE coins of the Kingdom of Kuninda in northern Punjab, surmounting depictions of stupas, on some the coins of the Indo-Parthian king Abdagases, or the coins of some of the Kushan kings such as Vima Kadphises. The triratna can be further reinforced by being surmounted with three dharma wheels (one for each of the three jewels of Buddhism: the Buddha, the Dharma and the Sangha). The triratna symbol is also called *nandipada*, or "bull's hoof", by Hindus.

THERAVADA BUDDHISM

Theravada (pronounced — more or less — "terra-VAH-dah"), the "Doctrine of the Elders," is the school of Buddhism that draws its scriptural inspiration from the Tipitaka, or Pali canon, which scholars generally agree contains the earliest surviving record of the Buddha's teachings. For many centuries, Theravada has been the predominant religion of continental Southeast Asia (Thailand, Myanmar/Burma, Cambodia, and Laos) and Sri Lanka. Today Theravada Buddhists number well over 100 million worldwide. In recent decades Theravada has begun to take root in the West.

Many Buddhisms, One Dhamma-vinaya

The Buddha — the "Awakened One" — called the religion he founded *Dhamma-vinaya* — "the doctrine and discipline." To provide a social structure supportive of the practice of Dhamma-vinaya (or *Dhamma* for short [Sanskrit: *Dharma]),* and to preserve these teachings for posterity, the Buddha established the order of *bhikkhus* (monks) and *bhikkhunis* (nuns) — the *Sangha* — which continues to this day to pass his teachings on to subsequent generations of laypeople and monastics, alike.

As the Dhamma continued its spread across India after the Buddha's passing, differing interpretations of the original teachings arose, which led to schisms within the Sangha and the emergence of as many as eighteen distinct sects of Buddhism. One of these schools eventually gave rise to a reform movement that called itself *Mahayana* (the "Greater Vehicle") and that referred to the other schools disparagingly as *Hinayana* (the "Lesser Vehicle"). What we call Theravada today is the sole survivor of those early non-Mahayana schools. To avoid the pejorative tone implied by the terms Hinayana and Mahayana, it is common today to use more neutral language to distinguish between these two main branches of Buddhism. Because Theravada historically dominated southern Asia, it is sometimes called "Southern" Buddhism, while Mahayana, which migrated northwards from India into China, Tibet, Japan, and Korea, is known as "Northern" Buddhism.

The Language of Theravada Buddhism

The language of the Theravada canonical texts is Pali (lit., "text"), which is based on a dialect of Middle Indo-Aryan that was probably spoken in central India during the Buddha's time. Ven. Ananda, the Buddha's cousin and close personal attendant, committed the Buddha's sermons *(suttas)* to memory and thus became a living repository of these teachings. Shortly after the Buddha's death *(ca.* 480 BCE), five hundred of the most senior monks — including Ananda — convened to recite and verify all the sermons they had heard during the Buddha's forty-five year teaching career. Most of these sermons therefore begin with the disclaimer, *"Evam me sutam"* — "Thus have I heard."

After the Buddha's death the teachings continued to be passed down orally within the monastic community, in keeping with an Indian oral tradition that long predated the Buddha. By 250 BCE the Sangha had systematically arranged and compiled these teachings into three divisions: the Vinaya Pitaka (the "basket of discipline" — the texts concerning the rules and customs of the Sangha), the Sutta Pitaka (the "basket of discourses" — the sermons and utterances by the Buddha and his close disciples), and the Abhidhamma Pitaka (the "basket of special/higher doctrine" — a detailed psycho-philosophical analysis of the Dhamma). Together these three are known as the Tipitaka, the "three baskets." In the third century BCE Sri Lankan monks began compiling a series of exhaustive commentaries to the Tipitaka; these were subsequently collated and translated into Pali beginning in the fifth century CE. The Tipitaka plus the post-canonical texts (commentaries, chronicles, etc.) together constitute the complete body of classical Theravada literature.

Pali was originally a spoken language with no alphabet of its own. It wasn't until about 100 BCE that the Tipitaka was first fixed in writing, by Sri Lankan scribe-monks, who wrote the Pali phonetically in a form of early Brahmi script. Since then the Tipitaka has been transliterated into many different scripts (Devanagari, Thai, Burmese, Roman, Cyrillic, to name a few). Although English translations of the most popular

Tipitaka texts abound, many students of Theravada find that learning the Pali language — even just a little bit here and there — greatly deepens their understanding and appreciation of the Buddha's teachings.

No one can prove that the Tipitaka contains any of the words actually uttered by the historical Buddha. Practicing Buddhists have never found this problematic. Unlike the scriptures of many of the world's great religions, the Tipitaka is not regarded as gospel, as an unassailable statement of divine truth, revealed by a prophet, to be accepted purely on faith. Instead, its teachings are meant to be assessed firsthand, to be put into practice in one's life so that one can find out for oneself if they do, in fact, yield the promised results. It is the truth towards which the words in the Tipitaka point that ultimately matters, not the words themselves. Although scholars will continue to debate the authorship of passages from the Tipitaka for years to come (and thus miss the point of these teachings entirely), the Tipitaka will quietly continue to serve— as it has for centuries — as an indispensable guide for millions of followers in their quest for Awakening.

3

THE BUDDHA'S TEACHINGS

THE FOUR NOBLE TRUTHS

Shortly after his Awakening, the Buddha delivered his first sermon, in which he laid out the essential framework upon which all his later teachings were based. This framework consists of the Four Noble Truths, four fundamental principles of nature (Dhamma) that emerged from the Buddha's radically honest and penetrating assessment of the human condition. He taught these truths not as metaphysical theories or as articles of faith, but as categories by which we should frame our direct experience in a way that conduces to Awakening:

1. *Dukkha:* suffering, unsatisfactoriness, discontent, stress;
2. The cause of *dukkha:* the cause of this dissatisfaction iscraving *(tanha)* for sensuality, for states of becoming, and states of no becoming;
3. The cessation of *dukkha:* the relinquishment of that craving;
4. The path of practice leading to the cessation of *dukkha:* the Noble Eightfold Path of right view, right resolve, right speech, right action, right livelihood, right effort, right mindfulness, and right concentration.

Because of our ignorance *(avijja)* of these Noble Truths, because of our inexperience in framing the world in their terms, we remain bound to *samsara,* the wearisome cycle of birth, aging, illness, death, and rebirth. Craving propels this process onward, from one moment to the next and over the course of countless lifetimes, in accordance with *kamma* (Skt. *karma),* the universal law of cause and effect. According to this immutable law, every action that one performs in the present moment — whether by body, speech, or mind itself — eventually bears fruit according to its skillfulness: act in unskilful and harmful ways and unhappiness is bound to follow; act skillfully and happiness will ultimately ensue. As long as one remains ignorant of this principle, one is doomed to an aimless existence: happy one moment, in despair the next; enjoying one lifetime in heaven, the next in hell.

The Buddha discovered that gaining release from samsara requires assigning to each of the Noble Truths a specific task: the first Noble Truth is to be *comprehended*; the second, *abandoned*; the third, *realized*; the fourth, *developed*. The full realization of the third Noble Truth paves the way for Awakening: the end of ignorance, craving, suffering, and kamma itself; the direct penetration to the transcendent freedom and supreme happiness that stands as the final goal of all the Buddha's teachings; the Unconditioned, the Deathless, Unbinding — Nibbana (Skt. *Nirvana).*

THE EIGHTFOLD PATH AND THE PRACTICE OF DHAMMA

Because the roots of ignorance are so intimately entwined with the fabric of the psyche, the unawakened mind is capable of deceiving itself with breathtaking ingenuity. The solution therefore requires more than simply being kind, loving, and mindful in the present moment. The practitioner must equip him-or herself with the expertise to use a range of tools to outwit, outlast, and eventually uproot the mind's unskilful tendencies. For example, the practice of generosity *(dana)* erodes the heart's habitual tendencies towards craving and teaches valuable lessons about the motivations behind, and the results of, skillful action. The practice of virtue *(sila)* guards one against straying wildly off-course and into harm's way. The cultivation of goodwill *(metta)* helps to undermine anger's seductive grasp. The ten recollections offer ways to alleviate doubt, bear physical pain with composure, maintain a healthy sense of self-respect, overcome laziness and complacency, and restrain oneself from unbridled lust. And there are many more skills to learn.

The good qualities that emerge and mature from these practices not only smooth the way for the journey to Nibbana; over time they have the effect of transforming the practitioner into a more generous, loving, compassionate, peaceful, and clear-headed member of society. The individual's sincere pursuit of Awakening is thus a priceless and timely gift to a world in desperate need of help.

DISCERNMENT (PANNA)

The Eightfold Path is best understood as a collection of personal qualities to be developed, rather than as a sequence of steps along a linear path. The development of right view and right resolve (the factors classically identified with wisdom and discernment) facilitates the development of right speech, action, and livelihood (the factors identified with virtue). As virtue develops so do the factors identified with concentration (right effort, mindfulness, and concentration). Likewise, as concentration matures, discernment evolves to a still deeper level. And so the process unfolds: development of one factor fosters development of the next, lifting the practitioner in an upward spiral of spiritual maturity that eventually culminates in Awakening.

The long journey to Awakening begins in earnest with the first tentative stirrings of right view — the discernment by which one recognizes the validity of the four Noble Truths and the principle of kamma. One begins to see that one's future well-being is neither predestined by fate, nor left to the whims of a divine being or random chance. The responsibility for one's happiness rests squarely on one's own shoulders. Seeing this, one's spiritual aims become suddenly clear: to relinquish the habitual unskilful tendencies of the mind in favour of skillful ones. As this right resolve grows stronger, so does the heartfelt desire to live a morally upright life, to choose one's actions with care.

At this point many followers make the inward commitment to take the Buddha's teachings to heart, to become "Buddhist" through the act of taking refuge in the Triple Gem: the Buddha (both the historical Buddha and one's own innate potential for Awakening), the Dhamma (both the Buddha's teachings and the ultimate Truth towards which they point), and the Sangha (both the unbroken monastic lineage that has preserved the teachings since the Buddha's day, and all those who have achieved at least some degree of Awakening). With one's feet thus planted on solid ground, and with the help of an admirable friend or teacher *(kalyanamitta)* to guide the way, one is now well-equipped to proceed down the Path, following in the footsteps left by the Buddha himself.

VIRTUE (SILA)

Right view and right resolve continue to mature through the development of the path factors associated with *sila,* or virtue — namely, right speech, right action, and right livelihood. These are condensed into a very practical form in the five precepts, the basic code of ethical conduct to which every practicing Buddhist subscribes: refraining from killing, stealing, sexual misconduct, lying, and using intoxicants. Even the monks' complex code of 227 rules and the nuns' 311 ultimately have these five basic precepts at their core.

CONCENTRATION (SAMADHI)

Having gained a foothold in the purification of one's outward behaviour through the practice of *sila,* the essential groundwork has been laid for delving into the most subtle and transformative aspect of the path: meditation and the development of *samadhi,* or concentration. This is spelled out in detail in the final three path factors: right effort, by which one learns how to favour skillful qualities of mind over unskilful ones; right mindfulness, by which one learns to keep one's attention continually grounded in the present moment of experience; and right concentration, by which one learns to immerse the mind so thoroughly and unwaveringly in its meditation object that it enters *jhana,* a series of progressively deeper states of mental and physical tranquillity.

Right mindfulness and right concentration are developed in tandem through *satipatthana* ("frames of reference" or "foundations of mindfulness"), a systematic approach to meditation practice that embraces a wide range of skills and techniques. Of these practices, mindfulness of the body (especially mindfulness of breathing) is particularly effective at bringing into balance the twin qualities of tranquillity *(samatha)* and insight *(vipassana),* or clear-seeing.

Through persistent practice, the meditator becomes more adept at bringing the combined powers of *samatha-vipassana* to bear in an exploration of the fundamental nature of mind and body. As the meditator masters the ability to frame his immediate experience in terms of *anicca* (inconstancy), *dukkha,* and *anatta* (not-self), even the subtlest manifestations of these three characteristics of experience are brought into exquisitely sharp focus. At the same time, the root cause of *dukkha* — craving— is relentlessly exposed to the light of awareness. Eventually craving is left with no place to hide, the entire karmic process that fabricates *dukkha* unravels, the eightfold path reaches its noble climax, and the meditator gains, at long last, his or her first unmistakable glimpse of the Unconditioned — Nibbana.

AWAKENING

This first enlightenment experience, known as stream-entry *(sotapatti),* is the first of four progressive stages of Awakening, each of which entails the irreversible shedding or weakening of several fetters *(samyojana),* the manifestations of ignorance that bind a person to the cycle of birth and death. Stream-entry marks an unprecedented and radical turning point both in the practitioner's current life and in the entirety of his or her long journey in samsara. For it is at this point that any lingering doubts about the truth of the Buddha's teachings disappear; it is at this point that any belief in the purifying efficacy of rites and rituals evaporates; and it is at this point that the long-cherished notion of an abiding personal "self" falls away. The stream-enterer is said to be assured of no more than seven future rebirths (all of them favorable) before eventually attaining full Awakening.

But full Awakening is still a long way off. As the practitioner presses on with renewed diligence, he or she passes through two more significant landmarks: once-returning *(sakadagati)*, which is accompanied by the weakening of the fetters of sensual desire and ill-will, and non-returning *(agati)*, in which these two fetters are uprooted altogether. The final stage of Awakening— *arahatta* — occurs when even the most refined and subtle levels of craving and conceit are irrevocably extinguished. At this point the practitioner — now an *arahant*, or "worthy one" — arrives at the end-point of the Buddha's teaching. With ignorance, suffering, stress, and rebirth having all come to their end, the arahant at last can utter the victory cry first proclaimed by the Buddha upon his Awakening:

> *"Birth is ended, the holy life fulfilled, the task done! There is nothing further for the sake of this world." [MN 36]*

The arahant lives out the remainder of his or her life inwardly enjoying the bliss of Nibbana, secure at last from the possibility of any future rebirth. When the arahant's aeons-long trail of past kamma eventually unwinds to its end, the arahant dies and he or she enters into *parinibbana* — total Unbinding. Although language utterly fails at describing this extraordinary event, the Buddha likened it to what happens when a fire finally burns up all its fuel.

THE SERIOUS PURSUIT OF HAPPINESS

Buddhism is sometimes naively criticized as a "negative" or "pessimistic" religion and philosophy. Surely life is not all misery and disappointment: it offers many kinds of happiness and sublime joy. Why then this dreary Buddhist obsession with unsatisfactoriness and suffering?

The Buddha based his teachings on a frank assessment of our plight as humans: there is unsatisfactoriness and suffering in the world. No one can argue this fact. Dukkha lurks behind even the highest forms of worldly pleasure and joy, for, sooner or later, as surely as night follows day, that happiness must come to an end. Were the Buddha's teachings to stop there, we might indeed regard them as pessimistic and life as utterly hopeless. But, like a doctor who prescribes a remedy for an illness, the Buddha offers both a hope (the third Noble Truth) and a cure (the fourth).

The Buddha's teachings thus give cause for unparalleled optimism and joy. The teachings offer as their reward the noblest, truest kind of happiness, and give profound value and meaning to an otherwise grim existence. One modern teacher summed it up well: "Buddhism is the serious pursuit of happiness."

THERAVADA COMES WEST

Until the late 19th century, the teachings of Theravada were little known outside of southern Asia, where they had flourished for some two and one-half millennia. In the past century, however, the West has begun to take notice of Theravada's unique spiritual legacy in its teachings of Awakening. In recent decades this interest has swelled, with the monastic Sangha from various schools within Theravada establishing dozens of monasteries across Europe and North America.

Increasing numbers of lay meditation centres, founded and operated independently of the monastic Sangha, strain to meet the demands of lay men and women — Buddhist and otherwise — seeking to learn selected aspects of the Buddha's teachings.

The turn of the 21st century presents both opportunities and dangers for Theravada in the West: Will the Buddha's teachings be patiently studied and put into practice, and allowed to establish deep roots in Western soil, for the benefit of many generations to come? Will the current popular Western climate of "openness" and cross-fertilization between spiritual traditions lead to the emergence of a strong new form of Buddhist practice unique to the modern era, or will it simply lead to confusion and the dilution of these priceless teachings? These are open questions; only time will tell.

Spiritual teachings of every description inundate the media and the marketplace today. Many of today's popular spiritual teachings borrow liberally from the Buddha, though only rarely do they place the Buddha's words in their true context. Earnest seekers of truth are therefore often faced with the unsavory task of wading through fragmentary teachings of dubious accuracy. How are we to make sense of it all?

Fortunately the Buddha left us with some simple guidelines to help us navigate through this bewildering flood. Whenever you find yourself questioning the authenticity of a particular teaching, heed well the Buddha's advice to his stepmother:

> *The teachings that promote] the qualities of which you may know, 'These qualities lead to passion, not to dispassion; to being fettered, not to being unfettered; to accumulating, not to shedding; to self-aggrandizement, not to modesty; to discontent, not to contentment; to entanglement, not to seclusion; to laziness, not to aroused persistence; to being burdensome, not to being unburdensome': You may definitely hold, 'This is not the Dhamma, this is not the Vinaya, this is not the Teacher's instruction.'*
>
> *As for the teachings that promote] the qualities of which you may know, 'These qualities lead to dispassion, not to passion; to being unfettered, not to being fettered; to shedding, not to accumulating; to modesty, not to self-aggrandizement; to contentment, not to discontent; to seclusion, not to entanglement; to aroused persistence, not to laziness; to being unburdensome, not to being burdensome': You may definitely hold, 'This is the Dhamma, this is the Vinaya, this is the Teacher's instruction.' [AN 8.53]*

The truest test of these teachings, of course, is whether they yield the promised results in the crucible of your own heart. The Buddha presents the challenge; the rest is up to you.

BUDDHIST DOCTRINE AND TERMINOLOGY

Is Buddhism a Religion or a Philosophy?

The Buddha referred to his teachings simply as *Dhamma-vinaya* — "the doctrine and discipline" — but for centuries people have tried to categorize the teachings in various ways, trying to fit them into the prevailing molds of cultural, philosophical, and religious thought. Buddhism is an ethical system — a way of life — that leads to a very specific goal and that possesses some aspects of both religion and philosophy:

It is a Philosophy: Like most philosophies, Buddhism attempts to frame the complexities of human existence in a way that reassures us that there is, in fact, some underlying order to the Universe.

In the Four Noble Truths the Buddha crisply summarizes our predicament: there is suffering, it has a cause, it has an end, and there is a way to reach the end. The teachings on kamma provide a thorough and logically self-consistent description of the nature of cause-and-effect. And even the Buddhist view of cosmology, which some may at first find farfetched, is a logical extension of the law of kamma. According to the Dhamma, a deep and unshakable logic pervades the world.

It is not a Philosophy: Unlike most philosophical systems, which rely on speculation and the power of reason to arrive at logical truths, Buddhism relies on the direct observation of one's personal experience and on honing certain skills in order to gain true understanding and wisdom. Idle speculation has no place in Buddhist practice.

Although studying in the classroom, reading books, and engaging in spirited debate can play a vital part in developing a cognitive understanding of basic Buddhist concepts, the heart of Buddhism can never be realized this way. The Dhamma is not an abstract system of thought designed to delight the intellect; it is a roadmap to be *used,* one whose essential purpose is to lead the practitioner to the ultimate goal, nibbana.

It is a Religion: At the heart of each of the world's great religions lies a transcendent ideal around which its doctrinal principles orbit. In Buddhism this truth is nibbana, the hallmark of the cessation of suffering and stress, a truth of utter transcendence that stands in singular distinction from anything we might encounter in our ordinary sensory experience. Nibbana is the *sine qua non* of Buddhism, the guiding star and ultimate goal towards which all the Buddha's teachings point. Because it aims at such a lofty transcendent ideal, we might fairly call Buddhism a religion.

It is not a Religion: In stark contrast to the world's other major religions, however, Buddhism invokes no divinity, no supreme Creator or supreme Self, no Holy Spirit or omniscient loving God to whom we might appeal for salvation.

Instead, Buddhism calls for us to hoist ourselves up by our own bootstraps: to develop the discernment we need to distinguish between those qualities within us that are unwholesome and those that are truly noble and good, and to learn how to nourish the good ones and expunge the bad. This is the path to Buddhism's highest perfection, nibbana. Not even the Buddha can take you to that goal; you alone must do the work necessary to complete the journey:

> *"Therefore, Ananda, be islands unto yourselves, refuges unto yourselves, seeking no external refuge; with the Dhamma as your island, the Dhamma as your refuge, seeking no other refuge."— DN 16*

Despite its non-theistic nature, however, Buddhist practice does call for a certain kind of faith. It is not blind faith, an uncritical acceptance of the Buddha's word as transmitted through scripture.

Instead it is *saddha,* a confidence born of taking refuge in the Triple Gem; it is a willingness to trust that the Dhamma, when practiced diligently, will lead to the rewards promised by the Buddha. Saddha is a provisional acceptance of the teachings, that is ever subject to critical evaluation during the course of one's practice, and which must be balanced by one's growing powers of discernment.

For many Buddhists, this faith is expressed and reinforced through traditional devotional practices, such as bowing before a Buddha statue and reciting passages from the early Pali texts.

Despite a superficial resemblance to the rites of many theistic religions, however, these activities are neither prayers nor pleas for salvation directed towards a transcendent Other. They are instead useful and inspiring gestures of humility and respect for the profound nobility and worth of the Triple Gem.

Is Vipassana the same as Theravada?

The Pali word *vipassana* — often translated as "insight"— has a variety of meanings. First, it refers to the flash of liberating intuitive understanding that marks the culmination of Buddhist meditation practice. In the Pali discourses *vipassana* also refers to the mind's ability to witness clearly as events unfold in the present moment. In this sense it is a skill that a meditator develops using a broad arsenal of meditative tools and techniques. With practice, this skill can bring the meditator to the threshold of liberating insight.

In its third meaning, one that has become especially popular in the West in recent years, "Vipassana" (usually with a capital "V") refers to a system of meditation — *vipassana bhavana,* or "Insight Meditation" — that is based on an interpretation of the Satipatthana Sutta (MN 10), the Buddha's concise "how-to" guide to the development of mindfulness *(sati).* Followers of the popular Vipassana movement often cite the Satipatthana Sutta as the essence of the Buddha's teachings; some even claim that the instructions it contains are the *only* ones necessary for achieving liberating insight.

Theravada Buddhism, by contrast, embraces the thousands of discourses of the Pali canon, each highlighting a different aspect of the Buddha's teachings. In Theravada each discourse supports, depends upon, reflects, and informs all the others; even a discourse as important as the Satipatthana Sutta is seen as but a single thread in the Buddha's complex tapestry of teachings.

Although many students do find all they want in Vipassana, some have a nagging sense that something fundamental is missing. This reaction is hardly surprising, as the Satipatthana discourse itself was delivered to a group of relatively advanced students who were already quite experienced and well established in the path of Dhamma practice. Happily, all those missing pieces can be found in the Pali canon. In the Canon we find the Buddha's teachings on generosity and virtue, the twin pillars upon which all spiritual practice is built. His teachings on the recollection of the Buddha, Dhamma, and Sangha serve to strengthen the development of *saddha* (faith, confidence), which provides a potent fuel to sustain Dhamma practice long after we return home from that meditation retreat.

In the Canon we also find his teachings on the drawbacks of sensuality and the value of renunciation; on developing *all* the factors in the Eightfold Path, including those that are seldom explored during organized Vipassana retreats: right speech, right livelihood, right effort, and right concentration (meaning jhana). And there is much, much more.

In Theravada, the path to liberating insight does not boil down to a single meditation technique or to being continuously mindful. The path to Awakening is full of surprising twists and turns but, thankfully, the Buddha left for us an assortment of tools to use and skills to learn to help us safely make the journey. If we're all reborn when we die, how does Buddhism explain the world's increasing population?

According to Buddhist cosmology, when a living being passes away he or she is reborn into one of thirty-one distinct "planes" or "realms" of existence, of which the human realm is just one. An increase in the human population simply implies that creatures from other planes are being reborn into the human realm at a rate faster than humans are dying. Likewise, a decline in the human population would imply that humans, upon death, are taking rebirth in other planes (or exiting samsara altogether) at a rate faster than other creatures are taking rebirth as humans. These sorts of population shifts have been occurring for countless eons and in themselves hold little cosmic significance.

If there's no self, then who gets enlightened?

If there's no self, then what gets reborn?

If there's no self, then why...?

Nowhere in the Pali canon does Buddha categorically declare, without qualification, "There is no self." Any question that begins along the lines of, "If there's no self..." is thus inherently misleading, dooming the questioner to a hopeless tangle of confusion — "a thicket of [wrong] views" [MN 2]. Such questions are best put aside altogether in favour of more fruitful lines of questioning. I hear the word "sangha" used a lot these days in Buddhist circles. What does it really mean?

The Pali word "sangha" literally means "group" or "congregation," but when it is used in the suttas, the word usually refers to one of two very specific kinds of groups: either the community of Buddhist monastics *(bhikkhus* and *bhikkhunis),* or the community of people who have attained at least the first stage of Awakening.

In recent decades, a new usage of the word has emerged in the West, one that seems to have no basis in classical Theravada Buddhist teachings: the usage of the word "sangha" to describe a meditation group or any sort of spiritual community. It sounds innocent enough, but this particular usage can — and often does — lead to profound confusion concerning one of the most fundamental underpinnings of the Buddha's teachings, the going for refuge in the Triple Gem.

The act of going for refuge in the Buddha, Dhamma, and Sangha marks a major turning point in one's spiritual development, the real start of the journey down the Buddhist path. It helps foster a healthy attitude towards Buddhist practice by encouraging the development of right view, and serves as a constant reminder both of the goal of practice and of the means to achieve that goal. It is therefore crucial to be clear and precise about the meaning of the refuges, lest we end up heading down a road quite different from the one the Buddha had in mind.

In taking refuge in the Sangha, we set our inner sights on the ideal community of Noble Ones *(ariya-sangha)* — those monks, nuns, laywomen, and laymen who, throughout history, have by their own diligent efforts successfully carried out the Buddha's instructions and gained at least a glimpse of the supreme happiness of nibbana. If this is the direction in which we also wish to go, then it is to these individuals that we should turn for refuge:

The Sangha of the Blessed One's disciples who have practiced well... who have practiced straight-forwardly... who have practiced methodically... who have practiced masterfully — in other words, the four types [of noble disciples] when taken as pairs, the eight when taken as individual types — they are the Sangha of the Blessed One's disciples: worthy of gifts, worthy of hospitality, worthy of offerings, worthy of respect, the incomparable field of merit for the world. — AN 11.12

But going for refuge doesn't stop there. We are also asked to turn to the monastic community *(bhikkhu-sangha)* for refuge, for it is thanks to the unbroken lineage of this 2,600-year-old institution that we are fortunate enough today to be able to hear the teachings.

Moreover, the living example of the monastic community serves to remind us of the immense value of generosity, of living a morally upright life, of renunciation — in short, it reminds us that it is indeed possible to live a life fully in tune with every aspect of the Buddha's teachings. In reality, of course, not every monk or nun necessarily lives up to the Buddha's high standards of conduct. For this reason it is to the *institution* of the Sangha that we turn to refuge, not to the individual members themselves. This is the Sangha to which lay people have turned since the time of the Buddha:

I go to Master Gautama for refuge, to the Dhamma, and to the Sangha of monks. May Master Gautama remember me as a lay follower who has gone to him for refuge, from this day forward, for life. — DN 2, MN 72, SN 51.15, AN 4.184, etc.]

So it is these exceptional groups of people — the *ariya-sangha* and the *bhikkhu-sangha* — that define the Third Gem and Refuge; it is to *these* groups that we are asked to turn for refuge, not to some vaguely defined community of like-minded Dhamma friends and fellow meditators. In which group would you rather put your trust? In an effort to resolve this confusion, some writers have proposed various alternatives to the word "sangha" to describe gatherings and communities of Dhamma companions. But this still leaves me wondering why we must invoke the Pali language here at all. Does a meditation group really need a special name? Why not simply call it a "meditation group" and leave it at that?

"Sangha" is an important term with a rich and precise meaning. It stands for something truly extraordinary and brilliant that can constantly remind us of the highest and most excellent possibilities the Path has to offer. Let's use it well.

What's the Difference between a Buddha and an Arahant?

The attainment of arahantship and Buddha-hood are identical: the attainment of the Deathless (Nibbana) and the complete and irreversible eradication of the defilements, the underlying cause of suffering. It is the Buddha who (re-)discovers the Dhamma on his own; it is the arahant who puts his teachings into practice and follows in his footsteps.

Here is the Buddha's answer to this very question:

> [The Buddha:] *"So what difference, what distinction, what distinguishing factor is there between one rightly self-awakened and a monk discernment-released?"*
>
> A group of monks: *"For us, lord, the teachings have the Blessed One as their root, their guide, & their arbitrator. It would be good if the Blessed One himself would explicate the meaning of this statement. Having heard it from the Blessed One, the monks will remember it."*
>
> *"In that case, monks, listen & pay close attention. I will speak."*
>
> *"As you say, lord," the monks responded.*

The Blessed One said, "The Tathagata — the worthy one, the rightly self-awakened one — is the one who gives rise to the path (previously) unarisen, who engenders the path (previously) unengendered, who points out the path (previously) not pointed out. He knows the path, is expert in the path, is adept at the path. And his disciples now keep following the path and afterwards become endowed with the path.

> *"This is the difference, this the distinction, this the distinguishing between one rightly self-awakened and a monk discernment-released." — SN 22.58*

MAITREYA (METTEYYA)

Have there been other Buddhas?

What's a "Private Buddha" (paccekabuddha)?: According to Theravada tradition, many Buddhas have come and gone over countless eons. Every once in a great while, after a long period of spiritual darkness blankets the world, an individual is eventually born who, through his own efforts, rediscovers the long-forgotten path to Awakening and liberates himself once and for all from the long round of rebirth, thereby becoming an arahant ("worthy one," one who has fully realized Awakening).

If such a being lacks the requisite development of the paramis (perfections of character), he is unable to articulate his discovery to others and is known as a "Silent" or "Private" Buddha *(paccekabuddha)*. If, however, his paramis are fully developed, he is able to deliver his message *(sasana)* to the world and is called, simply, a Buddha.

Some of a Buddha's followers may themselves become arahants, but they are not Buddhas, because they required a Buddha to show them the way to Awakening. (All Buddhas and paccekabuddhas are arahants, but not all arahants are Buddhas or paccekabuddhas) No matter how far and wide the *sasana* spreads, sooner or later it succumbs to the inexorable law of *anicca* (impermanence), and fades from memory. The world descends again into darkness, and the eons-long cycle repeats. The most recent Buddha was born Siddhattha Gautama in India in the sixth century BCE. He is the one we usually mean when we refer to "The Buddha."

The next Buddha due to appear is said to be Maitreya (Skt; Pali: Metteyya), a bodhisatta currently residing in the Tusita heavens. Legend has it that at some time in the far distant future, once the teachings of the current Buddha have long been forgotten, he will be reborn as a human being, rediscover the Four Noble Truths, and teach the Noble Eightfold Path once again.

Although he plays an important role in some Mahayana Buddhist traditions, whose followers appeal to him for favourable rebirth and salvation, he plays an insignificant role in Theravada. I believe he's mentioned only once in the entire Tipitaka, in the Cakkavatti-Sihanada Sutta (DN 26; The Lion's Roar on the Turning of the Wheel):

> *The Buddha: And in that time of the people with an eighty-thousand-year life-span, there will arise in the world a Blessed Lord, an arahant fully enlightened Buddha named Metteyya, endowed with wisdom and conduct, a Well-farer, Knower of the worlds, incomparable Trainer of men to be tamed, Teacher of gods and humans, enlightened and blessed, just as I am now.—The Long Discourses of the Buddha (formerly Thus Have I Heard), Maurice Walshe, trans. (Boston: Wisdom Publications, 1987), p 403f.*

That jolly fellow with the large belly who appears in Chinese and Japanese art—and who serves as a fashionable ornament in countless lawns and gardens—represents Maitreya from a previous lifetime.

THE BUDDHA

On the fullmoon day of May, in the year 623 BC, there was born in the district of Nepal an Indian Sakya Prince named Siddhattha Gautama, who was destined to be the greatest religious teacher in the world. Brought up in the lap of luxury, receiving an education befitting a prince, he married and had a son. His contemplative nature and boundless compassion did not permit him to enjoy the fleeting material pleasures of a Royal household. He knew no woe, but he felt a deep pity for sorrowing humanity. Amidst comfort and prosperity, he realized the universality of sorrow. The palace, with all its worldly amusements, was no longer a congenial place for the compassionate prince. The time was ripe for him to depart. Realizing the vanity of sensual enjoyments, in his twenty-ninth year, he renounced all worldly pleasures and donning the simple yellow garb of an ascetic, alone, penniless, wandered forth in search of Truth and Peace.

It was an unprecedented historic renunciation; for he renounced not in his old age but in the prime of manhood, not in poverty but in plenty. As it was the belief in the ancient days that no deliverance could be gained unless one leads a life of strict asceticism, he strenuously practiced all forms of severe austerities. "Adding vigil after vigil, and penance after penance," he made a superhuman effort for six long years.

His body was reduced to almost a skeleton. The more he tormented his body, the farther his goal receded from him. The painful, unsuccessful austerities which he strenuously practiced proved absolutely futile. He was now fully convinced, through personal experience, of the utter futility of self-mortification which weakened his body and resulted in lassitude of spirit.

Benefiting by this invaluable experience of his, he finally decided to follow an independent course, avoiding the two extremes of self-indulgence and self-mortification. The former retards one's spiritual progress, and the latter weakens one's intellect. The new way which he himself discovered was the Middle Path, *Majjhima Patipada,* which subsequently became one of the salient characteristics of his teaching. One happy morning, while He was deeply absorbed in meditation, unaided and unguided by any supernatural power and solely relying on His efforts and wisdom, He eradicated all defilements, purified Himself, and, realizing things as they truly are, attained Enlightenment (Buddhahood) at the age of 35. He was not born a Buddha, but He became a Buddha by His own striving. As the perfect embodiment of all the virtues He preached, endowed with deep wisdom commensurate with His boundless compassion. He devoted the remainder of His precious life to serve humanity both by example and precept, dominated by no personal motive whatever.

After a very successful ministry of 45 long years the Buddha, as every other human being, succumbed to the inexorable law of change, and finally passed away in His 80th year, exhorting His disciples to regard His doctrine as their teacher.

The Buddha was a human being. As a man He was born, as a man He lived, and as a man His life came to an end. Though a human being, He became an extraordinary man *(Acchariya Manussa),* but He never arrogated to Himself divinity. The Buddha laid stress on this important point and left no room whatever for anyone to fall into the error of thinking that He was an immortal divine being. Fortunately there is no deification in the case of the Buddha. It should, however, be remarked that there was no Teacher, "ever so godless as the Buddha, yet none so god-like."

The Buddha is neither an incarnation of the Hindu God Vishnu, as is believed by some, nor is He a saviour who freely saves others by His personal salvation. The Buddha exhorts His disciples to depend on themselves for their deliverance, for both purity and defilement depend on oneself. Clarifying His relationship with His followers and emphasizing the importance of self-reliance and individual striving, the Buddha plainly states: "You should exert yourselves, the Tathagatas are only teachers."

The Buddhas point out the path, and it is left for us to follow that path to obtain our purification.

"To depend on others for salvation is negative, but to depend on oneself is positive." Dependence on others means a surrender of one's effort.

In exhorting His disciples to be self-dependent the Buddha says in the *Parinibbana Sutta:* "Be ye islands unto yourselves, be ye a refuge unto yourselves, seek not for refuge in others." These significant words are self-elevating. They reveal how vital is self-exertion to accomplish one's object and, how superficial and futile it is to seek redemption through benignant saviours and to crave for illusory happiness in an after life through the propitiation of imaginary Gods or by irresponsive prayers and meaningless sacrifices.

Furthermore, the Buddha does not claim the monopoly of Buddhahood which, as a matter of fact, is not the prerogative of any specially graced person. He reached the highest possible state of perfection any person could aspire to, and without the close-fist of a teacher he revealed the only straight path that leads thereto. According to the Teaching of the Buddha anybody may aspire to that supreme state of perfection if he makes the necessary exertion. The Buddha does not condemn men by calling them wretched sinners, but, on the contrary, He gladdens them by saying that they are pure in heart at conception. In His opinion the world is not wicked but is deluded by ignorance. Instead of disheartening His followers and reserving that exalted state only to Himself, He encourages and induces them to emulate Him, for Buddhahood is latent in all. In one sense all are potential Buddhas.

One who aspires to become a Buddha is called a Bodhisatta, which, literally, means a wisdom-being. This Bodhisatta ideal is the most beautiful and the most refined course of life that has ever been presented to this ego-centric world, for what is nobler than a life of service and purity?

As a Man He attained Buddhahood and proclaimed to the world the latent inconceivable possibilities and the creative power of man. Instead of placing an unseen Almighty God over man who arbitrarily controls the destinies of mankind, and making him subservient to a supreme power, He raised the worth of mankind. It was He who taught that man can gain his deliverance and purification by his own exertion without depending on an external God or mediating priests. It was he who taught the ego-centric world the noble ideal of selfless service. It was He who revolted against the degrading caste system and taught equality of mankind and gave equal opportunities for all to distinguish themselves in every walk of life.

He declared that the gates of success and prosperity were open to all in every condition of life, high or low, saint or criminal, who would care to turn a new leaf and aspire to perfection.

Irrespective of caste, colour or rank He established for both deserving men and women a democratically constituted celibate Order. He did not force His followers to be slaves either to His Teachings or to Himself but granted complete freedom of thought.

He comforted the bereaved by His consoling words. He ministered to the sick that were deserted. He helped the poor that were neglected. He ennobled the lives of the deluded, purified the corrupted lives of criminals. He encouraged the feeble, united the divided, enlightened the ignorant, clarified the mystic, guided the benighted, elevated the base, dignified the noble. Both rich and poor, saints and criminals loved Him alike. Despotic and righteous kings, famous and obscure princes and nobles, generous and stingy millionaires, haughty and humble scholars, destitute paupers, down-trodden scavengers, wicked murderers, despised courtesans — all benefited by His words of wisdom and compassion.

His noble example was a source of inspiration to all. His serene and peaceful countenance was a soothing sight to the pious eyes. His message of Peace and Tolerance was welcomed by all with indescribable joy and was of eternal benefit to every one who had the fortune to hear and practice it.

Wherever His teachings penetrated it left an indelible impression upon the character of the respective peoples. The cultural advancement of all the Buddhist nations was mainly due to His sublime Teachings. In fact all Buddhist countries like Ceylon, Burma, Thailand, Cambodia, Vietnam, Laos, Nepal, Tibet, China, Mongolia, Korea, Japan, etc., grew up in the cradle of Buddhism. Though more than 2500 years have elapsed since the passing away of this greatest Teacher, yet his unique personality exerts a great influence on all who come to know Him.

His iron will, profound wisdom, universal love, boundless compassion, selfless service, historic renunciation, perfect purity, magnetic personality, exemplary methods employed to propagate the Teachings, and his final success — all these factors have compelled about one-fifth of the population of the world today to hail the Buddha as their supreme Teacher.

Paying a glowing tribute to the Buddha Sri Radhakrishnan states: "In Gautama the Buddha we have a master-mind from the East second to none so far as the influence on the thought and life of the human race is concerned, and, sacred to all as the founder of a religious tradition whose hold is hardly less wide and deep than any other. He belongs to the history of the world's thought, to the general inheritance of all cultivated men, for, judged by intellectual integrity, moral earnestness, and spiritual insight, He is undoubtedly one of the greatest figures in history. In *The Three Greatest Men in History* H.G. Wells writes: "In the Buddha you see clearly a man, simple, devout, lonely, battling for light — a vivid human personality, not a myth. He too gave a message to mankind universal in character. Many of our best modern ideas are in closest harmony with it. All the miseries and discontents are due, he taught, to selfishness. Before a man can become serene he must cease to live for his senses or himself.

Then he merges into a great being. Buddha in different language called men to self-forgetfulness 500 years before Christ. In some ways he is nearer to us and our needs. He was more lucid upon our individual importance and service than Christ and less ambiguous upon the question of personal immortality."

St. Hilaire remarks "The perfect model of all the virtues He preaches. His life has not a stain upon it."

Fausboll says — "The more I know of Him, the more I love Him."

A humble follower of his would say — "The more I know Him, the more I love Him; the more I love Him, the more I know Him."

THE DHAMMA

The non-aggressive, moral and philosophical system expounded by the Buddha, which demands no blind faith from its adherents, expounds no dogmatic creeds, encourages no superstitious rites and ceremonies, but advocates a golden mean that guides a disciple through pure living and pure thinking to the gain of supreme wisdom and deliverance from all evil, is called the Dhamma and is popularly known as Buddhism.

The all-merciful Buddha has passed away, but the sublime Dhamma which He unreservedly bequeathed to humanity, still exists in its pristine purity.

Although the Master has left no written records of His Teachings, His distinguished disciples preserved them by committing to memory and transmitting them orally from generation to generation. Immediately after His demise 500 chief Arahats versed in the Dhamma and Vinaya, held a convocation to rehearse the Doctrine as was originally taught by the Buddha. Venerable Ananda Thera, who enjoyed the special privilege of hearing all the discourses, recited the Dhamma, while the Venerable Upali recited the Vinaya.

The *Tipitaka* was compiled and arranged in its present form by those Arahats of old.

During the reign of the pious Sinhala King Vattagamani Abhaya, about 83 BC, the Tipitaka was, for the first time in the history of Buddhism, committed to writing on palm leaves (ola) in Ceylon.

This voluminous *Tipitaka,* which contains the essence of the Buddha's Teaching, is estimated to be about eleven times the size of the Bible. A striking contrast between the Tipitaka and the Bible is that the former is not a gradual development like the latter.

As the word itself implies, the *Tipitaka* consists of three baskets. They are the Basket of Discipline *(Vinaya Pitaka),* the Basket of Discourses *(Sutta Pitaka),* and the Basket of Ultimate Doctrine *(Abhidhamma Pitaka).*

The *Vinaya Pitaka* which is regarded as the sheet anchor to the oldest historic celibate order — the Sangha — mainly deals with rules and regulations which the Buddha promulgated, as occasion arose, for the future discipline of the Order of monks *(Bhikkhus)* and nuns *(Bhikkunis).*

It described in detail the gradual development of the *Sasana* (Dispensation). An account of the life and ministry of the

Buddha is also given. Indirectly it reveals some important and interesting information about ancient history, Indian customs, arts, science, etc.

The Vinaya Pitaka consists of the five following books:

Vibhanga:

1. *Parajika* Pali — Major Offenses
2. *Pacittiya* Pali — Minor Offenses

Khandaka:

3. *Mahavagga* Pali — Greater Section
4. *Cullavagga* Pali — Shorter Section
5. *Parivara* Pali — Epitome of the Vinaya

The *Sutta Pitaka* consists chiefly of discourses, delivered by the Buddha himself on various occasions. There are also a few discourses delivered by some of His distinguished disciples such as the Venerable Sariputta, Ananda, Moggallana, etc., included in it. It is like a book of prescriptions, as the sermons embodied therein were expounded to suit the different occasions and the temperaments of various persons. There may be seemingly contradictory statements, but they should not be misconstrued as they were opportunely uttered by the Buddha to suit a particular purpose: for instance, to the self-same question He would maintain silence (when the inquirer is merely foolishly inquisitive), or give a detailed reply when He knew the inquirer to be an earnest seeker. Most of the sermons were intended mainly for the benefit of Bhikkhus and they deal with the Holy life and with the expositions of the doctrine. There are also several other discourses which deal with both the material and moral progress of His lay followers.

This Pitaka is divided into five Nikayas or collections, viz:

1. *Digha Nikaya* (Collection of Long Discourses).
2. *Majjhima Nikaya* (Collection of Middle-Length Discourses).
3. *Samyutta Nikaya* (Collection of Kindred Sayings).
4. *Anguttara Nikaya* (Collection of Discourses arranged in accordance with numbers).
5. *Khuddaka Nikaya* (Smaller Collection).

The fifth is subdivided into fifteen books:

1. *Khuddaka Patha* (Shorter texts)
2. *Dhammapada* (Way of Truth)
3. *Udana* (Paeans of Joy)
4. *Iti Vuttaka* ("Thus said" Discourses)

5. *Sutta Nipata* (Collected Discourses)
6. *Vimana Vatthu* (Stories of Celestial Mansions)
7. *Peta Vatthu (Stories of Petas)*
8. *Theragatha* (Psalms of the Brethren)
9. *Therigatha* (Psalms of the Sisters)
10. *Jataka* (Birth Stories)
11. *Niddesa* (Expositions)
12. *Patisambhida Magga* (Analytical Knowledge)
13. *Apadana* (Lives of Arahats)
14. *Buddhavamsa* (The History of the Buddha)
15. *Cariya Pitaka* (Modes of Conduct)

The *Abhidhamma Pitaka* is the most important and the most interesting of the three, containing as it does the profound philosophy of the Buddha's Teaching in contrast to the illuminating and simpler discourses in the Sutta Pitaka.

In the *Sutta Pitaka* is found the conventional teaching *(vohara desana)* while in the *Abhidhamma Pitaka* is found the ultimate teaching *(paramattha-desana).*

To the wise, Abhidhamma is an indispensable guide; to the spiritually evolved, an intellectual treat; and to research scholars, food for thought. Consciousness is defined. Thoughts are analyzed and classified chiefly from an ethical standpoint. Mental states are enumerated. The composition of each type of consciousness is set forth in detail. How thoughts arise, is minutely described. Irrelevant problems that interest mankind but having no relation to one's purification, are deliberately set aside. Matter is summarily discussed; fundamental units of matter, properties of matter, sources of matter, relationship between mind and matter, are explained.

The Abhidhamma investigates mind and matter, the two composite factors of the so-called being, to help the understanding of things as they truly are, and a philosophy has been developed on those lines. Based on that philosophy, an ethical system has been evolved, to realize the ultimate goal, Nibbana. The *Abhidhamma Pitaka* consists of seven books:

1. *Dhammasangani* (Classification of Dhammas)
2. *Vibhanga* (The book of Divisions)
3. *Katha-Vatthu* (Points of Controversy)
4. *Puggala-Pannatti* (Descriptions of Individuals)
5. *Dhatu-Katha* (Discussion with reference to elements)
6. *Yamaka* (The Book of Pairs),
7. *Patthana* (The Book of Relations)

In the Tipitaka one finds milk for the babe and meat for the strong, for the Buddha taught His doctrine both to the masses and to the intelligentsia. The sublime Dhamma enshrined in these sacred texts, deals with truths and facts, and is not concerned with theories and philosophies which may be accepted as profound truths today only to be thrown overboard tomorrow.

The Buddha has presented us with no new astounding philosophical theories, nor did He venture to create any new material science. He explained to us what is within and without so far as it concerns our emancipation, as ultimately expounded a path of deliverance, which is unique. Incidentally, He has, however, forestalled many a modern scientist and philosopher.

Schopenhauer in his "World as Will and Idea" has presented the truth of suffering and its cause in a Western garb. Spinoza, though he denies not the existence of a permanent reality, asserts that all phenomenal existence is transitory. In his opinion sorrow is conquered "by finding an object of knowledge which is not transient, not ephemeral, but is immutable, permanent, everlasting."

Berkeley proved that the so-called indivisible atom is a metaphysical fiction. Hume, after a relentless analysis of the mind, concluded that consciousness consists of fleeting mental states. Bergson advocates the doctrine of change. Prof. James refers to a stream of consciousness. The Buddha expounded these doctrines of Transiency, *(Anicca)*, Sorrow *(Dukkha)*, and

No-Soul *(Anatta)* some 2500 years ago while He was sojourning in the valley of the Ganges.

It should be understood that the Buddha did not preach all that He knew. On one occasion while the Buddha was passing through a forest He took a handful of leaves and said:

"O Bhikkhus, what I have taught is comparable to the leaves in my hand. What I have not taught is comparable to the amount of leaves in the forest."

He taught what He deemed was absolutely essential for one's purification making no distinction between an esoteric and exoteric doctrine. He was characteristically silent on questions irrelevant to His noble mission. Buddhism no doubt accords with science, but both should be treated as parallel teachings, since one deals mainly with material truths while the other confines itself to moral and spiritual truths. The subject matter of each is different.

The Dhamma He taught is not merely to be preserved in books, nor is it a subject to be studied from a historical or literary standpoint. On the contrary it is to be learned and put into practice in the course of one's daily life, for without practice one cannot appreciate the truth. The Dhamma is to be studied, and more to be practiced, and above all to be realized; immediate realization is its ultimate goal. As such the Dhamma is compared to a raft which is meant for the sole purpose of escaping from the ocean of birth and death *(Samsara).*

Buddhism, therefore, cannot strictly be called a mere philosophy because it is not merely the "love of, inducing the search after, wisdom." Buddhism may approximate a philosophy, but it is very much more comprehensive.

Philosophy deals mainly with knowledge and is not concerned with practice; whereas Buddhism lays special emphasis on practice and realization.

IS IT A RELIGION?

It is neither a religion in the sense in which that word is commonly understood, for it is not "a system of faith and worship owing any allegiance to a supernatural being."

Buddhism does not demand blind faith from its adherents. Here mere belief is dethroned and is substituted by confidence based on knowledge, which, in Pali, is known as *Saddha*. The confidence placed by a follower on the Buddha is like that of a sick person in a noted physician, or a student in his teacher. A Buddhist seeks refuge in the Buddha because it was He who discovered the Path of Deliverance.

A Buddhist does not seek refuge in the Buddha with the hope that he will be saved by His personal purification. The Buddha gives no such guarantee. It is not within the power of a Buddha to wash away the impurities of others. One could neither purify nor defile another. The Buddha, as Teacher, instructs us, but we ourselves are directly responsible for our purification.

Although a Buddhist seeks refuge in the Buddha, he does not make any self-surrender. Nor does a Buddhist sacrifice his freedom of thought by becoming a follower of the Buddha. He can exercise his own free will and develop his knowledge even to the extent of becoming a Buddha himself.

The starting point of Buddhism is reasoning or understanding, or, in other words, *Samma-ditthi.*

To the seekers of truth the Buddha says:

"Do not accept anything on (mere) hearsay — (i.e., thinking that thus have we heard it from a long time). Do not accept anything by mere tradition — (i.e., thinking that it has thus been handed down through many generations). Do not accept anything on account of mere rumours — (i.e., by believing what others say without any investigation). Do not accept anything just because it accords with your scriptures. Do not accept anything by mere suppositions. Do not accept anything by mere inference. Do not accept anything by merely considering the reasons. Do not accept anything merely because it agrees with your preconceived notions. Do not accept anything merely because it seems acceptable— (i.e., thinking that as the speaker seems to be a good person his words should be accepted). Do not accept

anything thinking that the ascetic is respected by us (therefore it is right to accept his word).

"But when you know for yourselves — these things are immoral, these things are blameworthy, these things are censured by the wise, these things, when performed and undertaken conduce to ruin and sorrow — then indeed do you reject them.

"When you know for yourselves — these things are moral, these things are blameless, these things are praised by the wise, these things, when performed and undertaken, conduce to well-being and happiness — then do you live acting accordingly."

These inspiring words of the Buddha still retain their original force and freshness.

Though there is no blind faith, one might argue whether there is no worshipping of images etc., in Buddhism.

Buddhists do not worship an image expecting worldly or spiritual favours, but pay their reverence to what it represents.

An understanding Buddhist, in offering flowers and incense to an image, designedly makes himself feel that he is in the presence of the living Buddha and thereby gains inspiration from His noble personality and breathes deep His boundless compassion. He tries to follow His noble example.

The Bo-tree is also a symbol of Enlightenment. These external objects of reverence are not absolutely necessary, but they are useful as they tend to concentrate one's attention. An intellectual person could dispense with them as he could easily focus his attention and visualize the Buddha.

For our own good, and out of gratitude, we pay such external respect but what the Buddha expects from His disciple is not so much obeisance as the actual observance of His Teachings. The Buddha says — "He honours me best who practices my teaching best." "He who sees the Dhamma sees me."

With regard to images, however, Count Kevserling remarks— "I see nothing more grand in this world than the image of the Buddha. It is an absolutely perfect embodiment of spirituality in the visible domain." Furthermore, it must be mentioned that there are not petitional or intercessory prayers in Buddhism. However much we may pray to the Buddha we cannot be saved. The Buddha does not grant favours to those who pray to Him. Instead of petitional prayers there is meditation that leads to self-control, purification and enlightenment. Meditation is neither a silent reverie nor keeping the mind blank. It is an active striving. It serves as a tonic both to the heart and the mind. The Buddha not only speaks of the futility of offering prayers but also disparages a slave mentality. A Buddhist should not pray to be saved, but should rely on himself and win his freedom.

> *"Prayers take the character of private communications, selfish bargaining with God. It seeks for objects of earthly ambitions and inflames the sense of self. Meditation on the other hand is self-change." — Sri Radhakrishnan*

In Buddhism there is not, as in most other religions, an Almighty God to be obeyed and feared. The Buddha does not believe in a cosmic potentate, omniscient and omnipresent. In Buddhism there are no divine revelations or divine messengers. A Buddhist is, therefore, not subservient to any higher supernatural power which controls his destinies and which arbitrarily rewards and punishes. Since Buddhists do not believe in revelations of a divine being Buddhism does not claim the monopoly of truth and does not condemn any other religion. But Buddhism recognizes the infinite latent possibilities of man and teaches that man can gain deliverance from suffering by his own efforts independent of divine help or mediating priests.

Buddhism cannot, therefore, strictly be called a religion because it is neither a system of faith and worship, nor "the outward act or form by which men indicate their recognition of the existence of a God or gods having power over their own destiny to whom obedience, service, and honour are due."

If, by religion, is meant "a teaching which takes a view of life that is more than superficial, a teaching which looks into life and not merely at it, a teaching which furnishes men with a guide to conduct that is in accord with this its in-look, a teaching which enables those who give it heed to face life with fortitude and death with serenity," or a system to get rid of the ills of life, then it is certainly a religion of religions.

BUDDHISM AS AN ETHICAL SYSTEM

It no doubt contains an excellent ethical code which is unparalleled in its perfection and altruistic attitude. It deals with one way of life for the monks and another for the laity. But Buddhism is much more than an ordinary moral teaching. Morality is only the preliminary stage on the Path of Purity, and is a means to an end, but not an end in itself. Conduct, though essential, is itself insufficient to gain one's emancipation. It should be coupled with wisdom or knowledge *(panna)*. The base of Buddhism is morality, and wisdom is its apex.

In observing the principles of morality a Buddhist should not only regard his own self but also should have a consideration for others we well — animals not excluded. Morality in Buddhism is not founded on any doubtful revelation nor is it the ingenious invention of an exceptional mind, but it is a rational and practical code based on verifiable facts and individual experience.

It should be mentioned that any external supernatural agency plays no part whatever in the moulding of the character of a Buddhist. In Buddhism there is no one to reward or punish. Pain or happiness are the inevitable results of one's actions. The question of incurring the pleasure or displeasure of a God does not enter the mind of a Buddhist. Neither hope of reward nor fear of punishment acts as an incentive to him to do good or to refrain from evil. A Buddhist is aware of future consequences, but he refrains from evil because it retards, does good because it aids progress to Enlightenment (Bodhi). There are also some who do good because it is good, refrain from evil because it is bad.

To understand the exceptionally high standard of morality the Buddha expects from His ideal followers, one must carefully read the Dhammapada, Sigalovada Sutta, Vyaggapajja Sutta, Mangala Sutta, Karaniya Sutta, Parabhava Sutta, Vasala Sutta,

Dhammika Sutta, etc. As a moral teaching it excels all other ethical systems, but morality is only the beginning and not the end of Buddhism.

- In one sense Buddhism is not a philosophy, in another sense it is the philosophy of philosophies.
- In one sense Buddhism is not a religion, in another sense it is the religion of religions.
- Buddhism is neither a metaphysical path nor a ritualistic path.
- It is neither sceptical nor dogmatic.
- It is neither self-mortification nor self-indulgence.
- It is neither pessimism nor optimism.
- It is neither eternalism nor nihilism.
- It is neither absolutely this-worldly nor other-worldly.
- It is a unique Path of Enlightenment.

The original Pali term for Buddhism is Dhamma, which, literally, means that which upholds. There is no English equivalent that exactly conveys the meaning of the Pali term.

The Dhamma is that which really is. It is the Doctrine of Reality. It is a means of Deliverance from suffering, and Deliverance itself. Whether the Buddhas arise or not the Dhamma exists. It lies hidden from the ignorant eyes of men, till a Buddha, an Enlightened One, realizes and compassionately reveals it to the world.

This Dhamma is not something apart from oneself, but is closely associated with oneself. As such the Buddha exhorts:

> *"Abide with oneself as an island, with oneself as a Refuge. Abide with the Dhamma as an island, with the Dhamma as a Refuge. Seek no external refuge." — Parinibbana Sutta*

SALIENT FEATURES OF BUDDHISM

The foundations of Buddhism are the four Noble Truths— namely, Suffering (the *raison d'etre* of Buddhism), its cause (*i.e.*, Craving), its end (*i.e.*, Nibbana, the Summum Bonum of Buddhism), and the Middle Way.

What is the Noble Truth of Suffering?

"Birth is suffering, old age is suffering, disease is suffering, death is suffering, to be united with the unpleasant is suffering, to be separated from the pleasant is suffering, not to receive what one craves for is suffering, in brief the five Aggregates of Attachment are suffering."

What is the Noble Truth of the Cause of Suffering?

"It is the craving which leads from rebirth to rebirth accompanied by lust of passion, which delights now here now there; it is the craving for sensual pleasures (Kamatanha), for existence (Bhavatanha) and for annihilation (Vibhavatanha)."

What is the Noble Truth of the Annihilation of Suffering?

"It is the remainderless, total annihilation of this very craving, the forsaking of it, the breaking loose, fleeing, deliverance from it."

What is the Noble Truth of the Path leading to the Annihilation of Suffering?

"It is the Noble Eightfold Path which consists of right understanding, right thoughts, right speech, right action, right livelihood, right endeavour, right mindfulness, and right concentration."

Whether the Buddhas arise or not these four Truths exist in the universe. The Buddhas only reveal these Truths which lay hidden in the dark abyss of time.

Scientifically interpreted, the Dhamma may be called the law of cause and effect. These two embrace the entire body of the Buddha's Teachings.

The first three represent the philosophy of Buddhism; the fourth represents the ethics of Buddhism, based on that philosophy. All these four truths are dependent on this body itself. The Buddha states: "In this very one-fathom long body along with perceptions and thoughts, do I proclaim the world, the origin of the world, the end of the world and the path leading to the end of the world." Here the term world is applied to suffering.

Buddhism rests on the pivot of sorrow. But it does not thereby follow that Buddhism is pessimistic. It is neither totally pessimistic nor totally optimistic, but, on the contrary, it teaches a truth that lies midway between them. One would be justified in calling the Buddha a pessimist if He had only enunciated the Truth of suffering without suggesting a means to put an end to it. The Buddha perceived the universality of sorrow and did prescribe a panacea for this universal sickness of humanity. The highest conceivable happiness, according to the Buddha, is Nibbana, which is the total extinction of suffering.

The author of the article on Pessimism in the Encyclopedia Britannica writes: "Pessimism denotes an attitude of hopelessness towards life, a vague general opinion that pain and evil predominate in human affairs. The original doctrine of the Buddha is in fact as optimistic as any optimism of the West. To call it pessimism is merely to apply to it a characteristically Western principle to which happiness is impossible without personality. The true Buddhist looks forward with enthusiasm to absorption into eternal bliss."

Ordinarily the enjoyment of sensual pleasures is the highest and only happiness of the average man. There is no doubt a kind of momentary happiness in the anticipation, gratification and retrospection of such fleeting material pleasures, but they are illusive and temporary. According to the Buddha non-attachment is a greater bliss.

The Buddha does not expect His followers to be constantly pondering on suffering and lead a miserable unhappy life. He exhorts them to be always happy and cheerful, for zest *(Piti)* is one of the factors of Enlightenment.

Real happiness is found within, and is not to be defined in terms of wealth, children, honours or fame. If such possessions are misdirected, forcibly or unjustly obtained, misappropriated or even viewed with attachment, they will be a source of pain and sorrow to the possessors.

Instead of trying to rationalize suffering, Buddhism takes suffering for granted and seeks the cause to eradicate it. Suffering exists as long as there is craving. It can only be annihilated by treading the Noble Eightfold Path and attaining the supreme bliss of Nibbana.

These four Truths can be verified by experience. Hence the Buddha Dhamma is not based on the fear of the unknown, but is founded on the bedrock of facts which can be tested by ourselves and verified by experience. Buddhism is, therefore rational and intensely practical.

Such a rational and practical system cannot contain mysteries or esoteric doctrines. Blind faith, therefore, is foreign to Buddhism. Where there is no blind faith there cannot be any coercion or persecution or fanaticism. To the unique credit of Buddhism it must be said that throughout its peaceful march of 2500 years no drop of blood was shed in the name of the Buddha, no mighty monarch wielded his powerful sword to propagate the Dhamma, and no conversion was made either by force or by repulsive methods. Yet, the Buddha was the first and the greatest missionary that lived on earth.

Aldous Huxley Writes: "Alone of all the great world religions Buddhism made its way without persecution censorship or inquisition."

Lord Russell Remarks: "Of the great religions of history, I prefer Buddhism, especially in its earliest forms; because it has had the smallest element of persecution."

In the name of Buddhism no altar was reddened with the blood of a Hypatia, no Bruno was burnt alive.

Buddhism appeals more to the intellect than to the emotion. It is concerned more with the character of the devotees than with their numerical strength.

On one occasion Upali, a follower of Nigantha Nataputta, approached the Buddha and was so pleased with the Buddha's exposition of the Dhamma that he instantly expressed his desire to become a follower of the Buddha. But the Buddha cautioned him, saying:

"Of a verity, O householder, make a thorough investigation. It is well for a distinguished man like you to make (first) a thorough investigation."

Upali, who was overjoyed at this unexpected remark of the Buddha, said:

"Lord, had I been a follower of another religion, its adherents would have taken me round the streets in a procession proclaiming that such and such a millionaire had renounced his former faith and embraced theirs. But, Lord, Your Reverence advises me to investigate further. The more pleased am I with this remark of yours. For the second time, Lord, I seek refuge in the Buddha, Dhamma and the Sangha."

Buddhism is saturated with this spirit of free enquiry and complete tolerance. It is the teaching of the open mind and the sympathetic heart, which, lighting and warming the whole universe with its twin rays of wisdom and compassion, sheds its genial glow on every being struggling in the ocean of birth and death.

The Buddha was so tolerant that He did not even exercise His power to give commandments to His lay followers. Instead of using the imperative, He said: "It behooves you to do this— It behooves you not to do this." He commands not but does exhort.

This tolerance the Buddha extended to men, women and all living beings.

It was the Buddha who first attempted to abolish slavery and vehemently protested against the degrading caste system which was firmly rooted in the soil of India. In the Word of the Buddha it is not by mere birth one becomes an outcast or a noble, but by one's actions. Caste or colour does not preclude one from becoming a Buddhist or from entering the Order. Fishermen, scavengers, courtesans, together with warriors and Brahmans, were freely admitted to the Order and enjoyed equal privileges and were also given positions of rank. Upali, the barber, for instance, was made in preference to all other the chief in matters pertaining to Vinaya discipline. The timid

Sunita, the scavenger, who attained Arhatship was admitted by the Buddha Himself into the Order.

Angulimala, the robber and criminal, was converted to a compassionate saint. The fierce Alavaka sought refuge in the Buddha and became a saint. The courtesan Ambapali entered the Order and attained Arhatship. Such instances could easily be multiplied from the Tipitaka to show that the portals of Buddhism were wide open to all, irrespective of caste, colour or rank.

It was also the Buddha who raised the status of downtrodden women and not only brought them to a realization of their importance to society but also founded the first celibate religious order for women with rules and regulations.

The Buddha did not humiliate women, but only regarded them as feeble by nature. He saw the innate good of both men and women and assigned to them their due places in His teaching. Sex is no barrier to attaining Sainthood.

Sometimes the Pali term used to denote women is *Matugama,* which means "mother-folk" or "society of mothers." As a mother, woman holds an honourable place in Buddhism. Even the wife is regarded as "best friend" *(parama sakha)* of the husband.

Hasty critics are only making ex parte statements when they reproach Buddhism with being inimical to women. Although at first the Buddha refused to admit women into the Order on reasonable grounds, yet later He yielded to the entreaties of His foster-mother, Pajapati Gotami, and founded the Bhikkhuni Order. Just as the Arahats Sariputta and Moggallana were made the two chief disciples in the Order of monks, even so he appointed Arahats Khema and Uppalavanna as the two chief female disciples. Many other female disciples too were named by the Buddha Himself as His distinguished and pious followers.

On one occasion the Buddha said to King Kosala who was displeased on hearing that a daughter was born to him:

A woman child, O Lord of men; may prove

Even a better offspring than a male.

Many women, who otherwise would have fallen into oblivion, distinguished themselves in various ways, and gained their emancipation by following the Dhamma and entering the Order. In this new Order, which later proved to be a great blessing to many women, queens, princesses, daughters of noble families, widows, bereaved mothers, destitute women, pitiable courtesans— all, despite their caste or rank, met on a common platform, enjoyed perfect consolation and peace, and breathed that free atmosphere which is denied to those cloistered in cottages and palatial mansions.

It was also the Buddha who banned the sacrifice of poor beasts and admonished His followers to extend their loving kindness *(Metta)* to all living beings — even to the tiniest creature that crawls at one's feet. No man has the power or the right to destroy the life of another as life is precious to all.

A genuine Buddhist would exercise this loving-kindness towards every living being and identify himself with all, making no distinction whatsoever with regard to caste, colour or sex.

It is this Buddhist Metta that attempts to break all the barriers which separate one from another. There is no reason to keep aloof from others merely because they belong to another persuasion or another nationality. In that noble Toleration Edict which is based on *Culla-Vyuha* and *Maha-Vyuha* Suttas, Ashoka says: "Concourse alone is best, that is, all should harken willingly to the doctrine professed by others." Buddhism is not confined to any country or any particular nation. It is universal. It is not nationalism which, in other words, is another form of caste system founded on a wider basis. Buddhism, if it be permitted to say so, is supernationalism.

To a Buddhist there is no far or near, no enemy or foreigner, no renegade or untouchable, since universal love realized through understanding has established the brotherhood of all living beings. A real Buddhist is a citizen of the world. He regards the whole world as his motherland and all as his brothers and sisters.

Buddhism is, therefore, unique, mainly owing to its tolerance, non-aggressiveness, rationality, practicability, efficacy and universality. It is the noblest of all unifying influences and the only lever that can uplift the world.

These are some of the salient features of Buddhism, and amongst some of the fundamental doctrines may be said — Kamma or the Law of Moral Causation, the Doctrine of Rebirth, Anatta and Nibbana.

KAMMA OR THE LAW OF MORAL CAUSATION

We are faced with a totally ill-balanced world. We perceive the inequalities and manifold destinies of men and the numerous grades of beings that exist in the universe. We see one born into a condition of affluence, endowed with fine mental, moral and physical qualities and another into a condition of abject poverty and wretchedness. Here is a man virtuous and holy, but, contrary to his expectation, ill-luck is ever ready to greet him. The wicked world runs counter to his ambitions and desires. He is poor and miserable in spite of his honest dealings and piety. There is another vicious and foolish, but accounted to be fortune's darling. He is rewarded with all forms of favours, despite his shortcomings and evil modes of life.

Why, it may be questioned, should one be an inferior and another a superior? Why should one be wrested from the hands of a fond mother when he has scarcely seen a few summers, and another should perish in the flower or manhood, or at the ripe age of eighty or hundred? Why should one be sick and infirm, and another strong and healthy? Why should one be handsome, and another ugly and hideous, repulsive to all? Why should one be brought up in the lap of luxury, and another in absolute poverty, steeped in misery? Why should one be born a millionaire and another a pauper? Why should one be born with saintly characteristics, and another with criminal tendencies? Why should some be linguists, artists, mathematicians or musicians from the very cradle? Why should some be congenitally blind, deaf and deformed? Why should some be blessed and others cursed from their birth?

These are some problems that perplex the minds of all thinking men. How are we to account for all this unevenness of the world, this inequality of mankind? Is it due to the work of blind chance or accident?

There is nothing in this world that happens by blind chance or accident. To say that anything happens by chance, is no more true than that this book has come here of itself. Strictly speaking, nothing happens to man that he does not deserve for some reason or another. Could this be the fiat of an irresponsible Creator? Huxley writes:

"If we are to assume that anybody has designedly set this wonderful universe going, it is perfectly clear to me that he is no more entirely benevolent and just in any intelligible sense of the words, than that he is malevolent and unjust."

According to Einstein:

"If this being (God) is omnipotent, then every occurrence, including every human action, every human thought, and every human feeling and aspiration is also his work; how is it possible to think of holding men responsible for their deeds and thoughts before such an Almighty Being.

"In giving out punishments and rewards, he would to a certain extent be passing judgment on himself. How can this be combined with the goodness and righteousness ascribed to him."

"According to the theological principles man is created arbitrarily and without his desire and at the moment of his creation is either blessed or damned eternally. Hence man is either good or evil, fortunate or unfortunate, noble or depraved, from the first step in the process of his physical creation to the moment of his last breath, regardless of his individual desires, hopes, ambitions, struggles or devoted prayers. Such is theological fatalism." — *Spencer Lewis*

As Charles Bradlaugh says:

"The existence of evil is a terrible stumbling block to the Theist. Pain, misery, crime, poverty confront the

advocate of eternal goodness and challenge with unanswerable potency his declaration of Deity as all-good, all-wise, and all-powerful."

In the words of Schopenhauer:

"Whoever regards himself as having become out of nothing must also think that he will again become nothing; for an eternity has passed before he was, and then a second eternity had begun, through which he will never cease to be, is a monstrous thought.

"If birth is the absolute beginning, then death must be his absolute end; and the assumption that man is made out of nothing leads necessarily to the assumption that death is his absolute end."

Commenting on human sufferings and God, Prof. J.B.S. Haldane writes:

"Either suffering is needed to perfect human character, or God is not Almighty. The former theory is disproved by the fact that some people who have suffered very little but have been fortunate in their ancestry and education have very fine characters. The objection to the second is that it is only in connection with the universe as a whole that there is any intellectual gap to be filled by the postulation of a deity. And a creator could presumably create whatever he or it wanted."

Lord Russell states:

"The world, we are told, was created by a God who is both good and omnipotent. Before He created the world he foresaw all the pain and misery that it would contain. He is therefore responsible for all of it. It is useless to argue that the pain in the world is due to sin. If God knew in advance the sins of which man would be guilty, He was clearly responsible for all the consequences of those sins when He decided to create man."

In "Despair," a poem of his old age, Lord Tennyson thus boldly attacks God, who, as recorded in Isaiah, says, "I make peace and create evil." (Isaiah, xiv. 7.)

"What! I should call on that infinite love that has served us so well? Infinite cruelty, rather that made everlasting hell, Made us, foreknew us, foredoomed us, and does what he will with his own. Better our dead brute mother who never has heard us groan."

Surely "the doctrine that all men are sinners and have the essential sin of Adam is a challenge to justice, mercy, love and omnipotent fairness."

Some writers of old authoritatively declared that God created man in his own image. Some modern thinkers state, on the contrary, that man created God in his own image. With the growth of civilization man's concept of God also became more and more refined.

It is however, impossible to conceive of such a being either in or outside the universe.

Could this variation be due to heredity and environment? One must admit that all such chemico-physical phenomena revealed by scientists, are partly instrumental, but they cannot be solely responsible for the subtle distinctions and vast differences that exist amongst individuals. Yet why should identical twins who are physically alike, inheriting like genes, enjoying the same privilege of upbringing, be very often temperamentally, morally and intellectually totally different?

Heredity alone cannot account for these vast differences. Strictly speaking, it accounts more plausibly for their similarities than for most of the differences. The infinitesimally minute chemico-physical germ, which is about 30 millionth part of an inch across, inherited from parents, explains only a portion of man, his physical foundation. With regard to the more complex and subtle mental, intellectual and moral differences we need more enlightenment. The theory of heredity cannot give a satisfactory explanation for the birth of a criminal in a long line of honourable ancestors, the birth of a saint or a noble man in a family of evil repute, for the arising of infant prodigies, men of genius and great religious teachers.

According to Buddhism this variation is due not only to heredity, environment, "nature and nurture," but also to our own kamma, or in other words, to the result of our own inherited past actions and our present deeds. We ourselves are responsible for our own deeds, happiness and misery. We build our own hells. We create our own heavens. We are the architects of our own fate. In short we ourselves are our own kamma. On one occasion a certain young man named Subha approached the Buddha, and questioned why and wherefore it was that among human beings there are the low and high states.

> *"For," said he, "we find amongst mankind those of brief life and those of long life, the hale and the ailing, the good looking and the ill-looking, the powerful and the powerless, the poor and the rich, the low-born and the high-born, the ignorant and the intelligent."*

The Buddha briefly replied: "Every living being has kamma as its own, its inheritance, its cause, its kinsman, its refuge. Kamma is that which differentiates all living beings into low and high states." He then explained the cause of such differences in accordance with the law of moral causation.

Thus from a Buddhist standpoint, our present mental, intellectual, moral and temperamental differences are mainly due to our own actions and tendencies, both past the present. Kamma, literally, means action; but, in its ultimate sense, it means the meritorious and demeritorious volition *(Kusala Akusala Cetana)*. Kamma constitutes both good and evil. Good gets good. Evil gets evil. Like attracts like. This is the law of Kamma. As some Westerners prefer to say Kamma is "action-influence."

We reap what we have sown. What we sow we reap somewhere or some when. In one sense we are the result of what we were; we will be the result of what we are. In another sense, we are not totally the result of what we were and we will not absolutely be the result of what we are. For instance, a criminal today may be a saint tomorrow.

Buddhism attributes this variation to Kamma, but it does not assert that everything is due to Kamma.

If everything were due to Kamma, a man must ever be bad, for it is his Kamma to be bad. One need not consult a physician to be cured of a disease, for if one's Kamma is such one will be cured. According to Buddhism, there are five orders or processes *(Niyamas)* which operate in the physical and mental realms:

(i) *Kamma Niyama*, order of act and result, e.g., desirable and undesirable acts produce corresponding good and bad results.

(ii) *Utu Niyama*, physical (inorganic) order, *e.g.*, seasonal phenomena of winds and rains.

(iii) *Bija Niyama*, order of germs or seeds (physical organic order); *e.g.*, rice produced from rice-seed, sugary taste from sugar cane or honey etc. The scientific theory of cells and genes and the physical similarity of twins may be ascribed to this order.

(iv) *Citta Niyama*, order of mind or psychic law, *e.g.*, processes of consciousness *(Citta vithi)*, power of mind etc.

(v) *Dhamma Niyama*, order of the norm, *e.g.*, the natural phenomena occurring at the advent of a Bodhisatta in his last birth, gravitation, etc.

Every mental or physical phenomenon could be explained by these all-embracing five orders or processes which are laws in themselves. Kamma is, therefore, only one of the five orders that prevail in the universe. It is a law in itself, but it does not thereby follow that there should be a law-giver. Ordinary laws of nature, like gravitation, need no law-giver. It operates in its own field without the intervention of an external independent ruling agency.

Nobody, for instance, has decreed that fire should burn. Nobody has commanded that water should seek its own level. No scientist has ordered that water should consist of H_2O, and that coldness should be one of its properties. These are their intrinsic characteristics. Kamma is neither fate nor predestination imposed upon us by some mysterious unknown power to which we must helplessly submit ourselves. It is one's own doing reacting on oneself, and so one has the possibility to divert the course of Kamma to some extent. How far one diverts it depends on oneself. It must also be said that such phraseology as rewards and punishments should not be allowed to enter into discussions concerning the problem of Kamma.

For Buddhism does not recognize an Almighty Being who rules His subjects and rewards and punishes them accordingly. Buddhists, on the contrary, believe that sorrow and happiness one experiences are the natural outcome of one's own good and bad actions. It should be stated that Kamma has both the continuative and the retributive principle. Inherent in Kamma is the potentiality of producing its due effect. The cause produces the effect; the effect explains the cause. Seed produces the fruit; the fruit explains the seed as both are inter-related. Even so Kamma and its effect are inter-related; "the effect already blooms in the cause." A Buddhist who is fully convinced of the doctrine of Kamma does not pray to another to be saved but confidently relies on himself for his purification because it teaches individual responsibility.

It is this doctrine of Kamma that gives him consolation, hope, self reliance and moral courage. It is this belief in Kamma "that validates his effort, kindles his enthusiasm," makes him ever kind, tolerant and considerate. It is also this firm belief in Kamma that prompts him to refrain from evil, do good and be good without being frightened of any punishment or tempted by any reward. It is this doctrine of Kamma that can explain the problem of suffering, the mystery of so-called fate or predestination of other religions, and above all the inequality of mankind. Kamma and rebirth are accepted as axiomatic.

REBIRTH

As long as this Kammic force exists there is rebirth, for beings are merely the visible manifestation of this invisible Kammic force. Death is nothing but the temporary end of this temporary phenomenon. It is not the complete annihilation of this so-called being. The organic life has ceased, but the Kammic force which hitherto actuated it has not been destroyed. As the Kammic force remains entirely undisturbed by the disintegration of the fleeting body, the passing away of the present dying thought-moment only conditions a fresh consciousness in another birth. It is Kamma, rooted in ignorance and craving, that conditions rebirth. Past Kamma conditions the present birth; and present Kamma, in combination with past Kamma, conditions the future. The present is the offspring of the past, and becomes, in turn, the parent of the future.

If we postulate a past, present, and a future life, then we are at once faced with the alleged mysterious problem — "What is the ultimate origin of life?" Either there must be a beginning or there cannot be a beginning for life.

One school, in attempting to solve the problem, postulates a first cause, God, viewed as a force or as an Almighty Being.

Another school denies a first cause for, in common experience, the cause ever becomes the effect and the effect becomes the cause. In a circle of cause and effect a first cause is inconceivable. According to the former, life has had a beginning, according to the latter, it is beginningless. From the scientific standpoint, we are the direct products of the sperm and ovum cells provided by our parents. As such life precedes life. With regard to the origin of the first protoplasm of life, or colloid, scientists plead ignorance.

According to Buddhism we are born from the matrix of action (Kammayoni). Parents merely provide an infinitesimally small cell. As such being precedes being. At the moment of conception it is past Kamma that conditions the initial consciousness that vitalizes the fetus. It is this invisible Kammic energy, generated from the past birth that produces mental phenomena and the phenomenon of life in an already extent physical phenomenon, to complete the trio that constitutes man. For a being to be born here a being must die somewhere. The birth of a being, which strictly means the arising of the five aggregates or psycho-physical phenomena in this present life, corresponds to the death of a being in a past life; just as, in conventional terms, the rising of the sun in one place means the setting of the sun in another place. This enigmatic statement may be better understood by imagining life as a wave and not as a straight line. Birth and death are only two phases of the same process. Birth precedes death, and death, on the other hand, precedes birth. The constant succession of birth and death in connection with each individual life flux constitutes what is technically known as *Samsara* — recurrent wandering.

THE ULTIMATE ORIGIN OF LIFE

The Buddha declares:

> *"Without cognizable end is this Samsara. A first beginning of beings, who, obstructed by ignorance and fettered by craving, wander and fare on, is not to be perceived."*

This life-stream flows *ad infinitum,* as long as it is fed by the muddy waters of ignorance and craving. When these two are completely cut off, then only, if one so wishes, does the stream cease to flow, rebirth ends as in the case of the Buddhas and Arahats. An ultimate beginning of this life-stream cannot be determined, as a stage cannot be perceived when this life-force was not fraught with ignorance and craving.

The Buddha has here referred merely to the beginning of the life-stream of living beings. It is left to scientists to speculate on the origin and the evolution of the universe. The Buddha does not attempt to solve all the ethical and philosophical problems that perplex mankind. Nor does He deal with theories and speculations that tend neither to edification nor to enlightenment. Nor does He demand blind faith from His adherents. He is chiefly concerned with the problem of suffering and its destruction. With but this one practical and specific purpose in view, all irrelevant side issues are completely ignored. But how are we to believe that there is a past existence?

The most valuable evidence Buddhists cite in favour of rebirth is the Buddha, for He developed a knowledge which enabled Him to read past and future lives. Following His instructions, His disciples also developed this knowledge and were able to read their past lives to a great extent.

Even some Indian Rishis, before the advent of the Buddha, were distinguished for such psychic powers as clairaudience, clairvoyance, thought-reading, remembering past births, etc.

There are also some persons, who probably in accordance with the laws of association, spontaneously develop the memory of their past birth, and remember fragments of their previous lives. Such cases are very rare, but those few well-attested, respectable cases tend to throw some light on the idea of a past birth. So are the experiences of some modern dependable psychics and strange cases of alternating and multiple personalities. In hypnotic states some relate experiences of their past lives; while a few others, read the past lives of others and even heal diseases. Sometimes we get strange experiences which cannot be explained but by rebirth. How often do we meet persons whom we have never met, and yet instinctively feel that they are quite familiar to us? How often do we visit places, and yet feel impressed that we are perfectly acquainted with those surroundings? The Buddha tells us:

> *"Through previous associations or present advantage, that old love springs up again like the lotus in the water."*

Experiences of some reliable modern psychics, ghostly phenomena, spirit communications, strange alternating and multiple personalities and so on shed some light upon this problem of rebirth. Into this world come Perfect Ones like the Buddhas and highly developed personalities. Do they evolve suddenly? Can they be the products of a single existence?

How are we to account for great characters like Buddhaghosa, Panini, Kalidasa, Homer and Plato; men of genius like Shakespeare, infant prodigies like Pascal, Mozart, Beethoven, Raphael, Ramanujan, etc.? Heredity alone cannot account for them. "Else their ancestry would disclose it, their posterity, even greater than themselves, demonstrate it."

Could they rise to such lofty heights if they had not lived noble lives and gained similar experiences in the past? Is it by mere chance that they are been born or those particular parents and placed under those favourable circumstances?

The few years that we are privileged to spend here or, for the most five score years, must certainly be an inadequate preparation for eternity. If one believes in the present and in the future, it is quite logical to believe in the past. The present is the offspring of the past, and acts in turn as the parent of the future. If there are reasons to believe that we have existed in the past, then surely there are no reasons to disbelieve that we shall continue to exist after our present life has apparently ceased. It is indeed a strong argument in favour of past and future lives that "in this world virtuous persons are very often unfortunate and vicious persons prosperous."

A Western writer says:

"Whether we believe in a past existence or not, it forms the only reasonable hypothesis which bridges certain gaps in human knowledge concerning certain facts of every day life. Our reason tells us that this idea of past birth and Kamma alone can explain the degrees of difference that exist between twins, how men like Shakespeare with a very limited experience are able to portray with marvelous exactitude the most diverse types of human character, scenes and so forth of which they could have no actual knowledge, why the work of the genius invariably transcends his experience, the existence of infant precocity, the vast diversity in mind and morals, in brain and physique, in conditions, circumstances and environment observable throughout the world, and so forth."

It should be stated that this doctrine of rebirth can neither be proved nor disproved experimentally, but it is accepted as an evidentially verifiable fact. The cause of this Kamma, continues the Buddha, is *avijja* or ignorance of the Four Noble Truths. Ignorance is, therefore, the cause of birth and death; and its transmutation into knowingness or *vijja* is consequently their cessation. The result of this analytical method is summed up in the *Paticca Samuppada.*

PATICCA SAMUPPADA

Paticca means because of, or dependent upon: *Samuppada* "arising or origination." *Paticca Samuppada,* therefore, literally means — "Dependent Arising" or "Dependent Origination."

It must be borne in mind that *Paticca Samuppada* is only a discourse on the process of birth and death and not a theory of the ultimate origin of life. It deals with the cause of rebirth and suffering, but it does not in the least attempt to show the evolution of the world from primordial matter.

Ignorance *(Avijja)* is the first link or cause of the wheel of life. It clouds all right understanding. Dependent on ignorance of the Four Noble Truths arise activities *(Sankhara)* — both moral and immoral. The activities whether good or bad rooted in ignorance which must necessarily have their due effects, only tend to prolong life's wandering. Nevertheless, good actions are essential to get rid of the ills of life. Dependent on activities arise rebirth-consciousness *(Vinnana)*. This links the past with the present. Simultaneous with the arising of rebirth-consciousness there come into being mind and body *(Nama-rupa)*.

The six senses *(Salayatana)* are the inevitable consequences of mind and body. Because of the six senses contact *(Phassa)* sets in. Contact leads to feeling *(Vedana)*.

These five — *viz.*, consciousness, mind and matter, six senses, contact and feeling — are the effects of past actions and are called the passive side of life. Dependent on feeling arises craving *(Tanha)*. Craving results in grasping *(Upadana)*. Grasping is the cause of Kamma *(Bhava)* which in its turn, conditions future birth *(Jati)*. Birth is the inevitable cause of old age and death *(Jara-marana)*.

If on account of cause effect comes to be, then if the cause ceases, the effect also must cease. The reverse order of the *Paticca Samuppada* will make the matter clear.

Old age and death are possible in and with a psychophysical organism. Such an organism must be born; therefore it presupposes birth. But birth is the inevitable result of past deeds or Kamma. Kamma is conditioned by grasping which is due to craving. Such craving can appear only where feeling exists. Feeling is the outcome of contact between the senses and objects. Therefore it presupposes organs of senses which cannot exist without mind and body. Where there is a mind there is consciousness. It is the result of past good and evil. The acquisition of good and evil is due to ignorance of things as they truly are.

The whole formula may be summed up thus: Dependent on Ignorance arise Activities (Moral and Immoral)

- Activities arises Consciousness (Rebirth Consciousness)
- Consciousness arise Mind and Matter
- Mind and Matter arise the six Spheres of Sense
- the Six Spheres of Sense arises Contact
- Contact arises Feeling
- Feeling arises Craving
- Craving arises Grasping
- Grasping arise Actions (Kamma)
- Actions arises Rebirth
- Birth arise Decay, Death, Sorrow, Lamentation, Pain, Grief, and Despair.

Thus does the entire aggregate of suffering arise. The first two of these twelve pertain to the past, the middle eight to the present, and the last two to the future. The complete cessation of Ignorance leads to the cessation of Activities. The cessation of Activities leads to the cessation of Consciousness.

- Consciousness leads to the cessation of mind and matter.
- Mind and Matter leads to the cessation of the six Spheres of Sense.
- The six Spheres of Sense leads to the cessation of Contact,
- Contact leads to the cessation of Feeling.
- Feeling leads to the cessation of Craving.
- Craving leads to the cessation of Grasping.
- Grasping leads to the cessation of Actions.
- Actions leads to the cessation of Rebirth.
- Rebirth leads to the cessation of Decay, Death, Sorrow, Lamentation, Pain, Grief, and Despair.

Thus does the cessation of this entire aggregate of suffering result. This process of cause and effect continues ad infinitum. The beginning of this process cannot be determined as it is impossible to say whence this life-flux was encompassed by nescience. But when this nescience is turned into knowledge, and the life-flux is diverted into *Nibbanadhatu,* then the end of the life process of *Samsara* comes about.

ANATTA OR SOUL-LESSNESS

This Buddhist doctrine of rebirth should be distinguished from the theory of re-incarnation which implies the transmigration of a soul and its invariable material rebirth. Buddhism denies the existence of an unchanging or eternal soul created by a God or emanating from a Divine Essence *(Paramatma).* If the immortal soul, which is supposed to be the essence of man, is eternal, there cannot be either a rise or a fall. Besides one cannot understand why "different souls are so variously constituted at the outset."

To prove the existence of endless felicity in an eternal heaven and unending torments in an eternal hell, an immortal soul is absolutely necessary. Otherwise, what is it that is punished in hell or rewarded in heaven?

> *"It should be said," writes Bertrand Russell, "that the old distinction between soul and body has evaporated quite as much because 'matter' has lost its solidity as mind has lost its spirituality. Psychology is just beginning to be scientific. In the present state of psychology belief in immortality can at any rate claim no support from science."*

Buddhists do agree with Russell when he says "there is obviously some reason in which I am the same person as I was yesterday, and, to take an even more obvious example if I simultaneously see a man and hear him speaking, there is some sense in which the 'I' that sees is the same as the 'I' that hears." Till recently scientists believed in an indivisible and indestructible atom. "For sufficient reasons physicists have reduced this atom to a series of events. For equally good reasons psychologists find that mind has not the identity of a single continuing thing but is a series of occurrences bound together by certain intimate relations. The question of immortality, therefore, has become the question whether these intimate relations exist between occurrences connected with a living body and other occurrence which take place after that body is dead."

As C.E.M. Joad says in "The Meaning of Life," matter has since disintegrated under our very eyes. It is no longer solid; it is no longer enduring; it is no longer determined by compulsive causal laws; and more important than all, it is no longer known. The so-called atoms, it seems, are both "divisible and destructible." The electrons and protons that compose atoms "can meet and annihilate one another while their persistence, such as it is, is rather that of a wave lacking fixed boundaries, and in process of continual change both as regards shape and position than that of a thing." Bishop Berkeley who showed that this so-called atom is a metaphysical fiction held that there exists a spiritual substance called the soul.

Hume, for instance, looked into consciousness and perceived hat there was nothing except fleeting mental states and concluded that the supposed "permanent ego" is non-existent.

> *"There are some philosophers," he says, "who imagine we are every moment conscious of what we call 'ourself,' that we feel its existence and its continuance in existence and so we are certain, both of its perfect identity and simplicity. For my part, when I enter most intimately into what I call 'myself' I always stumble on some particular perception or other — of heat or cold, light or shade, love or hatred, pain or pleasure. I never catch myself... and never can observe anything but the perception... nor do I conceive what is further requisite to make me a perfect non-entity."*

Bergson says, "All consciousness is time existence; and a conscious state is not a state that endures without changing. It is a change without ceasing, when change ceases it ceases; it is itself nothing but change." Dealing with this question of soul Prof. James says — "The soul-theory is a complete superfluity, so far as accounting for the actually verified facts of conscious experience goes. So far no one can be compelled to subscribe to it for definite scientific reasons." In concluding his interesting chapter on the soul he says: "And in this book the provisional solution which we have reached must be the final word: the thoughts themselves are the thinkers."

Watson, a distinguished psychologist, states: "No one has ever touched a soul or has seen one in a test tube or has in any way come into relationship with it as he has with the other objects of his daily experience. Nevertheless to doubt its existence is to become a heretic and once might possibly even had led to the loss of one's head. Even today a man holding a public position dare not question it." The Buddha anticipated these facts some 2500 years ago.

According to Buddhism mind is nothing but a complex compound of fleeting mental states. One unit of consciousness consists of three phases — arising or genesis *(uppada)* static or development *(thiti),* and cessation or dissolution *(bhanga).* Immediately after the cessation stage of a thought moment there occurs the genesis stage of the subsequent thought-moment.

Each momentary consciousness of this ever-changing life-process, on passing away, transmits its whole energy, all the indelibly recorded impressions to its successor. Every fresh consciousness consists of the potentialities of its predecessors together with something more. There is therefore, a continuous flow of consciousness like a stream without any interruption. The subsequent thought moment is neither absolutely the same as its predecessor — since that which goes to make it up is not identical — nor entirely another — being the same continuity of Kamma energy. Here there is no identical being but there is an identity in process.

Every moment there is birth, every moment there is death. The arising of one thought-moment means the passing away of another thought-moment and vice versa. In the course of one lifetime there is momentary rebirth without a soul.

It must not be understood that a consciousness is chopped up in bits and joined together like a train or a chain. But, on the contrary, "it persistently flows on like a river receiving from the tributary streams of sense constant accretions to its flood, and ever dispensing to the world without the thought-stuff it has gathered by the way." It has birth for its source and death for its mouth.

The rapidity of the flow is such that hardly is there any standard whereby it can be measured even approximately. However, it pleases the commentators to say that the time duration of one thought-moment is even less than one-billionth part of the time occupied by a flash of lightning. Here we find a juxtaposition of such fleeting mental states of consciousness opposed to a superposition of such states as some appear to believe. No state once gone ever recurs nor is identical with what goes before. But we worldlings, veiled by the web of illusion, mistake this apparent continuity to be something eternal and go to the extent of introducing an unchanging soul, an Atta, the supposed doer and receptacle of all actions to this ever-changing consciousness.

"The so-called being is like a flash of lightning that is resolved into a succession of sparks that follow upon one another with such rapidity that the human retina cannot perceive them separately, nor can the uninstructed conceive of such succession of separate sparks." As the wheel of a cart rests on the ground at one point, so does the being live only for one thought-moment. It is always in the present, and is ever slipping into the irrevocable past. What we shall become is determined by this present thought-moment.

If there is no soul, what is it that is reborn, one might ask. Well, there is nothing to be re-born. When life ceases the Kammic energy re-materializes itself in another form. As Bhikkhu Silacara says: "Unseen it passes whithersoever the conditions appropriate to its visible manifestation are present. Here showing itself as a tiny gnat or worm, there making its presence known in the dazzling magnificence of a Deva or an Archangel's existence.

When one mode of its manifestation ceases it merely passes on, and where suitable circumstances offer, reveals itself afresh in another name or form." Birth is the arising of the psycho-physical phenomena. Death is merely the temporary end of a temporary phenomenon.

Just as the arising of a physical state is conditioned by a preceding state as its cause, so the appearance of psycho-physical phenomena is conditioned by cause anterior to its birth. As the process of one life-span is possible without a permanent entity passing from one thought-moment to another, so a series of life-processes is possible without an immortal soul to transmigrate from one existence to another.

Buddhism does not totally deny the existence of a personality in an empirical sense. It only attempts to show that it does not exist in an ultimate sense. The Buddhist philosophical term for an individual is *Santana, i.e.*, a flux or a continuity. It includes the mental and physical elements as well. The Kammic force of each individual binds the elements together. This uninterrupted flux or continuity of psycho-physical phenomenon, which is conditioned by Kamma, and not limited only to the present life, but having its source in the beginningless past and its continuation in the future — is the Buddhist substitute for the permanent ego or the immortal soul of other religions.

NIBBANA

This process of birth and death continues *ad infinitum* until this flux is transmuted, so to say, to Nibbanadhatu, the ultimate goal of Buddhists. The Pali word Nibbana is formed of *Ni* and *Vana*. *Ni* is a negative particle and *Vana* means lusting or craving. "It is called Nibbana, in that it is a departure from the craving which is called *Vana,* lusting." Literally, Nibbana means non-attachment.

It may also be defined as the extinction of lust, hatred and ignorance, "The whole world is in flames," says the Buddha. "By what fire is it kindled? By the fire of lust, hatred and ignorance, by the fire of birth, old age, death, pain, lamentation, sorrow, grief and despair it is kindled."

It should not be understood that Nibbana is a state of nothingness or annihilation owing to the fact that we cannot perceive it with our worldly knowledge. One cannot say that there exists no light just because the blind man does not see it. In that well known story, too, the fish arguing with his friend, the turtle, triumphantly concluded that there exists no land. Nibbana of the Buddhists is neither a mere nothingness nor a state of annihilation, but what it is no words can adequately express. Nibbana is a Dhamma which is "unborn, unoriginated, uncreated and unformed." Hence, it is eternal *(Dhuva)*, desirable *(Subha)*, and happy *(Sukha)*. In Nibbana nothing is "eternalized," nor is anything "annihilated," besides suffering.

According to the Books references are made to Nibbana as *Sopadisesa* and *Anupadisesa*. These, in fact, are not two kinds of Nibbana, but the one single Nibbana, receiving its name according to the way it is experienced before and after death.

Nibbana is not situated in any place nor is it a sort of heaven where a transcendental ego resides. It is a state which is dependent upon this body itself. It is an attainment (Dhamma) which is within the reach of all. Nibbana is a supramundane state attainable even in this present life. Buddhism does not state that this ultimate goal could be reached only in a life beyond. Here lies the chief difference between the Buddhist conception of Nibbana and the non-Buddhist conception of an eternal heaven attainable only after death or a union with a God or Divine Essence in an after-life. When Nibbana is realized in this life with the body remaining, it is called *Sopadisesa Nibbana-dhatu*. When an arahant attains Parinibbana, after the dissolution of his body, without any remainder of physical existence it is called *Anupadisesa Nibbana-dhatu*.

In the words of Sir Edwin Arnold:

"If any teach Nirvana is to cease

Say unto such they lie.

If any teach Nirvana is to love

Say unto such they err."

From a metaphysical standpoint Nibbana is deliverance from suffering. From a psychological standpoint Nibbana is the eradication of egoism. From an ethical standpoint Nibbana is the destruction of lust, hatred and ignorance. Does the arahant exist or not after death? The Buddha replies:

"The arahant who has been released from the five aggregates is deep, immeasurable like the mighty ocean. To say that he is reborn would not fit the case. To say that he is neither reborn nor not reborn would not fit the case."

One cannot say that an arahant is reborn as all passions that condition rebirth are eradicated; nor can one say that the arahant is annihilated for there is nothing to annihilate. Robert Oppenheimer, a scientist, writes:

"If we ask, for instance, whether the position of the electron remains the same, we must say 'no'; if we ask whether the electron's position changes with time, we must say 'no'; if we ask whether the electron is at rest, we must say 'no'; if we ask whether it is in motion, we must say 'no.'

"The Buddha has given such answers when interrogated as to the conditions of man's self after death; but they are not familiar answers from the tradition of the 17th and 18th century science."

THE PATH TO NIBBANA

How is Nibbana to be Attained?

It is by following the Noble Eightfold Path which consists of Right Understanding *(Samma-ditthi),* Right Thoughts *(samma-sankappa),* Right Speech *(samma-vaca),* Right Actions *(samma-kammanta),* Right Livelihood *(samma-ajiva),* Right Effort *(samma-vayama),* Right Mindfulness *(samma-sati),* and Right Concentration *(samma-samadhi).*

1. *Right Understanding,* which is the key-note of Buddhism, is explained as the knowledge of the four Noble Truths. To understand rightly means to understand things as they really are and not as they appear to be. This refers primarily to a correct understanding of oneself, because, as the Rohitassa Sutta states, "Dependent on this one-fathom long body with its consciousness" are all the four Truths. In the practice of the Noble Eightfold Path, Right

Understanding stands at the beginning as well as at its end. A minimum degree of Right Understanding is necessary at the very beginning because it gives the right motivations to the other seven factors of the Path and gives to them correct direction. At the culmination of the practice, Right Understanding has matured into perfect Insight Wisdom *(vipassana-panna),* leading directly to the Stages of Sainthood.

2. Clear vision of right understanding leads to clear thinking. The second factor of the Noble Eightfold Path is therefore, *Right Thoughts (samma-sankappa),* which serves the double purpose of eliminating evil thoughts and developing pure thoughts. Right Thoughts, in this particular connection, are three fold. They consist of:

   i. Nekkhamma—Renunciation of worldly pleasures or the virtue of selflessness, which is opposed to attachment, selfishness, and possessiveness;

   ii. Avyapada—Loving-kindness, goodwill, or benevolence, which is opposed to hatred, ill-will, or aversion; and

   iii. Avihimsa—Harmlessness or compassion, which is opposed to cruelty and callousness.

3. Right Thoughts lead to *Right Speech,* the third factor. This includes abstinence from falsehood, slandering, harsh words, and frivolous talk.

4. Right Speech must be followed by *Right Action* which comprises abstinence from killing, stealing and sexual misconduct.

5. Purifying his thoughts, words and deeds at the outset, the spiritual pilgrim tries to purify his *livelihood* by refraining from the five kinds of trade which are forbidden to a lay-disciple. They are trading in arms, human beings, animals for slaughter, intoxicating drinks and drugs, and poisons. For monks, wrong livelihood consists of hypocritical conduct and wrong means of obtaining the requisites of monk-life.

6. *Right Effort* is fourfold, namely:
   i. The endeavour to discard evil that has already arisen;
   ii. The endeavour to prevent the arising of unarisen evil;
   iii. The endeavour to develop unarisen good;
   iv. The endeavour to promote the good which has already arisen.
7. *Right Mindfulness* is constant mindfulness with regard to body, feelings, thoughts, and mind-objects.
8. Right Effort and Right Mindfulness lead to *Right Concentration*. It is the one-pointedness of mind, culminating in the Jhanas or meditative absorptions.

Of these eight factors of the Noble Eightfold Path the first two are grouped under the heading of Wisdom *(panna),* the following three under Morality *(sila),* and the last three under Concentration *(samadhi)*. But according to the order of development the sequence is as follows:

I. Morality *(sila)*
Right Speech
Right Action
Right Livelihood

II. Concentration *(samadhi)*
Right Effort
Right Mindfulness
Right Concentration

III. Wisdom *(panna)*
Right Understanding
Right Thoughts

Morality *(sila)* is the first stage on this path to Nibbana.

Without killing or causing injury to any living creature, man should be kind and compassionate towards all, even to the tiniest creature that crawls at his feet. Refraining from stealing, he should be upright and honest in all his dealings.

Abstaining from sexual misconduct which debases the exalted nature of man, he should be pure. Shunning false speech, he should be truthful. Avoiding pernicious drinks that promote heedlessness, he should be sober and diligent.

These elementary principles of regulated behaviour are essential to one who treads the path to Nibbana. Violation of them means the introduction of obstacles on the path which will obstruct his moral progress. Observance of them means steady and smooth progress along the path. The spiritual pilgrim, disciplining thus his words and deeds, may advance a step further and try to control his senses.

While he progresses slowly and steadily with regulated word and deed and restrained senses, the Kammic force of this striving aspirant may compel him to renounce worldly pleasures and adopt the ascetic life. To him then comes the idea that,

> *"A den of strife is household life, And filled with toil and need; But free and high as the open sky, Is the life the homeless lead."*

It should not be understood that everyone is expected to lead the life of a Bhikkhu or a celibate life to achieve one's goal. One's spiritual progress is expedited by being a Bhikkhu although as a lay follower one can become an arahant. After attaining the third state of Sainthood, one leads a life of celibacy. Securing a firm footing on the ground of morality, the progressing pilgrim then embarks upon the higher practice of Samadhi, the control and culture of the mind—the second stage on this Path.

Samadhi—is the "one-pointedness of the mind." It is the concentration of the mind on one object to the entire exclusion of all irrelevant matter. There are different subjects for meditation according to the temperaments of the individuals. Concentration on respiration is the easiest to gain the one-pointedness of the mind. Meditation on loving-kindness is very beneficial as it is conducive to mental peace and happiness. Cultivation of the four sublime states—loving-kindness *(Metta)*, compassion *(Karuna)*, sympathetic joy *(Mudita)*, and equanimity *(Upekkha)* — is highly commendable.

After giving careful consideration to the subject for contemplation, he should choose the one most suited to his temperament. This being satisfactorily settled, he makes a persistent effort to focus his mind until he becomes so wholly absorbed and interested in it, that all other thoughts get ipso facto excluded from the mind.

The five hindrances to progress—namely, sense-desire, hatred, sloth and torpor, restlessness and brooding and doubts are then temporarily inhibited. Eventually he gains ecstatic concentration and, to his indescribable joy, becomes enwrapt in Jhana, enjoying the calmness and serenity of a one-pointed mind.

When one gains this perfect one-pointedness of the mind it is possible for one to develop the five Supernormal Powers *(Abhinna):* Divine Eye *(Dibbacakkhu),* Divine Ear *(Dibhasota),* Reminiscence of past births *(Pubbenivasanussati-nana).* Thought Reading *(Paracitta vijanana)* and different Psychic Powers *(Iddhividha).* It must not be understood that those supernormal powers are essential for Sainthood.

Though the mind is now purified there still lies dormant in him the tendency to give vent to his passions, for by concentration, passions are lulled to sleep temporarily. They may rise to the surface at unexpected moments. Both Discipline and Concentration are helpful to clear the Path of its obstacles but it is Insight *(Vipassana Panna)* alone which enables one to see things as they truly are, and consequently reach the ultimate goal by completely annihilating the passions inhibited by Samadhi. This is the third and the final stage on the Path of Nibbana.

With his one-pointed mind which now resembles a polished mirror he looks at the world to get a correct view of life. Wherever he turns his eyes he sees nought but the Three Characteristics—*Anicca* (transiency), *Dukkha* (sorrow) and *anatta* (soul-lessness) standing out in bold relief.

He comprehends that life is constantly changing and all conditioned things are transient. Neither in heaven nor on earth does he find any genuine happiness, for every form of pleasure is a prelude to pain. What is transient is therefore painful, and where change and sorrow prevail there cannot be a permanent immortal soul.

Whereupon, of these three characteristics, he chooses one that appeals to him most and intently keeps on developing Insight in that particular direction until that glorious day comes to him when he would realize Nibbana for the first time in his life, having destroyed the three Fetters—self-illusion *(Sakkaya-ditthi)*, doubts *(Vicikiccha)*, indulgence in (wrongful) rites and ceremonies *(Silabbataparamasa)*. At this stage he is called a *Sotapanna* (stream-winner)—one who has entered the stream that leads to Nibbana. As he has not eradicated all Fetters he is reborn seven times at the most.

Summoning up fresh courage, as a result of this glimpse of Nibbana, the Pilgrim makes rapid progress and cultivating deeper Insight becomes a *Sakadagami* (onnce-returner) by weakening two more Fetters—namely Sense-desire *(Kamaraga)* and ill-will *(Patigha)*. He is called a Sakadagami because he is reborn on earth only once in case he does not attain Arhatship.

It is in the third state of Sainthood—*Anagama* (never-returner) that he completely discards the aforesaid two Fetters. Thereafter, he neither returns to this world nor does he seek birth in the celestial realms, since he has no more desire for sensual pleasures. After death he is reborn in the "Pure Abodes" *(Suddhavasa)* a congenial Brahma plane, till he attains Arhatship. Now the saintly pilgrim, encouraged by the unprecedented success of his endeavours, makes his final advance and, destroying the remaining Fetters—namely, lust after life in Realms of Forms *(Ruparaga)* and Formless Realms *(Aruparaga)*, conceit *(Mana)*, restlessness *(Uddhacca)*, and ignorance *(Avijja)*—becomes a perfect Saint: an arahant, a Worthy One.

Instantly he realizes that what was to be accomplished has been done, that a heavy burden of sorrow has been relinquished, that all forms of attachment have been totally annihilated, and that the Path to Nibbana has been trodden. The Worthy One now stands on heights more than celestial, far removed from the rebellious passions and defilements of the world, realizing the unutterable bliss of Nibbana and like many an arahant of old, uttering that paean of joy:

"Goodwill and wisdom, mind by method trained,

The highest conduct on good morals based,

This maketh mortals pure, not rank or wealth."

As T.H. Huxley states—"Buddhism is a system which knows no God in the Western sense, which denies a soul to man, which counts the belief in immortality a blunder, which refuses any efficacy to prayer and sacrifice, which bids men to look to nothing but their own efforts for salvation, which in its original purity knew nothing of vows of obedience and never sought the aid of the secular arm: yet spread over a considerable moiety of the world with marvelous rapidity—and is still the dominant creed of a large fraction of mankind."

4

THE CREED OF BUDDHA

The religions of the civilized world may be divided into two great groups, those of which the paramount deity is the Jewish Jehovah, and those of which the paramount deity is the Indian Brahma. Jehovah reigns, under the title of God the Father, over Europe and the continents which Europe has colonized; and, under the title of Allah, over western Asia and northern Africa.

Brahma reigns in the far East, India being under his direct rule, while Indo-China, China, and Japan belong to his "sphere of influence." Even in India he receives but little formal recognition. But he is content that this should be so. He is content that men should worship other gods until the time comes for them to give their hearts to him.

Between these two worlds, which I will call—loosely and inaccurately—the Western and the Eastern, there is a great gulf fixed, a gulf which few minds can pass over from either side. This gulf has been hollowed out by the erosive action of speculative thought. Western thought, which has always been dominated by the crude philosophy of the "average man," instinctively takes for granted the reality of outward things. Eastern thought, which, so far as it has been alive and active, has been mainly esoteric, instinctively takes for granted the reality of the "soul," or inward life. Such at least is the general trend of thought, on its various levels, in each of these dissevered worlds.

As is a man's conception of reality, so is the God whom he worships. Jehovah, the God of the Western world, is an essentially outward deity. Debarred by its instinctive disbelief in the soul from seeking for God in the world within, constrained by the same cause to identify "Nature" with the world without, the Western mind has conceived of a natural order of things which is real because God has made it so, and of a supernatural order of things which is the dwelling-place of God. But because the Western mind, in its quest of reality, must needs look outward, this supernatural order of things is conceived of as a glorified and etherealized replica of the natural order; and God, though veiled from sight by a cloud of splendour and mystery, is made in the image of man. Thus in the Western cosmology there are two worlds, the natural and the supernatural; and two bases of reality, lifeless matter and supernatural will.

In the East, where the soul is the supreme and fundamental reality, the identification of God with the world-soul, or soul of universal Nature, is the outcome of a movement of thought which is at once natural and logical. This divine soul is the only real existence: by comparison with it all outward things are shadows, and all inward things, so far as they hold aloof from the all-embracing consciousness, are dreams. Thus in the Eastern cosmology there is one world, and one centre of reality, the world of our experience seen as it really is, seen by the soul, which, passing inward, in its quest of absolute reality, from veil to veil, and gathering within itself all things that seem to bar its way, arrives at last at the very fountain-head of its being, at its own true self.

There are evils incidental to the worship of each of these sovereign deities. The despotism of the supernatural God tends to reduce to a minimum the spiritual freedom of his subjects. To tell men in precise detail what they are to believe and what they are to do, is to prohibit (under tremendous penalties) all spiritual initiative, and to pander to one of the most demoralizing of all human weaknesses,—the spiritual indolence of the "average man." And as in the higher stages of soul-growth freedom is not merely one of the first conditions of life, but is scarcely to be distinguished from life itself, the autocratic restriction of the spontaneous energies of the soul by codes and creeds, by scriptures and churches, must needs bear deadly fruit. In the present condition of the Mahometan world we see what devastation can be wrought by centuries of blind devotion to the irresponsible Lord of Fate.

In Christendom the character of Jehovah has been profoundly modified (though the change which has been effected is as yet potential rather than actual) by the influence of the Founder of Christianity, whose ideas, whatever may have been the history of their development in his mind, belong in their essence to the creed of the Far East. The gospel of spiritual freedom which Christ consistently preached was long ignored by Christianity—so potent was the sway of Jehovah—and has not yet been consciously accepted; but the leaven of Christ's teaching is now producing a visible ferment, and the struggle of the European mind for freedom bears witness to the efficacy of its action. Yet even in the development of that life-giving and soul-redeeming struggle one can trace the baneful influence of the commonplace and unimaginative philosophy which underlies the worship of Jehovah. The deification of the Supernatural too often ends, as it always begins, in the despiritualization of Nature; and the rejection by progressive thought of a supernatural deity prepares the way for the conscious acceptance of a materialistic "theory of things."

There is another way in which the shadow of the Supernatural tends to blight human life. If freedom is to be strangled, love, which is the most expansive and emancipative of all forces, must first be Wounded and disarmed. Dogmatism, intolerance, and uncharitableness are by-products of the worship of Jehovah. The people or the church which believes itself to have received a supernatural revelation, naturally claims to have exclusive possession of "the truth," and therefore regards all who are beyond the pale of its faith as either outcasts from God's presence or rebels against his will. The attitude of the Jew towards the Gentile, of the Christian towards the "Heathen," of the Mahometan towards the "Infidel," is an attitude of spiritual intolerance in which the "believer" reproduces towards his fellow men the supposed attitude of the "jealous God" whom he worships towards all but a faithful remnant of mankind. In this way supernaturalism tends to introduce hatred—the most anti-spiritual of all passions—into the most sacred of all spheres. The history of the Western world, since it accepted Jehovah as its Lord and Master, has been in the main the history of religious persecutions and religious wars; and men, in perfect good faith, have proved their zeal for God by devoting the bodies of their fellow men to the flames, and their souls to the torments of Hell.

The evils to which the worship of Brahma is exposed are of an entirely different order. Of the creed of him who gives his whole heart to the all-embracing Life I will not attempt to speak. Silence is the true language of cosmic adoration; and it is in sympathetic silence that one should contemplate so pure and profound a creed. When the Western mind accuses the Eastern of pantheism, it instinctively assumes that the Eastern standpoint is the same as its own. In point of fact the "higher pantheism" of the East is an entirely different thing from the materialistic pantheism into which Western thought, in its seasons of revolt from the worship of a supernatural God, is liable to relapse. The only fault that can be found with the former is that very few persons can breathe freely on its exalted heights. To give his heart to One who is not merely supremely real but alone real, and who is therefore in very truth the All of Being, "exceeds man's might." For all but a chosen few the figure of Brahma must needs recede into the dim background. As it recedes, lesser Gods—some beautiful, some terrible, some loathsome, some grotesque—emerge from the darkness and claim man's homage.

The further it recedes, the lowlier are the Gods that man worships. In China and Japan, where faith in the individual soul is strong but the "intuition of totality" is weak, Brahma (or his equivalent) becomes the mere shadow of a shade, and the souls that are worshipped are those of departed men. Thus the creed of the East tends to degenerate either into polytheism, which becomes at last the dead worship of dead Gods, or into ancestor-worship, which is indeed within its limits a living faith and does much for the stability of social life, but which, even in its most exalted moods, can present no higher ideal than that of patriotism to the aspiring souls of its votaries. From the uncharitableness of supernaturalism the creed of the East is, in theory at least, entirely free. All men, without exception, are near and dear to the Universal Soul, for all are sparks from its central fire. More than that, life as such, be it high or low, is sacred because of the fountain from which it issues. Not religious toleration only, but all-embracing charity is of the very essence of the faith that directs itself towards the All. One needs but a superficial acquaintance with the sacred writings of the East to convince oneself that, unlike his Western rival, Brahma is not, in any sense of the word, a "jealous" God. Jehovah's jealousy of other Gods and vindictiveness towards those who worship them suggest that he is conscious of his own limitations and is not secure of his position. Brahma knows that the lesser Gods whom men worship are his Viceroys,—embodiments in their several ways of the ever-changing dream of him, who is All in All, which possesses the growing soul of Humanity; and, far from resenting the worship that is paid to them, he accepts it as meant for himself:

Nay, and of hearts which follow other Gods

In simpler faith, their prayers arise to me,

O Kunti's Son! though they pray wrongfully;

For I am the Receiver and the Lord

Of every sacrifice.

Religions have indeed been persecuted in the East, but always for social or political reasons. Of Buddhism, the dominant creed of the East, one may say more than this; one may say that it has never persecuted, that, in practice as well as principle, it is an entirely tolerant creed. "Throughout the long history of Buddhism," says Dr. Rhys Davids, "... the Buddhists have been uniformly tolerant; and have appealed, not to the sword, but to intellectual and moral suasion. We have not a single instance, throughout the whole period, of even one of those religious persecutions which loom so largely in the history of the Christian church. Peacefully the Reformation began; and in peace, so far as its own action is concerned, the Buddhist church has continued till today." The idea of torturing a fellow-man to death because his theology happens to differ from one's own, is wholly alien from the Eastern tone and temper of thought, as alien as is the assumption which makes religious persecution possible,—the atheistical assumption that Divine Truth can be imprisoned in a form of words.

Each of these dominant types of religion has, as might be expected, its own psychology, its own eschatology, and its own moral and social life. The West regards the soul as dependent on the body, coming into being with the latter, growing with its growth, and either dying at its death or surviving it by the grace of the Supernatural God. The immediate destiny of the departed soul is a matter with regard to which Western theology is, speaking generally, in a state of complete bewilderment. That survival is not regarded as a natural process is proved by the fact that, both in Christendom and in Islam, the immortality to which the believer is taught to look forward is supernatural and quasi-material.

On some future day the outward and visible world (which Western thought identifies with "Nature") will pass away, and a supernatural order of things, also outward and visible, will take its place. The bodies of the dead will then be raised from the grave, and their souls, which meanwhile have been leading a dubious twilight kind of existence, will be restored to them, and will dwell in them for ever, either in the light of God's visible presence or in the lurid darkness of Hell. So the two great religions which sprang from the parent stem of Judaism have authoritatively taught, and so for many centuries the whole of Christendom and the whole of Islam were content to believe.

Supernaturalism is now being slowly undermined; but wherever belief in the Supernatural is dying, belief in survival is dying with it. Modern scepticism, which is based, like the faith that it repudiates, on an instinctive belief in the reality of the outward world and an instinctive disbelief in the reality of the inward life, sees in death the extinction of the soul (which indeed has never been anything but a name) as well as the dissolution of the body. Morality is a function of many variables, of which psychology and eschatology are perhaps the most important. The Soul, which is at once One and Many, is the real bond of union among men; and all communal sentiments, such as attachment to country, clan, or family, are ultimately rooted in the sense of oneness in and through the Universal Self. The Western disbelief in the reality of the soul has hastened the dissolution of communal bonds and interests, and has helped to bring in, perhaps prematurely, the regime of individualism,—a necessary stage in the development of the soul, but one in which selfishness is not merely permitted but directly fostered.

The Western belief in the reality of the outward world, and therefore in the intrinsic worth of outward goods, has made the struggle for wealth, both by nations and individuals, one of the most prominent features of Western civilization. Against this materialistic individualism, this regime of "competitive selfishness," the moral precepts of the founders of Christianity and (in a lesser degree) of Islamism have waged an honourable warfare. But in this struggle they have found the eschatological teaching of the churches a hindrance rather than a help. The idea of a natural connection between this life and the after life, or lives, has been almost wholly lost sight of in the West. A mechanical interpretation has been placed upon each of the rival doctrines of salvation, "faith" having been degraded to the level of belief, and "works" to the level of ceremonial observance. The false dualism (so characteristic of Western thought) which divides the future world into Heaven and Hell, has borne its inevitable fruit.

However tamely the Western mind may have seemed to acquiesce in the formal conceptions of infinite bliss and infinite misery, it has never failed (at any rate in more recent years) to rise in secret revolt against the assumption that in a single brief earth-life either extreme can fairly be earned. The shadow of Hell has at times fallen heavily on human life; but each man in turn has managed to persuade himself that so tremendous and unjust a penalty was not for him. The doctrine of eternal punishment, when steadily faced, is so intolerable as to become at last incredible; and as there are no intermediate states between Heaven and Hell (Purgatory being merely the anteroom of the halls of Heaven), the instinctive recoil of the soul from the latter throws open to all men the portals of the former. The average man of today too readily flatters himself that somehow or other he and his friends will all be "saved." But a Heaven which can be so cheaply earned is scarcely worth striving for. The practical abolition of Hell carries with it the practical abolition of Heaven, for in proportion as the former ceases to deter the latter ceases to attract. Even among those who call themselves believers there is an ever-growing tendency to live wholly in the present, and to turn away from the contemplation of death and its consequences.

Yet the very materialism of the West has been, in a sense, its salvation. The soul of man has grown in the Western world, not because religion has directly fostered its growth, but because circumstances which the very irreligiousness of popular thought—its very indifference to what is inward and spiritual—has helped to create, have actually compelled it to grow. The intense interest which the Western mind takes in the outward world, has caused it to devote itself with whole-hearted energy to the study of physical science. Scientific research prepares the way for practical discoveries and inventions; and these are ever tending to modify—some of them have in recent years revolutionized—the material conditions of human life.

In its efforts to adapt itself to the never-ending changes in its environment which Western inventiveness tends to produce, the soul is not only kept alive and awake, but must needs make considerable growth in certain directions. That the growth which it makes is inharmonious and one-sided; that the spiritual side of it has not kept pace, in its development, with the intellectual; that its spiritual faculties have been to some extent atrophied by the diversion of its vital energies into the channel of mental growth, is unhappily true.

But the fact remains that the sap of life is running strongly in the soul of the Western world; and from this one may perhaps infer that it will make vigorous growth in the right direction, when the higher impulses and the higher guidance for which it is waiting are given to it. Even that strong and ever-growing individualism which, for the time being, seems to have raised selfishness and ambition to the rank of virtues, has a moral value which cannot well be over-estimated. It is in the soil of social individualism that the seeds of freedom and of the love of freedom must be sown; and though in its earlier stages the struggle for freedom may take the form of selfish rebellion against wise and lawful restraint, it is certain that, with the gradual growth of the soul, man's conception of freedom will be expanded and purified, till at last the prize of which he dreams will reveal itself to him as the first condition, nay, as the very counterpart, of spiritual life. In this way—so ready is Nature to turn her loss to gain—the social individualism which is one of the by-products of Western philosophy, tends to become the champion of spiritual freedom against the tyrannical encroachments of supernaturalism,—itself one of the more direct and obvious products of the selfsame tendency of thought.

The psychology of the East is as simple as it is profound. The soul, or inward life, alone is real. Eternity is a vital aspect of reality. Birthlessness and deathlessness are the temporal aspects of eternity. The present existence of the soul is not more certain than its pre-existence and its future existence; and these three—the past, the present, and the future lives—are stages in an entirely natural process. The present life is always brief and fleeting; but the past begins, as the future ends, in eternity, in the timeless life of God himself. Issuing from the Universal Soul, and passing through axons of what I may call pre-natal existence, the soul at last becomes individualized, and enters on a career of conscious activity.

Far from being dependent on the body, it accretes to itself, on whatever plane it may energize, the outward form that it needs and deserves; and, in each of its many deaths, it is the body that dies, deprived of the vitalizing presence that animated it,—not the soul.

Never the spirit was born; the spirit shall cease to be never;

Never was time it was not; End and Beginning are dreams!

Birthless and deathless and changeless remaineth the spirit for ever;

Death has not touched it at all, dead though the house of it seems!

The destiny of the soul is determined by its origin. Issuing from the Universal Soul, it must eventually be reabsorbed into its divine source. Beginning its individualized career as a spiritual germ, it passes through innumerable lives on its way to the goal of spiritual maturity. The development of the germ-soul takes the form of the gradual expansion of its consciousness and the gradual universalization of its life. As it nears its goal, the chains of individuality relax their hold upon it; and at last,—with the final extinction of egoism, with the final triumph of selflessness, with the expansion of consciousness till it has become all-embracing,—the sense of separateness entirely ceases, and the soul finds its true self, or, in other words, becomes fully and clearly conscious of its oneness with the living Whole.

This pure and exalted creed, besides placing before man the highest and truest of all ideals—that of utter selflessness—has the merit of bringing the whole of human life under the dominion of natural law. Indeed, it applies to the life of the soul that great natural law, the discovery of which in the sphere of physical life has been one of the foremost achievements of modern thought,—the law of evolution.

One consequence of this is that the notions of arbitrariness, favouritism, and caprice, which cling, de facto if not de jure, to the conception of a supernatural God, and which introduce a gambling element—a readiness to take risks, a tendency to put off things to the eleventh hour—into the practical morality of the West, have no place in the ethical philosophy of the East.

The Catholic belief in the efficacy of the last rites of the Church, the Protestant belief that a deathbed repentance may open the door of Salvation to one who has led an impious life, bear witness, each in its own way, to the presence in the religious atmosphere of the West of a fantastic conception of God which is absolutely irreconcilable with the primary assumption of Eastern thought. It is of Brahma rather than of Jehovah that the words of the Lawgiver hold good: "God is not a man that he shall lie, neither the son of man that he shall repent." The successive lives of the soul, to which Eastern thought looks backward and forward, are linked together by a chain of natural causation. What a man sows that shall he reap, not in this earth-life only but also in the lives that are yet to be. The primary relation between the individual and the Universal Self is an essentially natural relation; and through this vast conception the whole spiritual world is brought under the dominion of natural law.

So pure, and so exalted is the inner faith of the East, that the excess of these qualities is perhaps its only defect. The ideas that it embodies immensely transcend the normal range of human desire and human thought, with the result that it has ever been and will long continue to be an esoteric creed. Yet the life of the masses in the East owes much to its occult influence. Besides investing the ethics of half the human race with an atmosphere of natural law, the Brahmanic ideal of duty, though beyond the apprehension of ordinary mortals, makes two contributions of inestimable value to the popular morality,—the sentiment of devotion to impersonal causes, and the kindred sense of detachment from material aims and interests. We have seen that, as the figure of Brahma recedes into the dim background, lesser Gods come forth and claim man's homage.

So too, as the Brahmanic ideal (devotion to, culminating in reunion with, the Universal Self) fades into the background, lesser ideals, such as patriotism, tribal loyalty, filial piety, and the like, come forth and claim man's devotion. In Japan, whose people during the past 50 years have transferred to their country the devotion which they formerly gave to the family and the clan, patriotism—as widespread as it is intense—has transformed an obscure, remote, and apparently helpless country into one of the foremost nations of the world. In China, where patriotism has but an embryonic existence, filial piety will move a man to sell himself into slavery or to devote himself to certain death.

Men who value life lightly will set but little store on those perishable accessories of life which the Western world esteems so highly. Among the personal desires which the sentiment of devotion to impersonal causes tends to suppress, the first and most obvious is the desire for material possessions,—the thirst for wealth. One might wander far and wide through Europe and America without finding such calm indifference to the charms of property, on the part of a man of business, as the Burmese contractor displayed who spent five-sixths of his modest income in charity, and was ready to retire from business because he had enough to live on quietly (his personal wants being very few) for the rest of his life. "His action," says the writer who tells of him, "is no exception, but the rule."

But the very disinterestedness of the Oriental mind may well become the cause of its undoing. Just as the West has the qualities of its defects, so the East has the defects of its qualities. The communism and idealism of the East have been unfavourable to the growth of physical science (the nidus of which has been in the main utilitarian), and to the development by man of the material resources of the earth. As science and industrialism are among the chief causes of change in the external conditions of human life, and as the endeavour to adapt itself to a changing environment is one of the chief causes of the development of the human spirit, we seem to be driven to the paradoxical conclusion that the periodic immobility of the East, which arrests the growth of the soul, both by denying it the opportunities for growth and making it revere custom for its own dead sake, is due in no small measure to the very strength of the Eastern faith in the soul.

So too, though the suppression of individuality is the last and highest achievement of the soul in its struggle for spiritual freedom, the war which Eastern thought has ever waged against individualism tends to keep the mass of men in leading strings, and to deny them that initial boon of social freedom without which the struggle for spiritual freedom—a struggle in which the soul is schooled by its very blunders, and taught to conquer by its very failures—cannot well be begun.

Separated from each other for thousands of miles by impassable mountain-chains and pathless deserts, the two worlds—the Eastern and Western—have had so little intercourse with each other, that each in turn has been free to develop, without let or hindrance, its own type of civilization, its own philosophy, its own ideal of life. Of late years, intercourse between the two worlds has been fostered by various causes, and there is reason to believe that it will become closer and more continuous as time goes on.

With the removal of the barriers that held the two worlds apart, their respective ideals will begin to influence each other; and one may venture to hope, or at least to dream, that in the far-off future a new ideal, higher and truer than either of these "mighty opposites," will be evolved by their reciprocal action, and will become the common possession of the whole human race. Meanwhile, it is essential that an attempt should be made by the more advanced spirits in each world to understand the thoughts, the dreams, the aims, the aspirations of the other. Recognition of the profundity of the abyss that parts the two types of mind, is the first step in the direction that I have indicated. Recognition of the possible one-sidedness and inadequacy of one's own spiritual prejudices, is the second.

The thinker of either world who cannot divest himself, even provisionally and hypothetically, of his own habits of thought will never be initiated into the mysteries of the other world. The abyss between East and West is not to be crossed by any bridge of controversial argument; for, owing to the two philosophies having, as philosophies, no common ground of agreement, the piers that should support the bridge could never get down to the bedrock of proof. It is only by outsoaring the abyss on the wings of imaginative sympathy that one may hope to span its depths.

EAST'S WISDOM

There were mighty warriors before the days of Agamemnon, and mighty thinkers before the days of Socrates and Plato. Greatest of all the forgotten thinkers of antiquity, greatest, as it seems to me, of all who have ever consecrated their mental powers to the service of Humanity, was the sage whose vision of reality found expression in the parables and aphorisms of the Upanishads. So lofty was the plane on which his spirit moved that, however high the fountain of idealistic speculation may ascend in its periodic outbursts of activity, it can never do more than seek the level of his thought.

Philosophy is, in its essence, the quest of reality. In the attempt to determine what is real, one has to choose, in the first instance, between the percipient self and the things that it perceives. This choice may seem to be purely metaphysical, but sooner or later it becomes a moral choice and one which is decisive of the chooser's destiny. For him who can face the problem steadily there is, in the last resort, but one possible solution of it. If we may assume that each term of the given antithesis has some measure of reality, we need be in no doubt as to which is the more real.

The problem solves itself, for the simple reason that the decision as to whether the self or the outward world is (relatively) real rests with the self, not with the outward world. It is I who have to make the choice between myself and the world that surrounds me; and I have to make it to my own satisfaction. Is it possible for me to remain impartial? Am I not inevitably prejudiced in favour of myself? If I invest the outward world with reality of any degree or kind, if I persuade myself that it is more real than I am, if, by some metaphysical tour de force, I go so far as to regard it as the substance of which I am merely the shadow, the fact remains that it is I who am guaranteeing its reality; and, that being so, the question inevitably suggests itself: If the guarantor is metaphysically insolvent, what is the value of his guarantee?

The man who can allow himself to say: "I can see the outward world; therefore it is real. But I cannot see my self; therefore I am non-existent": is obviously the victim of a singular confusion of thought. It is sometimes said that the idealist starts with himself, and never gets to the outward world. There are certain dialectical developments of idealism of which this criticism may perhaps hold good; but, as a general criticism of idealism, it is, I think, entirely untrue. The idealist starts, where every thinker must start, with provisional acceptance of the outward world as well as of the percipient self; and, in common with all his fellow men, he invests the former with some measure or degree of reality; but, in the act of guaranteeing its reality, he guarantees (as he has discernment enough to realize) a fuller measure and a higher degree of reality to himself. Nor is the value of the latter guarantee impaired by the patent fact that it is illogical to go surety for oneself. To prove the reality of what alone enables one to prove reality is, for obvious reasons, impossible. But the Universe (as I know it) would melt into a dream-world if I could not place my self at the centre of it; and my inability to prove, or even begin to prove, that my self is real, matters little so long as Nature herself constrains me—with or without the consent of my consciousness—to postulate its reality.

In the choice between the percipient self and the objects of its perception, the thinkers of India threw the whole weight of their thought on the side of the former. The philosophy of the Far East, which has ever been dominated by the "ancient wisdom" of India, bases itself on acceptance of the self or soul, just as the philosophy of the West bases itself on acceptance of the outward world. This is a point on which I have already dwelt, and need not further enlarge. What it now concerns us to notice is that there are vast philosophical conceptions implicit in the germinal assumption of Eastern thought, and that the thinker who speaks to us in of the Upanishads, proved his greatness by the profound insight and the speculative daring with which he developed those conceptions into a world-embracing system of thought.

"The grand, sonorous, long-linked lines"

Let us, with the aid of the Upanishads, attempt to do his thinking for him. If in the microcosm, the world which directly and obviously centres in the individual, the self or conscious subject is real and the objects of its knowledge are by comparison unreal, must it not be the same—one instinctively argues—in the macrocosm, or totality of things?

Is there not at the heart of the Universe a conscious life, and is not this all-conscious life—this Universal Self, as we may call it the supreme reality by reference to which all existent things, when their claims to reality are tested, take their several "stations and degrees"? To argue from one's own experience (whether rightly or wrongly interpreted) to the world at large is permissible, for the simple but sufficient reason that it is inevitable. The man who inclines to materialism when he makes his choice between his own self and the world that environs him, will be a materialist in his general conception of the Universe. The transition from personal to impersonal idealism is equally natural and necessary.

The truth is that the distinction between the microcosm and the macrocosm is a tentative and provisional one, which readily melts away under the solvent influence of speculative thought. The microcosm, as we try to define its boundaries, gradually expands into the macrocosm; and the relation between the two is seen to be one, not of analogy merely, but of ultimate identity. The reality of the Universal Self is as certain as the reality of the individual self; and in the act of accepting the latter we accept the former, with all that it implies.

For Indian thought, then, which started with acceptance of the individual self, Brahma—the Universal Soul or Self—was and is alone real. The first thing that we can say about him is that he is unknown and unknowable. In the world which centres in me, it is I, the knower, who am unknown and unknowable. It is the same in the Cosmos. We must either keep silence when we meditate on Brahma, or speak of him (as the Upanishads habitually do) in the language of paradox and negation. Speech cannot reveal him, for he makes speech possible. Thought cannot reveal him, for he makes thought possible. Sight cannot reveal him, for he makes sight possible. Hearing cannot reveal him, for he makes hearing possible. He is afar and yet near. He is innermost and outermost. Though swifter than the mind, he moves not. All things are in him, and he is in everything. Allow opposites are harmonized in him,—being and non-being, wisdom and unwisdom, right and wrong. He is beyond sight, beyond speech, beyond mind, beyond the known, beyond the unknown. "If thou thinks 'I know him well,' but little sure of Brahma does thou know."

"He is unknown to whoso think they know,

But known to whoso know they know him not."

But though he is in very truth the Unknown and Unknowable, he is not "the Unknowable" of modern European thought. In the "synthetic" philosophy the Unknowable is a background of unreality which brings out into strong belief the reality of the phenomenal world. Or, again, it is a convenient hypothesis which bears, like the scapegoat of old, the sins and follies of idealism, and takes them away into the wilderness of non-existence, and so sets the thinker free to develop, without let or hindrance, a materialistic system of thought. But the Unknowable of Indian philosophy is the most real of all realities. Indeed it is the sum total of reality, the beginning and end of all that really is.

"This is that ultimate and uttermost

Which shall not be beheld, being in a

The unbeholden essence!"

Brahma, then, far from being the pale reflection of our own complacent ignorance, is the innermost reality, in the sense that all existent things have their life and their power in him. This conception finds fitting expression in the parable of Brahma and the Gods. The story goes that Brahma once won a victory for the Gods,—Wind, Fire, and the rest. They thought, "Ours is this victory, our very own the triumph." Knowing their thought, Brahma stood before them. They knew him not, and wondered who he was. They said to Fire, "Find out, all-knowing one, who that wondrous Being is." Fire did their bidding, and, as he drew near to the stranger, was greeted with the words, "Who art thou?" "Why, I am Fire," he answered, "all-knowing Fire am I." "What power is in thine I-ness, then?" said the stranger. "Why, I can burn up everything on earth," said Fire.

Then the stranger set a straw before him, and bade him burn it. He smote it with all his might, but could not even scorch it. So he returned and said, "I could not find out who that wondrous Being is." Then Air was sent on the same quest, and he too was asked, "Who art thou?" "Why, I am Air," he answered, "breather in mother space am I." "What power is in thine I-ness, then?" said the stranger. "Why, I can blow away all things on earth," said Air. Then the stranger set a straw before him, and bade him blow it away. He smote it with all his might, but could not stir it. So he too returned and said, "I could not find out who that wondrous Being is." Then "the Lord" (Indra) was sent; but the stranger, as he drew near to him, vanished from his sight, and where he had been standing there stood a beautiful woman arrayed in gold. Of her the Lord asked who the stranger was. "Brahma," she said. "In Brahma's conquest do ye triumph."

The moral of this story is plain. Individuality is the negation of reality. Apart from the One the individual is nothing. Even the high Gods triumph in Brahma's might. Left to themselves, they have no power, no life. Their selfhood, when severed from the Universal selfhood, is a pure delusion. Fire cannot of himself burn a straw. Air cannot of himself blow a straw away. The Universal Self is the true self of each of the high Gods. It follows, a fortiori, that it is the true self of each individual man. We have seen that the microcosm, as we try to define its boundaries, gradually expands into the macrocosm, and that the relation between the two worlds is one, not of analogy merely, but of ultimate identity.

There is a corollary to this general conception of things, which Indian thought did not fail to draw. As the microcosm expands into the macrocosm, so does what is real in the former—the individual self—expand into what is real in the latter,—the Universal Self.

The relation between the two selves, like the relation between the two worlds, is one, not of analogy merely, but of ultimate identity. As I try to determine what my self really is, I find that it begins to melt into the Universal Self; and at last the idea begins to dawn upon me that the Universal Self, the All-Consciousness, is the real self of each individual man, and that until I have found the Universal Self, made myself one with it, made it in some sort my own, I am not really free to say, "I am I."

This grand conception is the keystone of the whole arch of Indian thought. Let us consider its bearing on human life. We must first remind ourselves that the philosophy of ancient

India brings the whole Universe under the dominion of natural law. The Divine Self does not dwell above or apart from the world of Nature, but at the very heart of it, being indeed the vital essence of Nature,—the revelation to him whose inward eyes are open, of what Nature really is.

It follows that the natural order of things is the expression, or at any rate an expression, of the Divine Self; that the central forces of Nature are a manifestation of the Divine Will; and that through the whole system of natural law the One, who "remains," proves his presence in and through the Many, which "change and pass." The physical science of the West believes itself to have evolved the conception of natural law, and claims to have exclusive rights in it.

But in this, as in other matters, we must distinguish between the conscious and the unconscious apprehension of a philosophic truth. The sense of law and order in Nature is not only common to all human beings, from the savant in his laboratory to the "burnt child" that "dreads the fire," but is also present, however dimly or inchoately, in every organism, however lowly, which adapts itself with any measure of success to the world in which it lives.

But, whereas in the West the conception of natural law has in the main been applied to the outward and visible world, in the East, where the outward and visible world owes such reality as it possesses to its own inward and spiritual life, the conception of law has not merely been applied to the inward and spiritual life, but has been more intimately associated with it than with any other aspect of Nature.

In the Universe, as the popular thought of the West conceives of it, there are two worlds,—the natural, which is under the dominion of law, and the supernatural, which is under the sway of an arbitrary and irresponsible despot, who can also suspend or modify at will the laws of the natural world.

But Eastern thought, in conceiving of the inward life as the real self of Nature, conceived of it also as the ultimate and eternal source of all natural law. Indeed, it is in and through the inward life that Nature—the totality of things—is transformed from a chaos into a Cosmos, from an aggregate of atoms into an organic Whole.

Now the Universal Soul is not only the real self of the whole Universe, but is also, more particularly, the real self of each individual soul. This fundamental fact determines the destiny of Humanity, and the duty (or individualized destiny) of each particular man.

Applying to the life of the human soul the highest of all natural laws—that of organic growth—the thinkers of the East evolved a sublime idealism which may be said to have centred in the following "sovereign dogma." As the destiny of every animal and plant is to find its true self, or, in other words, advance towards the perfection of which its nature is capable,—so the destiny of man, as a "living soul," is to find his true self, by growing into oneness with the Divine or Universal Soul, which is in very truth the ideal perfection of all soul-life.

Having set man this tremendous task, they gave him ample time in which to accomplish it. There is no respect in which the Eastern mind differs so widely from the Western as in the range of their respective visions.

The temporal horizon of Western thought had never, until the discoveries of physical science transformed its conceptions, been more than a few hundreds or, at most, thousands of years from the mental eye of the spectator. A generation ago, it was possible for learned men to believe, in all seriousness, that the Universe was created 4004 years before the birth of Christ. Nor did this grotesque belief begin to fall into discredit until Science had convinced men that the changes which are registered in the strata of the earth's surface had taken millions of years to accomplish.

The idea that cons are needed for the spiritual development of each individual man is one which is still foreign to the Western mind. That a single earth-life, or fraction of a life on earth (for it is never too late for the sinner to repent and be "saved"), can fit the soul for "eternal life," can fit it, in other words, either for immediate admission into the pure light of God's unclouded presence, or for entrance into that Purgatorial world which is the ante-room of Heaven,—this, with the correlative belief that one brief earth-life can earn for a man the tremendous penalty of eternal damnation, is one of the accepted doctrines of all the Christian churches. The very glibness with which the pious Christian talks of dwelling in Heaven "for ever," is the outcome of his spiritual myopia. Eternity, as he calls it, is but a high-sounding name for the wall of darkness which bounds his vision as he looks down the vista of soul-life.

But the Eastern mind has always moved with ease through vast cycles of time; and as its philosophy brings all things—spiritual as well as physical—under the dominion of natural law, and therefore forbids it, in any sphere of thought, to pass from finite causes to infinite effects, it has always instinctively assumed that the process of growth which is to transform the individual into the Universal Self is, speaking generally, of practically immeasurable duration.

In other words, it has always believed that the soul will pass through innumerable lives on its way to its divine goal. That many of these lives must be passed on earth has always been taken for granted.

The obvious fact that in one earth-life man can learn but little of what earth has to teach him, and the further fact that most men die with the desire for the goods and pleasures of earth still strong in their hearts, lead one to expect (once the idea of a plurality of lives has been accepted) that the soul, in the course of its wanderings, will return to earth again and again,—will return, partly in order to widen and enrich its experience, partly in response to attractive forces which it has not yet learned to control. It was in this way that the doctrine of re-incarnation—of a re-incarnating self or Ego—became one of the cardinal articles of the faith of the East.

Let us follow this doctrine into some of its momentous consequences. The prospect of attaining, in the fullness of time, to the infinite bliss of conscious union with the Divine Life must needs disparage the attractions of earth. Those who believe that they will never again return to earth may well cling fondly to this temporal life,—so fondly that they will even project it in imagination into the Heaven to which they look forward. But for the Eastern mind each temporal life was (and is) a stage in a long and toilsome journey,—a journey which seemed to grow ever longer and more toilsome, in proportion as the grandeur of the destiny that awaited the journeying soul was more and more vividly realized.

Hence it was that a kind of high-souled impatience, a "divine home-sickness" (to use Heine's beautiful words), took possession of the nobler spirits in the Eastern world; and the desire to shorten the journey, to escape as early as possible from the "whirlpool of rebirth," grew up and made its presence felt.

The Western mind, which is constitutionally incapable of seeing more than a few years into the future, finds much to satisfy it in the pleasures and pursuits of earth. But the far-sighted Eastern mind, looking beyond the immediate horizon of man's aims and interests, sees that disillusionment and disappointment are the inevitable sequels to success; sees that there is nothing of earth worth possessing, except what is intrinsically unattainable in any earth-life,—nothing, except those prizes which will not be won until the soul, after many wanderings, has entered into possession of its kingdom,—nothing, in fine, except Beauty and Love.

But how was the journey to the inward and spiritual Heaven to be shortened? It was by the actual growth of the soul, with the concomitant expansion of its consciousness, that the goal was to be reached. When the individual consciousness had become all-embracing, the union of the soul with God would obviously be complete.

What if the process of soul-expansion could be abridged? What if the soul could be made to realize—in this or in any future life—to realize fully, finally, and with unfaltering certitude, that all outward things are unsubstantial as shadows, that all the pleasures and interests of earth are evanescent as breaking bubbles, that its own individuality is an illusion,—that nothing, in fine, is real, either in the inward or in the outward world, except the Universal Self, the all-embracing One? If the hollowness and unreality of earth and its treasures could once be realized, would not the attractive force of earth—that subtle power by which it draws the soul back to itself again and again—have ceased to act? Would not the cycle of births and deaths have come to an end? Would not the "peace that passes all understanding" have been won?

The Upanishads are dominated by this idea. The beautiful story of Nachiketas and Death has one burden,—that "he who sees seeming difference" (he who thinks that differences are real, and cannot see the One for the Many) "goes from death to death," whereas he who knows the One, the "all-comprehending One" who is "far beyond distinction's power," escapes from death and inherits eternal life.

It is desire for the things of earth that draws man back to earth; and desire for the things of earth is generated by belief in their reality. Know that they are unreal, and you will cease to desire them. Cease to desire them, and they will no longer draw you back to earth.

"When all desires that linger in his heart are driven forth, the mortal immortal becomes, here Brahman he verily wins. When every knot of earth is here unloosed, then mortal immortal becomes." He who would escape from death must turn his eye away from outward things, and "behold the inner self." "After outward longings fools pursue, they tumble into death's wide-spreading net; whereas, the wise, sure deathlessness conceiving, want nothing here below among uncertain things."

The vision of the One discredits the reality of the Many, and in doing so frees the soul from bondage to desire, and therefore to death and rebirth. "Sole sovereign, inner self of all creation, who makes the one form manifold—the wise who gaze on him within their self, theirs and not others is the bliss that aye endures."

To say that knowledge of reality subdues desires for outward things, is to say, in simpler and homelier language, that reason teaches man self-control. "The man who is subject to reason and mindful, constantly pure, he unto that goal truly reaches from which he is not born again. Aye, the man who hath reason for driver, holding tight unto impulse's reins, he reaches the end of the journey, that home of the Godhead supreme." But the man "who is the prey of unreason, unmindful, ever impure, to that goal such a man never reaches, he goes to births and to deaths."

It is clear, from these and kindred passages, that the thinkers of the East attached immense importance to the effort and initiative of the individual soul. It is also clear that the highest achievement of the soul (as they conceived it) was to know the real from the unreal, and to translate that knowledge into feeling and action. Knowledge of reality was at once the goal of the soul's wanderings, and the path that led to the goal; and, that being so, the goal had but to become fully realized in order to make a sudden and final end of the path that led to itself.

The stress that the Sages of the Upanishads laid on knowledge, and the emancipative power that they ascribed to it, may seem strange to our Western minds. Our own ideas about knowledge have so long been dominated by the provisional assumptions of Physical Science, that there is now only one kind of knowledge—that which has scientific certitude for its counterpart—to which we are willing to apply the name.

But, in truth, the range of knowledge is as wide as that of Nature, and the word has as many shades of meaning as there are degrees in that "diameter of being" which leads from the pole of abstract and impersonal theory to the anti-pole of actual oneness with reality.

To know the supreme truth—that the Universal Self is the only reality, and is therefore the real self of each of us—delivers a man from the circle of life and death, and enables him to enter the great Peace. Were the thinkers of India justified in making salvation dependent on knowledge? Our answer to this question will depend on what we mean by knowledge. Such a truth as that in which the faith of India was rooted, may be apprehended in many ways. Let us consider four of these:

In the first place the truth may be apprehended notionally, as the conclusion to a chain of metaphysical argument.

In the second place it may be apprehended emotionally, as a living personal conviction, akin to the pious Christian's faith.

In the third place it may be apprehended intuitively, as the result of a sudden illumination of consciousness, which, while it lasts, gives a man perfect certitude, making him as sure of what he discerns as he is of his own existence.

In the fourth place it may be apprehended really. A man may become conscious—clearly, fully, and finally—of his own absolute oneness with the Universal Self. This is obviously the highest imaginable type of knowledge; and it is obviously the ultimate outcome of the whole process of soul-growth. It is not until the soul has become divine that it can realize its oneness with God.

Of these four types of knowledge, the sages of the East, in their quest of absolute truth, wavered between the first and the third. The second did not appeal to them, partly because the emotional apprehension of truth is generated and fed by personal influences and is therefore foreign to the impersonal mind of the East, and partly because the ultimate identity of the individual with the Universal Self is a truth too large and fundamental to be apprehended with anything of the nature of personal emotion.

The fourth type of knowledge was, in a sense, the goal of their desire; but they believed that there were short cuts to it; and it was their very endeavour to find those short cuts that led some into the path of metaphysical speculation, and others into the path of mental discipline and inward illumination.

The idea of at once following and abridging the path of soul-growth—the only path to the goal of real knowledge, and the one path which is open to all men—did not suggest itself to them. Yet one of the many advantages of that path is that by following it we necessarily abridge it; and it was inevitable that, sooner or later, some master-mind should discover and reveal to mankind this too obvious truth.

Meanwhile, those whose mental bias predisposed them to approach the sovereign dogma of Eastern philosophy from a dialectical standpoint, set to work to establish its truth by quasi-logical methods,—to demonstrate its soundness as a theory, to show that it was the last link in a flawless chain of metaphysical argument.

But as, in the region of speculative thought, theory and counter-theory are always equal and opposite, each in turn evoking and being evoked by the other, the attempt to grasp the truth of things in a purely "notional" form plunged those who made it into a whirlpool of metaphysical strife.

A truth which, if true at all, is the very counterpart of supreme reality, and which therefore needs, for its apprehension, an atmosphere of perfect mental serenity, became a war-cry in one of those dialectical controversies: and inflamed the angry passions of those whom it should have filled with inward peace. Apart from this, it is obvious that the "notional" apprehension of spiritual truth does not necessarily stimulate the soul to bring forth the fruits of good living; and that in any case it is far beyond the reach of ordinary men.

"Where friend and foe are shadows in the mist"

Other thinkers who had no turn for metaphysical speculation, or to whom the atmosphere of controversy was distasteful, tried to arrive at the truth of things by another and a more direct path.

In various ways—by mental discipline, by ascetic practices, by concentrated meditation—they tried to realize that rare but very real experience, a sudden illumination of consciousness, an experience which, while it lasts, solves all riddles and mysteries by making the inner meaning of life as clear as the light of noon. Such a mode of seeking truth may seem to our Western minds to savour of madness.

But there is always method in the madness of the East. It is possible that some of us, even in the West, have at one time or another experienced, if only for a fleeting moment, a feeling akin to that of which I speak; a feeling of absolute certitude with regard to the ultimate realities of existence; a sense of having been initiated into a mighty mystery, in which all the lesser mysteries that distress and bewilder us are obviously, and of inner necessity, summed up and solved; a sudden and overmastering conviction that the world has, after all, a real and sufficient meaning, and that life is, in its essence, a movement towards a glorious goal.

Generated, as it ordinarily is, by the shock of an overwhelming sorrow or of an overwhelming joy,—a shock which for the moment benumbs all the mental faculties of the ordinary self, and wakes to consciousness a higher and more inward self,—the feeling too often passes away before one has had time to realize its presence.

But, evanescent though it be, the memory of it is ineffaceable; and those who have once experienced it can understand the attraction which that esoteric pathway to reality had for the Indian sage.

Nor are we to assume off-hand that the labours of those who tried to find and follow the pathway were wasted. It is possible and even probable that, in the search for inward illumination, important "psychical" discoveries were made; that some at least among the seekers were enabled to realize, each for himself, the presence in man of clairvoyant senses and occult powers; and that by exercising these they gained, in exceptional cases, clear insight into the very heart of their cherished truth.

There is something in the philosophy of the East, even on its more popular and practical side, which suggests that those who expounded it spoke, not merely out of the abundance of their hearts and the conviction of their minds, but also out of a personal experience, which, though supernormal, was by no means supernatural, and which was at once convincingly actual and transcendently real. 1 But the pathway to the inward light is hard to find and easy to lose; and the methods by which recluses in Indian forests tried to acquire intuitive knowledge of the truth of truths, are not to be followed by ordinary men.

How, then, was that life-giving knowledge to be communicated to the rank and file of mankind? The solution which this problem received was in keeping with the esoteric tendency of Indian thought.

The grand ideas in which the Soul of the East had found refuge could not be communicated as ideas to the average man, who was, ex hypothesi, as incapable of high thinking as of self-culture and mental self-control. Personal faith such as that which the devout Christian reposes in Christ, and in God the Father for Christ's sake, was not expected from him; for it was a vast conception that was presented to him, not a personality or a life.

The truth of things must be taught to him, for he could neither evolve it nor discern it for himself; and though the notion of his growing, in the fulness of time, into oneness with that living truth of things which is the counterpart of supreme reality, was implicit in the creed of his teachers, the immediate bearing of the notion had not yet been realized.

The truth of things must be taught to him; but it was not to be taught to him as abstract truth. What then? One course only remained. The truth must be taught to him symbolically. It must be embodied for him in a ceremonial system, and he must express his belief in it by the due discharge of a series of prescribed rites. This is what happened in India; and the seed which was thus sown bore its inevitable fruit.

The inner meaning of the symbol was gradually forgotten, until at last the symbol was mistaken for the reality to which it bore witness. Then the forces in the East which periodically make for immobility asserted themselves without let or hindrance. The tyranny of ceremonialism—a tyranny which is inherent in the assumption that the truth of things is to be taught ab extra—extinguished spiritual feeling, and suspended, if it did not wholly destroy, the inner life of the people. "Deeper than ever plummet sounded," the Soul of India "lay (as it is lying now) inactive." The process of its evolution was arrested; and the last and safest pathway to reality—the pathway of soul-growth, of the actual expansion and vivification of consciousness—was closed to mankind.

What remedy was there for this state of things? There was a remedy; but it was too obvious to be easily found, and centuries had to pass before it could suggest itself to Eastern thought. The symbolical, equally with the formal, teaching of spiritual truth, ends at last in the substitution of machinery for life. The path of salvation lies elsewhere. If you want the rank and file of mankind to realize the truth of a given conception of life, get them to act—to order their own lives—on the assumption that it is true.

5

PATH OF THE LIFE

Let us suppose that a great prophet appeared on earth, one who was in equal degrees a lover of his kind and a dreamer of spiritual dreams. Let us suppose that this prophet had drunk at the pure fountain of Indian thought, that he had accepted and assimilated the ideas which found expression in the Upanishads, the idea of the reality of the soul, of the development of the individual soul through a chain of earth-lives, of the consummation of this process of development in the union of the individual with the Universal Soul and its consequent admission into a life of unimaginable peace and bliss. Let us further suppose that, when his heart and mind had become saturated with these ideas, he became possessed with the desire to communicate them to his fellow-men. Let us imagine him looking down, from the standpoint of his exalted faith, on the toiling, suffering masses of mankind.

Let us picture to ourselves the sorrow that must have pierced his heart when he saw how profoundly ignorant were the masses of the great truth which he had made his own; how entirely they were absorbed in the pursuit of what was material, trivial, perishable, unreal; how they were living, without knowing it, in a world of shadows and illusions; how even religion, which must once have had an inward meaning, had become for them a round of ceremonies and a network of formula; how dense, in fine, and how deadly were the mists that overhung their lives, and how seldom could those mists be parted by any breath of spiritual freedom, or pierced by any ray of spiritual hope and joy.

Let us suppose that he then looked forward into the future, and saw his fellow men returning to earth again and again, and leading lives as hollow, as purposeless, and as joyless as the lives which they were leading then; the process of their soul-growth being so slow, owing to their fundamental ignorance of reality, that for a long sequence of earth-lives no appreciable progress could be made. Would not the sympathetic sorrow which the vision of the present had awaked in him, be intensified by his vision of the future; and would not the longing to help his fellow men, to enlighten them, to lead them into the path of light and life, become at last an absorbing passion which left no room in his heart for any other desire?

But how could he give men the knowledge that they needed? It was ignorance of reality that had darkened and debased their lives. It was knowledge which they were waiting for, knowledge of what was real and what was true. How could he give them this most rare and most precious of all gifts? How could he transform their sense of reality, and quicken and purify their perception of truth? Philosophical knowledge of the truth of things is, for obvious reasons, beyond the reach of the masses. The average man has no turn for metaphysical speculation, and the worse service that one can render him is to tempt him to indulge in it; for in the atmosphere of verbal controversy reality becomes an abstraction, truth becomes a formula, while love, which is the real unsealer of all spiritual secrets, inevitably withers and dies.

The intuitive apprehension of the truth of things is equally, and for equally obvious reasons, beyond the reach of the masses. The "psychical" faculties, which generate that rare but vividly real type of knowledge, though potentially present in all men, are developed in an exceedingly small minority; and the premature attempt to develop them would end in hysteria being mistaken for inspiration, and hallucination for divine truth.

The emotional apprehension of the truth of things may seem to be within the reach of ordinary men. In reality it also is reserved for a chosen few; for it is only in the genuinely poetic nature that it can maintain its equable heat and pristine purity.

In lower natures it burns itself away in the pitchy flames of undisciplined sentiment, and dies out at last into formalism, dogmatism, and other "bodies of death." Moreover, the teacher who appeals to the spiritual emotion of his disciples, and who thereby enters into emotional relations with them, and through them with their disciples and spiritual descendants, runs one serious risk.

The chances are that, sooner or later, those who come under his influence, without having known him in the flesh, and who are therefore free to construct imaginary pictures of his life and person, will transfer to his personality the devotion which he wished them to give to his ideas, and will end by regarding his inevitable limitations, or rather the limitations of their own imagination—for by this time the teacher will have become a legendary hero—as the very boundaries of reality.

There remains what I have elsewhere called the real apprehension of ultimate truth. This, and this alone, is within the reach of all men. The actual expansion of the soul, in response to the forces in Nature that are making for its development, will give men, little by little, the knowledge that they need; for, as the soul expands, as it increases in wisdom and stature, its consciousness will enlarge its horizon, its vision will become clearer and deeper, and its sense of proportion will be transformed. When the knowledge of reality has been finally won, the attractive forces of earth, which will then be felt to be wholly illusory, will have ceased to act, and the end of the soul's pilgrimage will be at hand. The best service, then, that a man can render to his fellow men is to persuade them to enter the path of soul-growth. Or rather—for they entered it long ago—to follow it, no longer blindly and instinctively, but deliberately and of their own free will; and, by thus consciously cooperating with the expansive forces of Nature, to shorten the path of soul-growth, and to hasten the advent of its glorious goal.

That our prophet, looking at things from the standpoint of his own higher knowledge, should desire to render this service to his fellow men, may be taken for granted. But how should he persuade men that escape from the cycle of earth-lives was intrinsically desirable, that the path of soul-growth was the path of real life, that the goal to which it would lead them was worthy of their highest aspiration and their most strenuous endeavour? If their ignorance of reality was as dense as it seemed to be, to what faculty should he appeal and on what ground of admitted truth should he take his stand?

The relation between knowledge and action, in the sphere of moral life, presents a problem which is insoluble, except on one hypothesis. Our difficulty is that for right action we need right knowledge; that for right knowledge we need inward enlightenment; that for inward enlightenment we need the transforming influence of a life of right action. There is but one way of escape from this seemingly vicious circle. Apply the law of development to the inward life of the soul; and it will become clear that the sense of reality, like every other sense and power, exists in embryo in each individual man.

It is to this embryonic sense of reality that our prophet would make his appeal. In doing so, he would provide both for the development of that sense, and for the concurrent development in the soul of his disciple of the germ of his own teaching. For the sense of reality, like every other sense and power, grows by being exercised; and if it is to be exercised, it must be appealed to and called upon to exert itself. It follows that, in appealing to a man's sense of reality, one helps it to grow; and it follows that, in helping the sense to grow, one trains it to understand and respond to the appeal that is made to it.

We may conjecture, then, that the teacher who wished to lead men to the knowledge of reality would begin by assuming that the sense of reality was latent in every heart. He would say to them, "Does this earth-life really satisfy you? Cannot you see for yourselves that in the last resort it is hollow and unreal? Do the prizes for which you strive content you when you have won them?

Do they not crumble into dust as you grasp them? Everything that earth can give you—health, wealth, pleasure, power, success, fame—proves to be either transient or illusory. Health lasts a few years, and is then undermined by disease and decay.

Wealth has neither meaning nor value except so far as it enables you to buy pleasure, power, success, and fame. Pleasure palls upon you, and at last ceases to please. Or, if it does continue to please, age and disease forbid you to enjoy it. Power brings with it a weight of care and responsibility. Success has its counterpart in failure, for:

'Things won are done: joy's soul lies in the doing.'

Fame is 'Enjoyed no sooner but despised straight.'

Look down the vista of the years. If you continue to desire the things of earth, you will return to earth, drawn by the influences that now attract you, again and again. Does this prospect content you? Has your experience of earth been so happy that you wish to renew it again and again? Is it not true that the earth-life brings real happiness to those only who have found inward peace?

And is it not true that inward peace, though it can transfigure earth and make it spiritual and beautiful, is won by detachment from earth, not by devotion to it? This inward peace, in enjoying which you drink the only draught of real happiness that the earth-life can offer you, is a faint foretaste of what is in store for the soul when all its wanderings are over. Beyond all earth-lives a goal awaits you—a goal which crowns and completes the process of the soul's evolution—the goal of deep, perfect, inexhaustible bliss. This reward will be yours when you have broken the last of the ties by which earth attracts you, and in doing so have escaped, once and for ever, from the 'whirlpool of rebirth.'"

If there was anything in the heart of man which could respond to this appeal, the seed of the prophet's teaching would have been safely sown. His philosophy would have taught him that his appeal would not be made in vain. The germ of divine wisdom is implicit in the germ of soul-life; and the teacher who took for granted that men could see for themselves the inner truth of things, would find that the insight with which he credited them would evolve itself, little by little, in response to his appeal. But, be it carefully observed, he would make his appeal to the people as simple and direct as possible. He would not attempt to base it on metaphysical or theological grounds. He would not employ arguments which appeal to the intellectual faculties only, for he would know that the people have no capacity for abstract speculation, and he would infer from this that the more cogent a metaphysical or a theological argument might seem to be, when addressed to popular thought, the more certain it would be to delude and mislead. The reticence which he would thus impose upon himself might carry him very far, but he would respect all its obligations. He would make no attempt to lead the undeveloped minds of his hearers into the presence of what was ultimate, either in themselves or in the world at large. He would say nothing to them about the "Ego," nothing about God. He would put no truth before them which was not in some measure self-evident.

To say that life, as we know it, is full of pain, sorrow, and disappointment; that its pleasures are transitory and delusive; that its prizes are intrinsically worthless; that the inward peace which moral goodness generates is the only real happiness; and that to escape into a world of inward peace is, therefore, the highest imaginable bliss;—to advance such arguments as these is to appeal to an inward sense which exists potentially in all men. But to go beyond the limits of those simple yet profound conceptions, would be to lead men into a region of doubt, bewilderment, and wordy strife.

Having won from men some measure of assent to the self-evident truths which he had set before them, the teacher would proceed to draw for them the practical inferences from his premises. He would tell them that there was a path, by following which they would become gradually detached from earth and its shadows and delusions, and brought within sight of their spiritual goal; and he would then teach them how to enter that path and walk in it.

The path of deliverance is the path of soul-growth. As the soul grows, and its perceptive faculties widen and deepen, the unreality of the earth-life will become gradually apparent; and when this has been fully realized, the last chain that binds the soul to earth will snap of its own accord, and deliverance will be won. The one thing needful, then, the one thing which every man ought to do and which any man can do, is so to live as to make his soul grow. How is this to be done? We need not go far for an answer to this question. In the first place, all the influences which directly thwart the growth of the soul must be subdued and disarmed.

The lusts and passions of the animal self; the desires and ambitions, the moods and impulses, that are generated by petty egoism; the endencies, whatever they may be, that make for the contraction of the life of the soul, for the restriction of its vital energies to the plane of the lower self,—all these must, for obvious reasons, be kept under due control.

To allow the soul to identify itself with any of the lower selves which egoism seeks to magnify, would be fatal to its spiritual progress. Also, since it is of the essence of the new scheme of life to entrust to each man in turn the duty of ordering his own goings, it is clear that if any carnal or semi-carnal desire or passion were allowed to seize the helm of the will, the voyaging soul would make early shipwreck.

This is the negative side of soul-growth. The positive side is of even greater importance. If the soul is to grow, it must go out of itself into some sphere of being which seems for the moment to lie beyond its own.

Now there are many avenues of escape from the ordinary self; and each of these helps, in its own way, to foster the growth of the soul. But there is one and one only which is open to all men,—the avenue of sympathy, of living or beginning to live in the lives of other persons and other things.

In teaching men to live in the lives of others, our moralist would be content to lead them on from strength to strength, and would make no attempt to initiate them, while they were still in pupilage, into the esoteric mystery of an all-embracing, all-consuming love.

He would take for granted that the germ of sympathy was in every heart, and that the germ would evolve itself, under the stress of the natural forces that make for the expansion of the soul, when once the adverse influences that hindered its outgrowth had been removed or, at least, reduced to inaction. What hinders the outgrowth of sympathy is not the lust of cruelty (for that is a rare and artificial by-product of human development), but the reckless egoism which prompts the strong, in the general struggle for existence, to trample down the weak.

The impulse—half fear, half anger—which makes a man strike in self-defence; the "instinct to live" which makes him ready to sacrifice life in other beings in order that he may preserve it in himself; the desire for material comfort and well-being, which makes him reckless of the comfort and well-being of others, these tendencies are not in themselves incompatible with sympathy, though they may, if uncontrolled, develop into darker and deadlier passions, and generate an egoism more callous and more self-seeking than that from which they spring.

But the scheme of life which we are considering has provided for all the animal and semi-animal passions being placed under due control; and he who had laid this teaching to heart would be ready to receive the further lesson, that he ought to refrain from wanton unkindness, first to his fellow-men, and then to all other living things.

In other words, though he would be left free to take whatever steps might prove to be necessary for the protection and preservation of his life, he would be taught that no wound was to be wantonly inflicted, no life to be recklessly destroyed; and that, speaking generally, each man in turn was to make his pilgrimage on earth as free as might be possible from harm and offence to others.

Under the influence of this teaching, gentleness, kindness, and tolerance would gradually impregnate the atmosphere of man's daily life; and in that atmosphere the germ of sympathy would make strong and steady growth.

To trace the stages in the growth of that soul-expanding germ would be beside my present purpose. That the destiny of sympathy is to transform itself into the passion of spiritual love, can scarcely be doubted. It is of the essence of the individual life to seek to outgrow itself, to seek to mingle itself with other lives on its way to that Universal life which is its own true self; and when once the individual life has begun to lose itself in the lives of others, a process has been initiated, of which absorption into the Universal life—itself the highest imaginable development of love—is the natural and necessary consummation.

But one who was addressing himself to the rank and file of mankind, and was therefore taking thought for the earlier stages of soul-growth, would be careful to disabuse the minds of his disciples of the idea that there was any short cut to spiritual perfection.

The critic who looks at things from the standpoint of the "enthusiasm of humanity," may possibly condemn the gospel of sympathy as a cold and pallid substitute for the gospel of love; but the moralist who had taken upon himself to lead the average man into the path of life, would not allow this criticism to deflect him from his purpose.

Knowing that in the earlier stages of soul-growth self-control was the one thing needful, and that until the self-seeking desires had been mastered the outgrowth of the soul-expanding desires was not to be looked for; and knowing further that sympathy, which has much in common with self-control, and follows naturally from it, would gradually prepare the way for the outgrowth of spiritual love and the desires that are akin to it, or rather would itself, in the natural course of things, develop into these;—knowing this, the idealistic moralist would be content that men should aim in the first instance at the skyline which was visible to them, and that the heights which this hid from view should unfold themselves, little by little, as the soul surmounted the foothills of its life.

Herein he would show his practical wisdom and make good his claim to be a teacher of mankind. The premature development of the "enthusiasm of humanity" and other spiritual passions might well have fatal consequences; for experience has amply proved that the lower desires and impulses are all too ready to masquerade as the higher,—lust, for example, as love, race-hatred as patriotism, religious intolerance as spiritual devotion, egoism as self-respect, censoriousness and uncharitableness as moral zeal.

The truth is that in ordinary men the passion of love necessarily directs itself towards what is individual and quasi-concrete, whereas sympathy, just because it is a colder and paler sentiment, has an immeasurably wider and more abstract range.

There are indeed exceptional natures which can sublimate personal into impersonal love; but, speaking generally, if the impersonal passion of universal love is to be our goal, the safer path to it,—at any rate in the earlier stages of man's development,—will be that of the impersonal sentiment of sympathy rather than the personal passion of love.

The master principle, that deliverance from the illusions of earth is to be won by self-control and sympathy, would be embodied in a simple "Law."

It is in this form, and no other, that the new philosophy of life would have to be presented to the rank and file of mankind. It may be possible for ordinary men to see for themselves that escape from the "whirlpool of rebirth" into the calm haven of inward peace and spiritual bliss, is a desirable end; but the teacher who should try to explain to them that this end was to be compassed by the practice of self-control and the cultivation of sympathy, would find that his words had missed their mark.

The average man has no turn for abstract thinking; and to ask him to trace the logical connection between this or that moral principle and the paramount end of life, is to set him a task beyond his power. What is needed for his edification is to give him a few simple moral rules, and to tell him that these, if faithfully followed, will lead him to the goal that he desires to reach.

But the rules that are given him must be simple and few. In other words, they must be the axiomata media of morality, the broad rules of life which mediate between the master principles of moral action and those meticulous details into which the mind that values rules for their own sake is so ready to descend.

The force and authority of each rule must be self-evident. The teacher must be able to say to his disciples: "Cannot you see for yourselves that this course of action is better than that,—that continence (let us say) is better than incontinence, sobriety than intemperance, kindness than cruelty, gentleness than violence?"

In making this appeal to his disciples he would at once exercise and cultivate their spiritual intelligence and their power of moral choice. When we say that the force and authority of the axiomata media of morality are self-evident, we imply that they stand very near to the moral principles which are behind them, so near that, in yielding to their attractive force, the soul is brought into subconscious contact with the truth and beauty of the teacher's philosophy of life.

We imply, in other words, that the simple rules of a sane morality are in themselves a source of inward illumination, and that the soul which disregards them sins, in some sort, "against light and knowledge" and misuses its power of choice.

To this proposition there are corollaries which are of profound importance.

The growth of the soul, and its consequent absorption into itself of forces and influences which seem to be external to its life, are necessarily accompanied by the diminution of outward pressure and the consequent growth of freedom; and it stands to reason that, when the individual has become one with the Universal Self, so that all forces and all influences are gathered at last within the compass of its conscious life, absolute freedom will have been won.

It follows that freedom is the very counterpart of spiritual life. Now freedom is of two kinds,—freedom to know and freedom to do; and these two are in the last resort one. The teacher who would lead men into the path of life must assume at the outset that man is free, potentially if not actually,—free both to discern good from evil and to make his choice between the two; and he must so shape his teaching that this dual faculty shall be constantly exercised, and to that extent encouraged to grow.

It is because the teacher who limits himself, when framing his Law, to a few axiomata media and refuses to go further into detail, makes ample provision, first for the recognition and then for the culture of spiritual freedom,—it is for this, if for no other reason, that he must take rank as the wisest of Lawgivers.

The superiority of a simple to an elaborate Code of Law, in respect of the services that they respectively render to the cause of spiritual freedom, may be looked at from another point of view.

The connection between the broader rules of conduct and the goal by which obedience to those rules is at last to be rewarded, though possibly not directly traceable by the man of average insight and intelligence, is always felt by him to be natural and real. In an elaborate Code of Law, on the other hand, nine-tenths of the rules that men are directed to obey are so unreasonable and so unattractive that the man who obeys them can neither discern their moral significance, nor see that there is any natural connection between his obedience and his promised goal.

The consequence is that he gets to regard both the law and its reward as wholly alien from his own inward life. He is to obey such and such rules of conduct because he is told to obey them, and for no other reason; and if, and so far as, he is obedient to them, he is to reap such and such rewards, not because there is any natural connection between his conduct and its recompense, but because the irresponsible despot who framed the Code of Law chose, for reasons of his own, to attach certain prizes to obedience, and certain penalties to rebellion.

When such a conception of life and duty has fully established itself, spiritual freedom has been mortally wounded, and the soul has entered the valley of the shadow of death.

Against this danger the teacher who regarded soul-growth as both the way and the end of "salvation," would be ever on his guard.

Not only would he make his moral rules as few, as simple, and as broad as possible, but he would also impress upon his disciples that by obeying those rules, by following the path, which they marked out for them, they would, in the natural course of things, arrive in due season at the promised goal of inward peace and bliss;—a goal which is so vitally connected with the way of living that leads up to it, that those who seek it enjoy it in some measure before they reach it, its foreglow—"the peace which passes all understanding"—falling in ever deepening splendour on each successive stage in the path of life.

He would therefore warn his disciples against whatever scheme of conduct might tend to substitute a mechanical for a spiritual, a supernatural for a natural, conception of life and duty.

Thus he would teach them that "sacrifices and burnt offerings" could profit them nothing; that ceremonial observances had no intrinsic meaning or value; that obedience to rules, for the mere sake of obedience, far from strengthening their souls, would entangle them at last in the clinging meshes of the infinitesimal.

He would teach them, further, that actions produce their natural and necessary consequences, and that the most vital of these is the reaction of what is done on the soul of the doer.

Is the soul really growing? Are the earth-ties being strengthened or weakened? These are the questions which men must learn to ask themselves, and to answer. It is by the strictly natural process of growth, and in no other way, that the soul is to be "saved alive"; and the idealistic teacher would urge his disciples to repudiate the authority of his own law, if it set any other path or any other ideal than that of soul-growth before them.

Above all—and this is perhaps "the conclusion of the whole matter"—the teacher who preached the gospel of soul-growth would impress upon his disciples that each of them must work out his salvation for himself; that he must take the conduct of his life into his own hands; that he must enlist his will-power on the side of those natural forces which are ever making for the expansion of his life; that his will-power was in fact the last and the highest of those natural forces; that its outgrowth had come, gradually and naturally, with the outgrowth of his soul; that whatever tended to arrest its growth tended also, and in an equal degree, to arrest the growth of his soul; that in this, as in other matters, the end of life must control the way, and the way foreshadow the end; that in this, as in other matters, a man must achieve his ideal by applying it to the solution of his practical problems, and giving expression to it in the daily round of his life.

6

BUDDHA AND THE GENERAL MYTHS

In the Sixth Century before the birth of Christ, India, which had long been seething and fermenting with spiritual thought, gave to the world a great teacher. The son of an Indian chieftain, Gaudama Buddha strove for many years to find that inward illumination on "great matters," which was the cherished dream of every serious thinker in that remarkable era. After having followed, to no purpose, the paths of metaphysical speculation, of mental discipline, and of ascetic rigour, he reaped on one memorable night the fruit of his prolonged spiritual effort, the truth of things being of a sudden so clearly revealed to him that thenceforth he never swerved for a moment from devotion to his creed and to the mission that it imposed upon him.

What was the creed of Buddha? What did he teach mankind, and what were the dominant ideas on which he based his teaching? It is, I think, at once easier and more difficult to interpret the creed of Buddha than that of Christ. Unquestionably easier, within certain clearly defined limits. Perhaps more difficult, when once those limits have been passed.

That the moral teaching of Buddha was of such and such a character, that the carefully elaborated scheme of life which has always been attributed to him was really his, can scarcely be doubted. On this point it will suffice if I cite the authority of two well-known Buddhist scholars. "When it is recollected," says Dr. Rhys Davids, "that Gaudama Buddha did not leave behind him a number of deeply simple sayings, from which his followers subsequently built up a system or systems of their own, but had himself thoroughly elaborated his doctrine, partly as to details, after, but in its fundamental points even before, his mission began; that during his long career as teacher, he had ample time to repeat the principles and the details of the system over and over again to his disciples, and to test their knowledge of it; and finally that his leading disciples were, like himself, accustomed to the subtlest metaphysical distinctions, and trained to that wonderful command of memory which Indian ascetics then possessed; when these facts are recalled to mind, it will be seen that much more reliance may reasonably be placed upon the doctrinal parts of the Buddhist Scriptures than upon correspondingly late records of other religions."

Dr. Oldenberg speaks to the same general effect: "On the whole we shall be authorized to refer to Buddha himself the most essential trains of thought which we find recorded in the Sacred Texts, and in many cases it is probably not too much to believe that the very words in which the ascetic of the Sakya house couched his gospel of deliverance, have come down to us as they fell from his lips. We find that throughout the vast complex of ancient Buddhist literature which has been collected, certain mottoes and formulas, the expression of Buddhist convictions upon some of the weightiest problems of religious thought, are expressed over and over again in a standard form adopted once for all.

Why may not these be words which have received their currency from the founder of Buddhism, which had been spoken by him hundreds and thousands of times throughout his long life devoted to teaching?" Whatever else Buddha may have been, he was a serious and systematic teacher who was deeply impressed with the belief that it was his mission to lead men into the path of salvation,—a broad path, as he conceived it, but clearly defined; and as his missionary life lasted for forty-five years, and was one of incessant preaching and teaching; we may well believe that he mapped out the path with extreme care and accuracy, and that the chart of life which he thus elaborated was preserved in all its detail by the retentive memory of his listeners and their disciples, and has come down intact to the present day. We also assume with confidence that tradition has faithfully preserved that part of his teaching in which he gave reasons for the faith that was in him. It is certain that he urged men to enter and walk in the path in order that, by extinguishing all desire for earthly things, they might win deliverance from the earth-life, with its attendant suffering, and attain to that blessed state of being which he called Nirvana. It is further certain that he believed in re-incarnation, and took for granted that those who listened to him held the same belief; and that therefore he meant by deliverance from earth deliverance from the "whirlpool of rebirth," deliverance from the cycle of earth-lives which the unenlightened soul is bound to pass through.

This much is practically certain. But when we ask ourselves what Buddha meant by re-incarnation—a question which must be asked, and which obviously gives rise to other questions wider and deeper than itself—we come to the verge of what is obscure and dubious; and the very next step takes us into a region of pure conjecture in which at present there is neither path nor guide.

For this sudden and complete change there are two chief reasons. The first is that, even when a great teacher says much about the ultimate realities of existence (or what he regards as such), it is extremely difficult to make out what he really believes. In the realm of metaphysical speculation, whether we are thinking for ourselves or trying to interpret the ideas of others—the two enterprises are really one—we feel (if we have any qualification for either task) that our thoughts are utterly inadequate to the solution of our problems, and that our words, besides being of Protean instability, are utterly inadequate to the expression of our thoughts.

Who but the novice at speculative thinking would venture to make any statement with confidence when he had to use such words as Soul, Ego, Person, Consciousness, Being, Reality, Universe, God;—words that have different meanings for different minds; words that take new shades of meaning from each new standpoint which the thinker finds it needful to adopt, and even from each new context which the course of his thinking suggests to him; words that stand on guard at the portal of every metaphysical inquiry, and refuse to allow us to pass until we have read the riddle of their meaning and so answered their unanswerable challenge?

The second reason for our uncertainty as to the metaphysical grounds on which Buddha based his ethical teaching, is that he himself was so far from dogmatizing about what is ultimate as to preserve a deep and consistent silence with regard to it. The meaning and the significance of this silence will presently be considered.

Meanwhile I can but say, with Dr. Oldenberg, that in the Buddhist philosophy (as it is presented to us in the Sacred Scriptures) "we have a fragment of a circle, to, complete which and to find the centre of which, is forbidden, for it would involve an inquiry after things which do not contribute to deliverance and happiness."

Let us now set forth what is clear and certain in Buddha's teaching, and then advance from this in the direction of what is dubious and obscure. It is fitting that we should begin, as Buddha himself began, with the Four Sacred Truths. In the Sermon to Five Ascetics at Benares, which tradition gives as the opening act of the ministry of Buddha, the Fourfold Truth is set forth in the following words:

> *"There are two extremes, O monks, from which he who leads a religious life must abstain. What are those two extremes? One is a life of pleasure, devoted to desire and enjoyment; that is base, ignoble, unspiritual, unworthy, unreal. The other is a life of mortification; it is gloomy, unworthy, unreal. The Perfect One, O monks, is removed from both these extremes and has discovered the way which lies between them, the middle way which enlightens the mind, which leads to rest, to knowledge, to enlightenment, to Nirvana. And what, O monks, is this middle way, which the Perfect One has discovered, which enlightens the eye and enlightens the spirit, which leads to rest, to knowledge, to enlightenment, to Nirvana? It is this sacred eightfold path, as it is called: Right Faith, Right Resolve, Right*

Speech, Right Action, Right Living, Right Effort, Right Thought, Right Self-Concentration. This, O monks, is the middle way, which the Perfect One has discovered, which enlightens the eye and enlightens the spirit, which leads to rest, to knowledge, to enlightenment, to Nirvana.

"This, O monks, is the sacred truth of suffering; birth is suffering, old age is suffering, death is suffering, to be united with the unloved is suffering, to be separated from the loved is suffering, not to obtain what one desires is suffering, in short the fivefold clinging to the earthly is suffering.

"This, O monks, is the sacred truth of the origin of suffering; it is the thirst for being, which leads from birth to birth, together with lust and desire, which finds gratification here and there: the thirst for pleasures, the thirst for being, the thirst for power.

"This, O monks, is the sacred truth of the extinction of suffering; the extinction of this thirst by complete annihilation of desire, letting it go, expelling it, separating oneself from it, giving it no room.

"This, O monks, is the sacred truth of the path which leads to the extinction of suffering; it is this sacred, eightfold path, to wit, Right Faith, Right Resolve, Right Speech, Right Action, Right Living, Right Effort, Right Thought, Right Self-Concentration."

This is the Fourfold Truth, on which Buddha's whole scheme of life is hinged. Let us try to set it forth in other and fewer words:

(1) Life on earth is full of suffering.

(2) Suffering is generated by desire.

(3) The extinction of desire involves the extinction of suffering.

(4) The extinction of desire (and therefore of suffering) is the outcome of a righteous life.

There is one link in Buddha's teaching which seems to be missing. Why does desire generate suffering? The answer to this question is given in a discourse which Buddha is said to have held with the five ascetics shortly after he had expounded to them the Four Sacred Truths.

"'The Exalted One,' so the tradition narrates, "spake to the five monks thus:

> *'The material form, O monks, is not the self. If material form were the self, O monks, this material form could not be subject to sickness, and a man should be able to say regarding his material form: My body shall be so and so; my body shall not be so and so. But inasmuch, O monks, as material form is not the self, therefore is material form subject to sickness, and a man cannot say as regards his material form: My body shall be so and so.*

"'The sensations, O monks, are not the self'"—and then follows in detail regarding the sensations the very same exposition which has been given regarding the body. Then comes the same detailed explanation regarding the remaining three component elements, the perceptions, the conformations, the consciousness, which, in combination with the material form and the sensations, constitute man's sentient state of being. Then Buddha goes on to say:

> *"How think ye then, O monks, is material form permanent or impermanent?"*
>
> *"Impermanent, Sire."*
>
> *"But is that which is impermanent, sorrow or joy?"*
>
> *"Sorrow, Sire."*
>
> *"But if a man duly considers that which is impermanent, full of sorrow, subject to change, can he say: that is mine, that is I, that is myself?"*
>
> *"Sire, he cannot."*

Then follows the same exposition in similar terms regarding sensations, perceptions, conformations, and consciousness: after which the discourse proceeds:

> *"Therefore, O monks, whatever in the way of material form, sensations, perceptions, etc., respectively, has ever been, will be, or is, either in our case, or in the outer*

world, or strong or weak, or low or high, or far or near, it is not self: this must he in truth perceive, who possesses real knowledge. Whosoever regards things in this light, O monks, being a wise and noble hearer of the word, turns himself from sensation and perception, from conformation and consciousness. When he turns therefrom, he becomes free from desire; by the cessation of desire he obtains deliverance; in the delivered there arises a consciousness of his deliverance; rebirth is extinct, holiness is completed, duty is accomplished; there is no more a return to this world, he knows."

We now understand what the desire is that generates suffering, and why it generates it. It is the desire for what does not belong to "self"—the real self—that generates suffering; and the reason why such desire generates suffering is that what does not belong to the real self is impermanent, changeable, perishable, and that impermanence in the object of desire must needs cause disappointment, regret, disillusionment, and other forms of suffering to him who desires.

The tendency to identify self with what is material and temporal, and therefore to desire for oneself material and temporal goods and pleasures, is the chief cause of human suffering; for, when such goods and pleasures are desired, success in the pursuit of them is perhaps more hurtful and scarcely less painful than failure. And not only does this tendency, with its derivative desire, cause suffering in the present earth-life, but it also causes suffering to be reproduced for the self in future earth-lives; for it is desire for the goods and pleasures of earth which, acting as a strong magnetic force, draws the self back to earth again and again. Desire in itself is not evil.

On this point Buddha's teaching must not be misunderstood. His disciples are expressly told—this is the very sum and substance of his teaching—to desire and strive for enlightenment, deliverance, Nirvana. Desire for the pleasures, or rather for the joys, that minister to the real self, is wholly good. It is desire for the pleasures that minister to the lower self; it is the desire to affirm the lower self, to live in it, to cling to it, to rest in it; it is the desire to identify oneself with the individual self and the impermanent world which centres in it, instead of with the Universal Self and the eternal world of which it is at once the centre and the circumference;—it is this desire, taking a thousand forms, which is evil, and which proves itself to be evil by causing ceaseless suffering to mankind. If the self is to be delivered from suffering, desire for what is impermanent, changeable, and unreal must be extinguished; and the gradual extinction of unworthy desire must therefore be the central purpose of one's life.

But how is desire, with the suffering that it generates, to be extinguished? The answer to this question is the Fourth of the Sacred Truths: "This, O monks, is the sacred truth of the path which leads to the extinction of suffering: it is the sacred eightfold path, to wit, Right Faith, Right Resolve, Right Speech, Right Action, Right Effort, Right Thought, Right Self-Concentration."

There is no part of Buddha's teaching in which his wisdom shines out more clearly than in this. At first one might feel disposed to think that Right Action was everything. Buddha does not think so. Right Speech, Right Action, and Right Living may perhaps be grouped together under the general head of Right Conduct; but there are other elements of Righteousness which Buddha seems to regard as not less important than these, to wit, Right Faith, Right Resolve, Right Effort, Right Thought, Right Self-Concentration.

In other words, Buddha lays as much stress on the inward as on the outward side of morality; and he would have us realize that conduct, when divorced from faith and thought and purpose, is worth nothing. Under the Jewish Law—at any rate in the later developments of legalism—correct action was regarded as the one thing needful. The consequences of this assumption were disastrous in the extreme. A mechanical and quasi-material conception of life and duty was introduced into the very heart of religion and morality; and spiritual freedom was crushed out by an ever-growing burden of narrow, rigid, and despotic rules. Buddha, like other moral teachers, found it necessary to give men rules for the conduct of life; but not only did he make his rules as few, as simple, and as comprehensive as possible, but by associating faith, thought, and purpose with speech and action, by impressing on his disciples that the inward side of conduct counts for at least as much as the outward, he provided against that miserable pullulation of trivial rules, which is sure to arise whenever correct action is regarded as an end in itself; and in doing so he shielded spiritual freedom from the most oppressive and most deadly form of constraint.

Nevertheless, when we have once realized that the inward side of action—the inward approaches to it and the inward consequences of it—is to the full as real and as significant as the outward, we may safely affirm, what Buddha would not have denied, that Right Conduct is the aspect of Righteousness which concerns us most. What we do, besides being the outward and visible sign of our inward and spiritual state, reacts, naturally and necessarily, on what we are, and so moulds our character and controls our destiny—for "character is destiny"—both in this and in future earth-lives. That being so, and conduct being the aspect of a man's general bearing for which directions are at once most needed and most easy to give, it is not to be wondered at that Buddha should have thought it necessary to formulate moral rules for the guidance of his followers,—men who were presumably ignorant and unenlightened (for his message was addressed to all men) and therefore in need of some measure of ethical direction.

In framing his moral code, Buddha, according to his wont, departed widely from precedent, and showed that, as regards his outlook on life, he was far in advance of his age. The ethical legislators of antiquity addressed themselves to a comparatively narrow audience,—a city, a tribe, or a people; they went fully into detail, their rules being many and minute; and they went far beyond the limits of ethics proper, nine-tenths of their rules being civil or ceremonial rather than ethical (in the stricter, and yet broader and more spiritual sense of the word). Buddha, on the contrary, addressed himself to the widest of all audiences,—to the whole human race: he carefully abstained from going into detail, his rules being few, simple, and comprehensive; and he kept entirely within the limits of ethics proper, limits which he may almost be said—so original and so formative was his teaching—to have been the first to define.

Here is his Code of Moral Law.

The believer is required:

1. To kill no living thing.
2. Not to lay hands on another's property.
3. Not to touch another's wife.
4. Not to speak what is untrue.
5. Not to drink intoxicating drinks.

A simple code this, but as profound as it is simple. To begin with, its extreme simplicity means that its authority is in the main self-evident; in other words, that it makes a direct appeal to a man's latent moral sense, and, in appealing to it, trains it and helps it to grow. In the next place, the fact that the rules are all prohibitions means that the believer is, first and foremost, to exercise self-control. The reason why he is to exercise self-control is that deliverance from suffering is to be won by the suppression of unworthy desires, and that without the exercise of self-control desire cannot be suppressed.

The five rules indicate five arterial directions in which his self-control is to be exercised. Thus the first rule calls upon him to control the passion of anger; the second, the desire for material possessions; the third, the lusts of the flesh; the fourth, cowardice and malevolence (the chief causes of untruthfulness); the fifth, the craving for unwholesome excitement. It is to be noted that the desires and passions which the believer is called upon to suppress, are those which are most hurtful to his own inner life, most productive of suffering to himself, and most productive of suffering to his fellow men. By learning self-control with regard to these, he not only brings happiness to himself and to others, but he also strengthens himself for the more general work of suppressing unworthy desires of every sort and kind.

But the five rules are something more than mere prohibitions. Self-control necessarily prepares the way for the development of the more positive and active virtues. When the baser tendencies of man's nature are kept under such strict control that at least they lose their baseness and cease to obstruct the outgrowth of the nobler tendencies, the latter must needs begin to germinate.

Thus the control of anger will prepare the way for the outgrowth of gentleness and compassion; the control of covetousness, for the outgrowth of charitableness and generosity; the control of lust, for the outgrowth of purity and unselfish love; and so forth. "How does a monk become a partaker of uprightness?" asks Buddha. The answer is, "A monk abstains from killing living creatures; he refrains from causing the death of living creatures; he lays down the stick; he lays down weapons. He is compassionate and tender-hearted; he seeks with friendly spirit the welfare of all living things. This is part of his uprightness." Let a man abstain from unkindness to his fellow men and other "living creatures,"— and the germs of kindness, gentleness, and compassion which are lying dormant in his nature will begin to make spontaneous growth. And so with the other rules.

Yet Buddha was wise to limit his formulated law to negative commandments. If a positive commandment is to move men to well-doing, it must be in some sort a counsel of perfection; and there are few men who can receive a counsel of perfection in the spirit in which it is, or ought to be, given to them. Some natures are over-wrought by it, and lose their spiritual balance. Others interpret it literally, and so make nonsense of its transcendent sense. Others again (the majority) listen to it, but pay no heed to it.

For ordinary men it is best that the active, positive side of virtue should be approached—gradually and naturally— from the side of self-control. Also, it must be remembered that the formulation of a positive moral law tends, especially in an age of ceremonialism, to arrest the development of conscience,— the very faculty which, in the Buddhist scheme of life, there is most need for men to cultivate. When a man does kind and compassionate deeds (let us say), not because his better nature, acting through his moral sense, prompts him to do them, but because he is authoritatively commanded to do them, there is a danger lest the man's moral sense, finding that there was little or no work for it to do, either as a prompter or as a guide, should gradually cease to energize, and the man should at last become entirely dependent for moral guidance on formulated rules and their professional exponents.

Obedience to a negative commandment—provided that the commandment is sufficiently broad and simple for the spirit of it to appeal to one—can do no harm to him who obeys, and may do much good, for the discipline of self-control is one of the best of moral tonics. But when the self-control has done its work, when the soul, braced and disciplined, is ready to walk in the path of active virtue, it is in the highest degree desirable that it should be allowed to walk by itself (or with no more guidance than is implicit in the prohibitions which it has obeyed), and that nothing should be done to impair its insight or weaken its will.

There were weighty reasons, then, why Buddha's ethical teaching should have been mainly negative. There is, however, one positive virtue which is inculcated in all the Buddhist Scriptures—the virtue in which, in its embryonic stage, all other virtues are present in embryo—the virtue in which, in its ideal stage, all other virtues are crowned and consummated—love. Not the impersonal passion of universal love—that would come at the end of the Path, not at the beginning—but the impersonal sentiment of sympathy, with all that it involves,—kindness, gentleness, unselfishness, compassion. That this should have found a prominent place in the Buddhist scheme of life was inevitable, for, when egoism has been subdued, the self is constrained, by the expansive stress of its own inward nature, to find channels for the overflow of its abounding life; and the safest and most accessible channel of overflow is that of sympathy, first with other men and then with every living thing. But the process which is thus initiated—a process of self-realization through self-expansion—will not cease until sympathy has transformed itself into the passion of spiritual love, and the individual life has at once lost and found itself in the Universal Life, which is and has always been its own true self.When a teacher tries to bring salvation within the reach of all men, he is confronted by the difficulty that men are in various stages of spiritual development, and that rules of life which are sufficient for the many may prove to be too elementary for the few. Not that the few are to ignore those rules or neglect to observe them. That they observe them fully and faithfully, and would never dream of breaking them, is taken for granted. But the simpler rules of life need to be supplemented, in these exceptional cases, by others which are at once more elevating and more exacting. When the foothills of life have been surmounted, the more difficult and dangerous mountain heights will come in view, and directions for climbing these will be needed and will have to be given.

In the Eightfold Path there are Four Stages, each of which is marked by the breaking of some of the "Fetters"—ten in all—which bind man to earth and to self.

In the First Stage, the stage of "Conversion" or "entering upon the stream," three fetters are broken:

(1) The delusion of self; the delusive belief that the individual self is real and self-existent. This fetter is rightly placed at the head of the list; for the clinging to individuality, the desire to affirm the apparent or actual self instead of looking forward to its expansion into the real or universal self, has its ethical counterpart in egoism, and egoism is the beginning and end of sin.

(2) Doubt: doubt as to the wisdom of the teacher and the efficacy of the prescribed Path.

(3) Belief in the efficacy of good works and ceremonies. The disciple must free himself, first from the general delusion that correct outward action will ensure a man's salvation, and then from the particular delusion that religious rites and ceremonies have intrinsic value.

Having broken these fetters, the disciple enters the Second Stage, "the path of those who will return only once to earth." In this, and in the Third Stage, "the path of those who will never return to earth," two more fetters are broken:

(4) The fetter of sensuality or fleshly lust. The belief that fleshly lusts war against the soul is not peculiar to Buddhism. The difficulty for most religions, and indeed for most men, is to hit the man between rigorous asceticism and moral laxity. Buddha, who regarded the "life of mortification" as "unreal" and "unworthy," carefully abstained from overstraining human nature in that particular direction. It was only in the case of the "monk," or "religious devotee," that complete renunciation of the pleasures of the flesh was enjoined. But in the third stage, "the path, of those who will return to earth no more," every one is in a sense a religious devotee; and there can be little doubt, I think, that in that stage the final extinction of lust was contemplated. If so, that achievement would be the consummation of a long course—perhaps pursued through many lives—of continence and self-control.

(5) The fetter of ill-will. The disciple has to subdue all the feelings of anger, resentment, envy, jealousy, hatred, and the like, which spring from his sense of separateness from the rest of mankind, or rather from the rest of living things, and from his subsequent reluctance to identify himself with the Universal Life. In other to get rid of those feelings, a spiritual exercise was prescribed by the early Buddhists, which is eminently characteristic of the general spirit of Buddhism.

"He [the disciple] lets his mind pervade one quarter of the world with thoughts of love, and so the second, and so the third, and so the fourth. And thus the whole wide world, above, below, around and everywhere, does he continue to pervade with heart of love, far-reaching, grown great, and beyond measure. Just as a mighty trumpeter makes himself heard and without difficulty towards all the four directions, even so of all things that have shape or form, there is not one that he passes or leaves aside, but regards them all with mind set free and deep-felt love." The exercise is then repeated, substituting each time for love, first pity, then sympathy, then equanimity. By this means the strength of the fifth fetter is gradually weakened, and at last destroyed.

The whole of the Second and Third Stages is occupied with the struggle against the many enemies of the higher life who fight under the banners of sensuality and ill-will. When all of these have been finally conquered, the disciple enters the Fourth Stage, "the path of the Holy Ones, or Arahats." There he breaks, one by one, the five remaining fetters, to wit:

(6) The desire for life—for separate life—in the worlds of form.

(7) The desire for life—for separate life—in the formless worlds.

(8) Pride.

(9) Self-Righteousness.

Ought not the eighth and ninth fetters to have been broken long ago? Perhaps they ought; but Buddha knew that even in the last stage of the upward Path the shadow of egoism may fall on one's thought. The man who can say to himself: "It is I who have walked in the Path. It is I who have scaled these heights. It is I who have suppressed egoism. It is I who have won deliverance: "is still the victim of delusions. There are still fetters for him to break.

(10) Ignorance. The last fetter, like the first, is ignorance. As the Path begins with enlightenment, so it ends with it. It begins with potential enlightenment. It ends with actual enlightenment. It begins with partial enlightenment. It ends with perfect enlightenment. It is for the sake of knowledge—real, final, absolute knowledge—that the Path has been followed. To know that the Universal Self is one's own real self,—to know this truth, not as a theory, not as a conclusion, not as a poetic idea, not as a sudden revelation, but as the central fact of one's own inmost life,—to know this truth (in the most intimate sense of the word know) by

living it, by being it,—is the final end of all spiritual effort. The expansion of the Self, which is the outcome of spiritual effort, carries with it the expansion of consciousness; and when consciousness has become all-embracing, the fetter of ignorance has been finally broken, and the delusion of self is dead.

When the last fetter has been broken, the disciple—the "Arahat" or "Holy One" as he is now called—has reached his goal; in other words, he has attained to a state of perfect knowledge, perfect love, perfect peace, perfect bliss.

There is something esoteric, one feels inclined to say, in this Path of the Four Stages. One finds some difficulty in identifying it with the Eightfold Path of the Fourth Sacred Truth. From Buddha's day down to our own, there has never been an age in which the number of men who could really break even the first of the Ten Fetters was not exceedingly small. What of the rest of mankind? Was no provision made for them in Buddha's scheme of life? Was that scheme meant for recluses and "adepts"—or would-be "adepts"—only? Were ordinary men to be left to their own devices until the time came for them to be "converted" (by what miracle we cannot well conjecture), and to realize what is so hard for even the best of us to realize,—the unreality of the individual life?

Surely not. "Conversion" has been happily defined as the "effective realization of admitted truth." The process that leads up to "conversion" is carried on, for the most part, in silence and obscurity. There is always a long period of ante-natal growth before the new idea, the new way of looking at things, can come to the birth. The authorities on Buddhism whom I have consulted do not make it clear whether the First Fetter was to be broken at the entrance to the First Stage of the Path, or whether it was the first delusion to be got rid of after the soul had entered that stage. In the latter case the difficulty of identifying the Path of the Four Stages with the Eightfold Path vanishes; for it is quite conceivable that the soul should linger long in the First Stage, should even pass, during its sojourn in it, through a sequence of earth-lives, before it could realize that its sense of separateness was illusory. In the former case we must adopt another hypothesis. We must assume that, before the first of the Four Stages can be entered, there must be for most men a long preliminary stage of preparation, during which they follow, perhaps through a sequence of lives, the rules of Right Conduct—the simple rules of kindness, honesty, continence, truthfulness, temperance—until at last the reaction of Right Conduct on character, and the consequent expansion of the Self and enlargement of the field of its consciousness, makes it possible for them to enter the Path proper,—the Path which will lead them in the fullness of time to the goal of conscious union with the Living Whole. In either case we may take for granted that, before the First Fetter can be broken and flung aside, the soul must set itself to acquire the strength which will enable it to perform that initiatory act of renunciation, and that it is only by a course of "Right Conduct"—by the consistent exercise of self-control, and culture of sympathy—that it can acquire the strength which it needs.

In any case we are free to regard the Fourfold Truth as a message to the rank and file of mankind. Men might accept that message, and even begin, in their feeble, faltering way, to walk by it, before they were fit to advance into the more esoteric stages of the Path of Life. But those stages must be passed through—on this Buddha would have insisted with all the weight of his authority—before the goal can be reached. Miracles, in the supernatural sense of the word, are not to be looked for in the moral, any more than in the physical world. It is conceivable that my neighbour, whose spiritual development is far in advance of mine, may complete the Path in 50 years, whereas my sojourn in it may last for 50,000; but by him as by me, and by me as by him, every stage must be passed through and every fetter must be broken, if the promised prize is to be won.

It is sometimes said that for ordinary men the path of spiritual ascent is spiral, whereas for men of exceptional spiritual development it is direct. This may be so; or it may be that for all men the path is spiral up to a certain point, and beyond that point direct. But be it spiral or direct or both, it is certain that it must free us from every delusion that separates us from the Real Self, if it is to lead us to our goal. Whatever view we may take of Buddha's teaching, we must admit that in its essence it belongs to no one nation and no one age. Moses legislated for the Jews, Lycurgus for the Spartans, Zoroaster for the Persians, Confucius for the Chinese, Buddha for all men who have ears to hear. Man, as Buddha conceived of him, is not a citizen but a "living soul." The life which the scheme prescribed, though compatible with good citizenship and even conducive to it, is quite independent of it.

It is also quite independent of caste, of social gradation, of distinctions such as that between priest and layman, between the learned and the ignorant, between gentle and simple, between rich and poor. Dr. Oldenberg's contention that Buddha had no message for the poor and lowly, is scarcely tenable. The inward and spiritual life can be lived by the poorest of day-labourers not less than by the richest of millionaires. If anything, it is easier for the poor than for the rich to enter "the Kingdom of Heaven," for there are fewer earth-ties for the former to break. When Dr. Oldenberg quotes the saying "to the wise belongs the law, not to the foolish," and argues from it that "for children and those who are like children the arms of Buddha are not opened," he is playing on the word "wise." The wisdom which Buddha magnified was not the wisdom of the intellectual, the learned, the cultured, but the wisdom of those who have taught themselves, by walking in the Path of Life, to distinguish between shadows and realities.

The simplicity Of Buddha's ethical code brings it within the reach of the simplest natures. It is surely open to those "who are like children" to be kind to their fellow-men, to abstain from envy and covetousness, to control the lusts of the flesh, to be truthful in word and deed. If there are heights to be climbed beyond those which the "child-like" can dream of, the soul will not be asked to attempt these until, by the practice of the life of simple goodness, it has grown strong enough for the more arduous task.

The greatness of Buddha as a teacher is proved by the fact that his scheme of life, so simple and yet so complex, so obviously and yet so profoundly true, so modest in its aims and yet so daringly ambitious, so moderate and yet so extravagant in the demands that it makes on our spiritual resources,—provides for the needs of all men, in all stages of development, of all moulds of character, of all types of mind.

There is one feature of Buddha's teaching which demands our special attention because it seems to pervade, like an atmosphere, the whole of his scheme of life. We know from experience that our actions produce far-reaching consequences which we can follow out, both laterally and lineally, to a considerable distance. We know, for example, that our actions affect the material conditions of our own and of other lives; that they produce social consequences which have a wide circle of disturbance; that they affect, for good or for evil, our own characters, and—to a lesser extent—the characters of those with whom we are much in contact.

We know also, if we take the trouble to consider the matter, that these consequences are the natural and necessary effects of causes which our action sets in motion; and, if we follow out this line of thought, we shall probably come to the conclusion that the whole moral world, under both its aspects—the outward and the inward—is, like the physical world, under the dominion of natural law. It was to this aspect of morality that Buddha attached supreme importance. According to the law of Karma, which he was not the first to formulate but which he unreservedly accepted, the consequences of a man's action—foremost among which is its effect on his character—follow him, not merely through life (in the vulgar sense of the word) but also from life to life, until they have exhausted their influence.

The Books say well, my Brother! each man's life.

The outcome of his former living is." What we have done has made us what we are. What we are doing is moulding our character and determining the direction of its development. When a man dies, he takes his character away with him. When he returns to earth, he brings his character back with him,—a character which determines the very nature of his material surroundings, for the re-incarnating soul seeks (according to the doctrine of Karma), or has assigned to it, the particular environment which is at once most in keeping with its nature and most suitable for its development.

"That which ye sow, ye reap. See yonder fields!

The sesamum was sesamum, the corn

Was corn. The Silence and the Darkness knew!

So is a man's fate born.

"He comes, reaper of the things he sowed,... "

The idea that pervades the whole of Buddha's teaching is that whatever we sow we must reap; in particular, that nothing can come between our conduct and its inward consequences; that every thought, every word, every deed is either making or marring us; in fine, that our spiritual destiny, which after all is our real destiny, is in our own hands.

With characteristic wisdom Buddha made no attempt to reconcile human freedom with the supremacy of natural law. He probably saw that the opposition of freedom to law is a false antithesis,—one of the fatal by-products of the dualism of ordinary thought. One who looked at things from the standpoint of the philosophy of the Upanishads would know that the free-will riddle, which has tied Western thought into so many desperate tangles, is a mere "Idol of the Cave." He would know that the Real or Highest Self—being, ex hypothesi, universal and eternal, and therefore exempt from all external constraint—is absolutely free.

He would know that the Real Self is present in potency in each individual life, and that every "living soul" is, therefore, potentially free. He would know, further, that the development of the soul, in the direction of its own true self, is always marked by the outgrowth of freedom; and he would infer from this that freedom varies, in the degree of its development, from soul to soul, and that, speaking generally, it is lost or won by conduct.

But though no man is absolutely free, and though in most men freedom has but a rudimentary existence, he would realize that the best way to foster its growth is to postulate its existence and appeal to it, as the wise teacher always appeals (though here too he is probably appealing to what has but a rudimentary existence) to a man's better self. In fine, far from teaching that freedom is incompatible with law, he would realize that the law of the growth of freedom—the seemingly paradoxical law that freedom, without which moral action is impossible, is itself generated by moral action—is one of the master laws of human life.

Whether Buddha did or did not accept the ideas of the Upanishads, is a question which will presently be considered. Meanwhile, it is enough to know that, with his own practical ends in view, he not only postulated freedom in man, but—by bringing the inward life under the dominion of natural law, and so excluding from it all extraneous influences—he laid a tremendous burden on the human will; for he told men that it rested with them, and with them only, to determine what course the process of their development should take, and how long their pilgrimage on earth (from life to life) should last.

Now the first and last of Nature's laws is that of growth; and the teacher who brings the inner life of man under the dominion of natural law brings it also, by implication, under the dominion of the law of growth. Wherever there is life there is growth; in other words, there is a gradual passage from embryonic existence to maturity, from the seed-state, in which all the potentialities of future perfection are wrapped up, to perfection itself,—the perfection of the particular species or type. This law applies to the self, not less than to the animal or the plant. Indeed, it applies first and foremost to the self, and applies to the living things that surround us because, and just so far as, they too are manifestations of the one self-evolving life.

There is, however, a vital difference between the growth of the soul and the growth of any animal or plant. "The lilies of the field... toil not, neither do they spin: and yet... Solomon in all his glory was not arrayed like one of these." But if the soul is to be arrayed in glory it must both toil and spin. "Which of you," asks Christ, "by taking thought can add one cubit unto his stature?" Buddha's teaching bases itself on the assumption that by taking thought we can add to our spiritual stature, that the soul can make itself grow. Buddha would, I think, if we could question him, pass on from can to must. He would say that, when a certain stage in our development has been reached, the soul can make no further growth except what it wills to make, that it is only by the action of the will—itself one of Nature's master "streams of tendency"—that the expansive forces of Nature which are at work in the soul can be co-ordinated and made effective.

He would say that the power of the soul to make itself grow is the very fruit of the whole previous process of its growth; that its presence is the proof that the process has (thus far) been successfully accomplished; that if it be wanting, the preliminary process of growth has not been carried far enough; that if, having been won, it has become atrophied through disuse, the growth of the soul has been arrested and the counter-process of degeneration has begun.

That we may the better realize the meaning and ulterior bearing of this conception, let us contrast it with the conception which has long dominated the ethical philosophy of the West. Owing to the myopia of the Western mind, the doctrine that the soul can work out its eternal destiny in a single earth-life has been able to win general acceptance. This doctrine is obviously incompatible with the idea that the destiny of the soul is to be achieved by the actual vital process of growth; for it stands to reason that, in the natural order of things, neither utter depravity nor absolute perfection can be achieved in the brief space of a single life.

How then is "salvation" to be won? Israel, from whom the Western mind inherited its popular philosophy, persuaded himself that salvation was to be won by obedience to a formal Law. This Law was the work of the supernatural God, by whom it was miraculously delivered to man. There was no reason why all or even many of its commandments should be moral, in the stricter sense of the word. The supernatural God, whose ways are presumably inscrutable, might, for reasons of his own, order man to do things which were apparently trivial or unreasonable. If he did, man must obey. Apart from this, there was a special reason why many of the commandments of the Jewish Law should be non-moral. The frailty of man is such that he is always liable to disobey God. Disobedience is hateful to God, and draws down his wrath upon the sinner. In order to appease God and avert his wrath, man must offer up something which he himself especially values,—a bullock, a he-goat, or whatever the victim may be.

Thus the idea of propitiation through sacrifice is bound up with the idea of salvation through obedience to a divinely formulated Law. Sacrificial observances, being an important part of man's life, must be duly and formally regulated. In other words, ceremonial directions must always form an essential part of a Law which has come to man from a supernatural source. Now it is obvious that in matters of ceremonial punctilio there can be no inward standard of right and wrong. Correctness of outward action is all that is asked for; but absolute correctness is indispensable, and the general idea that action must be outwardly correct if it is to please God easily spreads from the ceremonial to the more strictly moral side of the Law. In the attempt to define correctness with perfect accuracy, rules and sub-rules spring up in rank profusion, until at last the burden of legalism threatens to extinguish spiritual life.

This is what happened to Israel in the days of his national decadence. Christianity inherited his ideas, but rejected the intolerable burden of his Law. It inherited the idea of salvation being won by obedience; but it started, under the stress of Christ's vivifying influence, by assuming that the Law which God wished men to obey was mainly, if not wholly, moral. To obey a moral law is, however, even more difficult than to obey a ceremonial law; and in the one case, as in the other, the penalty of disobedience, when the Law comes from God, is eternal death.

How then was the wrath of God to be averted from disobedient man? "By the Sacrifice of Christ, the Mediator between God and Man," is the answer which Christian theology gave and still gives to this question. In the Catholic Church the sacrifice of Christ is perpetually repeated by the priest. In the Protestant Churches the Sacrifice is supposed to have been performed once and for all; and faith in the efficacy of the Cross opens the door of salvation to the believer. The reappearance—the inevitable reappearance—of the sacrificial idea in the religions of the West tended, for obvious reasons, to discredit morality and to substitute machinery for life. A man might conceivably have climbed to the highest pinnacle of virtue (in the human sense of the word), he might even have climbed to the highest level of holiness (in the inward and spiritual sense of the word), and yet be doomed to eternal perdition, either because he had no faith in the efficacy of the Sacraments of the Church or because he rejected the doctrine of the imputed righteousness of Christ. Contrariwise, a man might have sinned deeply, basely, and consistently, and yet, having made a late repentance, be forgiven—and therefore "saved"—for Christ's sake.

Where such anomalies were possible, there could be no causal connection between conduct and its results. The doctrine of forgiveness of sin has ever tended to demoralize human life, by undermining the idea that virtue is rewarded by virtue, and vice punished by vice. A Heaven in the future is reserved by official Christianity for those who fulfil certain clearly prescribed conditions; a Hell in the future, for those who neglect to fulfil them. But neither in Heaven nor in Hell does a man reap the actual crop that he has sown. If he did, the false dualism of Heaven and Hell would disappear, and there would be millions of after-states instead of only two. Even when Hell has been fairly earned it may conceivably be evaded, for it is always open to the sinner to fall back on the uncovenanted mercies of God.

From first to last, this theory of things—a theory from which the ideas of natural law and natural growth are conspicuously absent—is wholly foreign to Buddha's scheme of life. Miraculous intervention, whatever form it may take, is beyond the horizon of his thought. The sacrificial system, ceremonialism, sacerdotalism, legalism,—all these he entirely rejects. Correct outward action counts for nothing in his eyes. The inward motive to and the inward consequences of action are all that he regards. Mediators count for nothing. Redeemers count for nothing. Priests count for nothing. Casuists and such like spiritual directors count for nothing. The most that one man can do for other men is to tell them of the Path of Life—the broad Path of self-development through self-surrender—and give them general directions for finding and following it. The true Saviour of men is he who does this. But each man in turn must walk in the Path, by using his own sight, his own strength, his own judgment, his own will.

"Therefore, O Ananda! bey lamps unto yourselves. Be ye a refuge to yourselves. Betake yourselves to no external refuge.... Look not for refuge to anyone except yourselves." External rewards are not to be looked for. External penalties are not to be feared.

It knows not wrath nor pardon; utter true

Its measures mete, its faultless balance weighs;

Times are as nought, tomorrow it will judge,

Or after many days. Virtue rewards itself by strengthening the will, by subduing unworthy desire, by generating knowledge of reality, by giving inward peace. Sin punishes itself by weakening the will, by inflaming unworthy desire, by generating delusions, by breeding fever and unrest. For sin to be "forgiven" is as impossible as for virtue to forego its reward. To walk in the Path is its own reward; for the Path is lit by the ever-deepening foreglow of its goal. To depart from the Path is its own punishment; for the erring steps must, at whatever cost, be retraced. Must be retraced,—for all the forces of Nature are making for the growth of the soul, as surely as in springtime all the forces of Nature are making for the outgrowth of flower and leaf. It is Nature herself that, acting through his sense

of right and wrong, constrains him who has left the Path to seek to regain it. But the Path is not to be regained, except by a steep and arduous ascent; and the longer the return to it is delayed, the more steep and arduous will the ascent prove to be.

This is, I think, the most inward conception of life, and the most intrinsic standard of moral worth, that has ever been presented to human thought. When Christ says: "Take heed that ye do not your alms before men, to be seen of them: otherwise ye have no reward of your Father which is in Heaven"; when he bids us pray and fast in secret so that we may be rewarded, not by the applause of men, but by "the Father, which sees in secret"; when the author of the "Imitation"—in some ways the most Christ-like of all Christians—reminds us that "what each man is in Thine eyes, that he is and no more,"—we are taken as far in the direction of pure inwardness and intrinsic reality as it is possible for men to go who worship and have long worshipped a "personal God."

That "the Father in Heaven" whom Christ adored coincides, in the last resort, with Brahma—the all-knowing, all-thinking Self, the all-embracing, all-sustaining Life—is more than probable.

But though the inspired teacher, whose thoughts are all poems, may be able to purify and spiritualize the conception of a personal God, the average man is quite sure to debase and externalize it.

If we could but listen to the prayers that at any moment were being addressed "in secret to the Father which sees in secret," we should realize how widely popular thought had departed from a really inward conception of life, and from a really intrinsic standard of moral worth. What is unique in Buddha's scheme of life is that every influence which might conceivably come between conduct and its consequences is rigidly excluded. God himself—if we are to continue to think and speak about God—"knows not wrath nor pardon." But can we continue to think and speak about so impersonal a God? Buddha must, I think, have asked himself this vital question.

A great spiritual life-work is always the outcome of a great renunciation; and it is possible that what Buddha renounced was something dearer than wealth or power, dearer even than wife or child. The austere inwardness of his teaching had its counterpart, as we shall presently see, in a deep silence about what is ultimate and innermost, a silence which he must have imposed upon himself at the beginning of his long ministry, and which he never broke.

A MISREADING OF BUDDHA

Set forth in as few words as possible, Buddha's message to man is an appeal to him to find his true self, with all that this can give him—joy, peace, knowledge, love—by suppressing egoism, with all the desires and delusions on which it feeds, and breaking, one by one, the fetters of the surface life and the lower self.

Those who have followed me thus far will, I think, admit that Buddha's scheme of life coincides, at all its vital points, with the scheme that I worked out by drawing practical deductions from the master ideas of that deeply spiritual philosophy which found its highest expression in the Upanishads. One who accepted the central idea of that philosophy—the idea that the Universal Soul is the real self of each one of us—and realized its spiritual consequences, and who at the same time saw clearly that none of the current modes of apprehending it—the metaphysical, the intuitional, the poetical, the symbolical—was available for ordinary, unenlightened, undeveloped men, would probably come to the conclusion that, if the world at large was to be brought under the influence of that great spiritual idea, a practical interpretation of it must be presented to and followed by the rank and file of mankind. Such a teacher would begin by appealing to the very sense which it was his most cherished desire to cultivate,—the sense of reality, which is present in embryo in every breast. He would tell men that life is full of suffering, and that the chief cause of suffering is the impermanence—and therefore the unreality—of the objects of man's desire; and he would expect them to assent to these propositions.

This is what Buddha did.

He would explain to them that the desire for unreal things not only caused suffering in this or that earth-life, but also caused the suffering to be reproduced in other earth-lives,—desire for the shadows and illusions of earth being the subjective side of the attractive force by which earth draws the unemancipated soul back to itself again and again; and he would ask them to infer from this that deliverance from suffering (now and in the future) was to be won by the subjugation, and at last by the extinction of desire,—not of desire as such, but of the base, carnal, worldly, self-seeking desires, which, by keeping the soul in ignorance of its true nature and destiny, cause it to eddy round and round in the "whirlpool of rebirth."

This is what Buddha did.

He would tell them—though not in so many words—that, if their baser desires were to be subdued, they must practise self-control and cultivate sympathy; and, with that end in view, he would give them a few simple rules for the conduct of life,—rules which would provide for the development of self-control and sympathy along the arterial lines of morality, and the authority of which would therefore be in a measure self-evident.

This is what Buddha did.

For those who had mastered their baser desires and passions, and who, by a parallel process, had cultivated the latent virtues of gentleness, kindness, and compassion, and, speaking generally, begun to live in the lives of others, he would make further provision; he would help them in various ways to conquer their hydra-headed enemy, the lower self; he would teach them to distinguish between the shadows and the realities of life, to rid themselves of every self-seeking desire and every self-affirming delusion, to quench lust and anger, to extend in every direction the radiating light of sympathy and good will.

This is what Buddha did.

He would tell them that, when the last taint of egoism and the last shadow of ignorance had disappeared, the happiness to which they had always had an indefeasible title, but a title which each man in turn had to make good for himself, would at last be theirs; that the Path which they had followed for so long would lead them at last to the fullness of knowledge, the fullness of peace, the fullness of love,—and therefore to unimaginable bliss.

This is what Buddha did.

But he would impress on them that they lived in a world in which causes always produce their natural and necessary effects; that the consequences of their conduct would therefore follow them wherever they went; that external rewards were not to be hoped for; that external punishments were not to be dreaded; that virtue was its own reward and vice its own punishment, in the sense that whatever is done or left undone inevitably reacts upon the character, and, through the character, affects for weal or for woe the destiny of the soul; that interference from without was in the nature of things impossible; that the whole sacrificial system was based on a delusion; that ceremonial observances were of no avail:—he would teach them, in fine, that each man in turn must take his life into his own hands and work out his destiny for himself.

This is what Buddha did.

But, while he taught them all this, he would make no attempt to explain to them the deepest mysteries of existence; he would deliberately disconnect his scheme of life, so far as his own exposition of it was concerned, from theology and metaphysics; he would keep silence as to what is "ultimate and uttermost"; for he would know that the average mind has no capacity for deep thinking, and that, if he tried to disclose to his fellow-men his ultimate reasons for the course of life which he wished them to follow, they would make nonsense, first of his philosophical teaching and then of his whole scheme of life, giving themselves wrong reasons for everything that they did or left undone, and so (in the last resort) misinterpreting and misapplying every detail of his teaching.

This too is what Buddha did (or forebore to do). That he kept silence about "great matters" is as certain as that his ethical teaching was clear, coherent, and systematic.

The coincidences between the two schemes of life—that which Buddha taught and that which follows logically (in the deeper sense of the word) from the philosophy of the Upanishads—are so many and so vital that they cannot be ascribed to chance. Even if the age in which Buddha lived had been separated by a thousand years from the age which gave birth to the stories of Brahma and the Gods, and Nachiketas and Death, we should feel justified, on internal evidence, in concluding that Buddha had somehow or other come under the influence of the ideas which those stories enshrined.

But we need not trust to internal evidence only. We know that the spiritual atmosphere of India in Buddha's day was impregnated with the ideas of the Upanishads. We know that those ideas must have appealed with peculiar force to a thinker of Buddha's exalted nature, whether he ended by emancipating himself from their influence or not. We know that the teachers who had expounded those ideas had utterly failed to bring them into connection with the daily life of the ordinary man, and had thereby left a gap in the philosophical teaching of India, which was waiting to be filled by some master mind. The cumulative evidence afforded by these facts, added to the internal evidence which has already been set forth in detail, seems to point with irresistible force to one conclusion, namely that Buddha accepted the idealistic teaching of the Upanishads—accepted it at its highest level and in its purest form—and took upon himself as his life's mission to fill the obvious gap in it,—in other words, to make the spiritual ideas which had hitherto been the exclusive possession of a few select souls, available for the daily needs of mankind.

If this conclusion is correct, we shall see in Buddhism, not a revolt against the "Brahmanic" philosophy as such, but an ethical interpretation of the leading ideas of that philosophy,—a following out of those ideas, not into the word-built systems of (so-called) thought which the metaphysicians of the day were constructing with fatal facility, but into their practical consequences in the inner life of man.

But is the conclusion correct? I must admit at once that there is a preponderance of opinion against it. The Orientalist scholars into whose hands the work of expounding the ideas and doctrines of Buddha has perforce fallen, seem to be agreed in holding that in Buddhism the mind of India broke away from the Brahmanic line of thought. Some indeed go further than this. They tell us that Buddha's teaching was directly and openly subversive of the "sovereign dogmas" of Brahmanism. They admit indeed, with considerable reluctance, that he believed in re-incarnation, but they contend that he did not believe in any re-incarnating self or ego; and they accept on his behalf all the philosophical consequences of this sweeping denial, the last of these being that Nirvana—the Buddhist effort and aspiration—is the prelude to annihilation.

Foremost among the distinguished scholars who have satisfied themselves that Buddha was a negative dogmatist—a metaphysician, whose propositions were all fundamental negations—is Dr. Rhys Davids, a writer on Buddhism whose works enjoy a well-deserved popularity, and whose influence in determining the attitude of contemporary opinion towards the Buddhist scheme of life is very great. In the following passages from his writings his own attitude is clearly defined. After expounding the hour Sacred Truths, he goes on to say, "The remarkable fact is that we have here set forth a view of religion entirely independent of the soul theories on which all the various philosophies and religions then current in India were based." Speaking of re-incarnation he says, "There is no passage of a soul or I in any sense from the one life to the other.

Their [the Buddhists'] whole view of the matter is independent of the time-honoured soul-theories held in common by all the followers of every other creed." Speaking of the interest that the Brahmans took in Buddha's speculations, he says that "his [Buddha's] rejection of the soul-theory and of all that it involved was really incompatible with the whole theology of the Vedas." Elsewhere he says that no other school of religious thought is "quite so frankly and entirely independent as Buddhism of the two theories of God and the soul." Other significant passages in his writings are the following: "The victory to be gained by the destruction of ignorance is, in Gautama's view, a victory which can be gained and enjoyed in this life and in this life only."

"Man is never the same for two consecutive moments, and there is within him no abiding principle whatever." "Another proof of the prominence of the doctrine of the non-existence of the soul is the fact that the Brahmans who have misunderstood many less important or less clearly expressed tenets of Buddhism recognize this as one of its distinctive features." "Would it be possible in a more complete and categorical manner to deny that there is any soul—anything of any kind which continues to exist, in any manner, after death?" If there is no soul or ego, in any sense of the word, what is the meaning of Nirvana? According to Dr. Rhys Davids, it is a state of blissful repose which precedes annihilation, with which, however, it must not be confounded. "Death, utter death, with no new life to follow, is then the result of, but it is not Nirvana."

These passages make it clear that Buddha, according to Dr. Rhys Davids' estimate of him, was a daring speculative thinker who had thought out all the master problems of existence and solved them to his own satisfaction, his solution in every case, or rather in the one case which is decisive of the rest, being an unqualified negation. The uncompromising denial of the soul, which Dr. Rhys Davids ascribes to Buddha, makes an end of all metaphysical speculation. If there is no soul, if the sense of self is wholly delusive, we may know, without further inquiry, that there is no God (in any spiritual sense of the word), no inward life, no former life, no after life. But what of the outward things which the (so-called) self perceives and, in the act of perceiving, certifies as existent, and even provisionally certifies as real?

According to Western thought these are real things; and the physical force which is behind them all, is the fundamental reality which it is the aim of speculation to discover. But, according to Buddha, outward things are all shadows and delusions; his primary aim, as a moral teacher, being to deliver men from belief in their reality,—a belief which is the source of all error, sorrow, and suffering. It is clear then that, if Dr. Rhys Davids' interpretation of Buddha's metaphysical system is correct, he (Buddha) was not a materialist, like those modern thinkers with whom he may seem to have much in common, but a philosophical nihilist, who could find no centre of reality, no principle of permanence, in that whirl and flux of phenomena which for him constituted the Universe.

It is true that in more than one passage in his American lectures Dr. Rhys Davids says that Buddha denied the existence of the soul in the Christian sense of the word: and one might infer from this that it was open to him to believe in the soul in some other sense of the word,—for example in the Brahmanic, which is diametrically opposite to the "Christian." But whether Dr. Rhys Davids has himself failed to distinguish between the Christian and the Brahmanic theories of the soul, or whether he regards the former as the only soul-theory which is in any degree compatible with mental sanity, I cannot pretend to say. What is certain is that he regards Buddha's rejection of the soul-theory as thorough-going and uncompromising.

The words "There is no passage of a soul or I in any sense from the one life to the other. Their [the Buddhists'] whole view of the matter is independent of the time-honoured soul-theories held in common by all the followers of every other creed," are decisive on this point. Besides, it stands to reason that if "death, utter death," is the inevitable sequel to Nirvana, there is no room in Buddha's philosophy for the soul, in any sense of the word.

My reason for setting forth in detail Dr. Rhys Davids' interpretation of Buddha's philosophy is that it happens to be the one interpretation which has found its way into the outer world. Ask the man in the street what he knows of Buddha. He will tell you that Buddha was a pessimist and an atheist, who denied the soul, denied a supreme cause, denied that the world had any centre of reality, and taught his followers to look forward to annihilation as the final deliverance from the woes of earth. This, if not identical with Dr. Rhys Davids' teaching, is at least an echo of it. Dr. Paul Carus, who has taken upon himself to popularize Buddhism and to vindicate it from the disparaging criticism of its "Christian critics," is in the main in full agreement with Dr. Rhys Davids, but is more ready than that distinguished scholar to accept the logical consequences of the dynamically atomistic philosophy which he ascribes to Buddha. Even the author of "The Soul of a People," a writer whose deep and delicate sympathy with, and insight into, the "soul" or inner life of a Buddhist people, besides investing his book with a charm which is all its own, entitles him to a respectful hearing whenever he speaks, in general terms, about Buddhism,—even he, when treating of the popular belief in re-incarnation, must needs shake his head over the credulity of the good, simple people, and remind them that belief in the survival of the "I" is "opposed to all Buddhism," the real teaching of Buddha—"that what survives death is not the 'I' but only the results of its action"—"being too deep for them to hold."

Such unanimity on the part of the popular exponents of Buddhism points to a large measure of unanimity on the part of its more learned interpreters and commentators. That Dr. Rhys Davids has given voice to a general consensus of opinion on the part of the Western students of Buddhism, can scarcely be doubted. From Barthelemy Saint-Hilaire to H. C. Warren, the Orientalists of Europe and America are agreed, with one or two notable exceptions, in holding that Buddha denied the Ego and regarded Nirvana as the prelude to annihilation; while the fact that the South Buddhist Church has given Dr. Paul Carus a certificate of orthodoxy suggests that on these points the general trend of official opinion in the Buddhist world itself coincides, mutatis mutandis, with the general trend of learned opinion in the West.

What evidence can Dr. Rhys Davids, and those who think with him, give in support of their thesis that Buddha was a negative dogmatist

"Who dropped his plummet down the broad

Deep Universe, and said 'No God'

There is this initial difficulty in the way of our accepting Dr. Rhys Davids' interpretation of Buddha's metaphysical—as distinguished from his ethical—philosophy, that, on our author's own showing, Buddha was a true and consistent agnostic, who was so far from dogmatizing about what is ultimate that he regarded all metaphysical speculation as vain and foolish, and all metaphysical strife as morally wrong. "There were a certain number of questions to which it was his habit to refuse to reply. These were questions the discussion of which, in his opinion, was apt to lead the mind astray, and so far from being conducive to a growth in insight, would be a hindrance to the only thing which was supremely worth aiming at—the perfect life in Arahat-ship.

Such questions as: What shall I be during the ages of the future? Do I after all exist, or am I not? are regarded as worse than unprofitable, and the Buddha not only refused to discuss them, but held that the tendency, the desire to discuss them was a weakness, and that the answers usually given were a delusion." With these words, which are to be found in Dr. Rhys Davids' American lectures on Buddhism, we may compare Dr. Oldenberg's statement that "the most serious obstacle in the way of our comprehending Buddhist dogmas is the silence with which everything is passed over which does not lead to the separation from the earthly, to the subjection of all desire, to the cessation of the transitory, to quietude, knowledge, illumination, to Nirvana."

Both writers are agreed in holding that the scheme of life which Buddhism set before its votaries was in all probability formulated by Buddha himself; but both writers are also agreed in holding that, though Buddha gave his followers what I may call the penultimate (or perhaps the ante-penultimate) reasons for entering "the Path," he not only carefully abstained from giving them the ultimate reasons, but positively forbade them to speculate as to what those reasons might be. What then becomes of Dr. Rhys Davids' confident and often repeated statement that Buddha's philosophy centred in a fundamental denial? To deny the Ego is to gather all metaphysical problems into one pregnant question, and to answer that question with an everlasting "No." In other words, it is to say the last word that can be said in metaphysical speculation. Is it possible for the same thinker to be, at the same time and on the same plane of thought, a true agnostic and an aggressive dogmatist? If this is not possible, which role are we to assign to Buddha?

The teaching of Buddha, as Dr. Rhys Davids presents it to us, may be divided into two parts,—an ethical scheme of life, and a metaphysical theory of things. Dr. Rhys Davids will scarcely contend that the authenticity of the latter is as strongly vouched for by external evidence as that of the former. That there are passages in the Buddhist Scriptures in which Buddha is represented as having authoritatively denied the Ego, may perhaps be provisionally admitted. But surely, in the light of

Dr. Rhys Davids' assertion that Buddha both abstained from and discountenanced metaphysical speculation, we are free to conjecture that, as statements of Buddha's own metaphysical teaching, these passages are entirely untrustworthy. It is surely conceivable that what is set forth in them is, not Buddha's own words or even his own opinions, but the writers' private interpretation of Buddha's deeper philosophy,—an interpretation which is based partly on what he said, partly on what he left unsaid (for his silence is both significant and suggestive), but chiefly on what the writers themselves happened to believe. It is conceivable that the writers felt, as Dr. Rhys Davids evidently feels and as we must all feel, that behind Buddha's silence there was a living creed; and that, feeling this, they succumbed to a temptation which it is always hard to resist—the temptation to bring the ideas of a great writer into line with one's own—and ascribed to Buddha conclusions and arguments which he had never formulated, but which, in their opinion, he would certainly have endorsed.

It is conceivable, to say the least, that many of the stories and discourses in the Buddhist Scriptures are as far from setting forth the inner creed of Buddha as the writings of Christian theologians in all ages are from setting forth the inner creed of Christ. At any rate, if I am to reconcile Dr. Rhys Davids' authoritative statement that Buddha abstained on principle from metaphysical speculation with his equally authoritative exposition of Buddha's metaphysical system, I must assume that he has based the latter on internal rather than on external evidence; I must assume, in other words, that his interpretation of Buddha's philosophy is, in the main, the outcome of his study of Buddha's scheme of life, is in fact his own private attempt "to complete and to find the centre of the circle" of which Buddha has given us only a "broken arc."

If this is what Dr. Rhys Davids has attempted to do, he has set us an example which I, for one, intend to follow. The specific passages to which he appeals in support of his general thesis will be considered in due course, and an attempt will be made to show that for the most part they admit of an interpretation which is the exact opposite of that which Dr. Rhys Davids has put upon them. But as, on his own showing, the internal evidence is far more weighty than the external (which indeed he has expressly debarred himself from regarding as conclusive), and as on this point I am in full accord with him, I will now study the internal evidence in the light of his interpretation of it. He tells me that Buddha broke away, abruptly and completely, from the deeper spiritual ideas of his own age and country. That he should have done this, that any great Teacher should ever do this, is improbable in a very high degree. Christ was in open revolt against the legalism of his age and nation; but, far from rejecting the grandly poetical conception of God which Israel had evolved in the days of his spiritual greatness, and to which his sacred writings owe their charm and influence, he went back to that conception, went back to what was most spiritual and most poetical in it, reaffirmed this against the materialism and formalism of the Scribes and Pharisees, and then transformed it into a deeper and more spiritual vision of God than Israel, at his best, had ever fashioned.

The relation of Christ to Judaism may well have been paralleled by the relation of Buddha to Brahmanism. That there was much in the Brahmanism of his day which Buddha rejected and even denounced, is certain; but it does not follow from this that he had broken away from the Brahmanic teaching at its highest level. On the contrary, the fact that the Brahmanism of his day had either forgotten that high teaching or deliberately betrayed it, makes it probable that in denouncing the former he was championing the cause of the latter. And the further fact that his own scheme of life, when surveyed from the standpoint of the Brahmanic philosophy, seems to be the practical application and expression of its spiritual ideas, raises to a high degree the probability of his having been in sympathy with those ideas, and raises to a still higher degree the improbability of his having formally renounced them.

Thus at the outset we are entitled to insist that the internal evidence which Dr. Rhys Davids brings forward in support of his general position shall be convincingly strong. It happens, however, that, as an interpreter of the inner creed of an Eastern thinker, he, in common with other European exponents of

Buddhism, labours under the disability of looking at "great matters" from standpoints which are exclusively Western. For example, that ultra-Stoical conception of life which makes it possible for him to say that "the true Buddhist saint does not mar the purity of his self-denial by lusting after a positive happiness, which he, himself, shall enjoy hereafter," and which gives a strong bias to the general attitude which he and others have instinctively adopted towards Buddhism, is wholly foreign to Eastern modes of thought, and is in no way countenanced by Buddha's own ethical teaching.

On this point there cannot be the shadow of a doubt. Buddha's own outlook on life, if, as all the commentators admit, it is faithfully mirrored in the "Four Sacred Truths," was not ultra-Stoical but essentially anti-Stoical. The two paramount ends which he set before his disciples, when he urged them to enter "the Path," were deliverance from suffering and the ultimate fruition of perfect bliss. In other words, his philosophy was hedonism of a pure and exalted type. It is true that he condemned the life of pleasure. But why? Not because those who led it were trying to be happy, but because they were trying to be happy in the wrong way,—because they had mistaken the shadow of happiness for the reality, because what they sowed as pleasure they were doomed to reap as pain. So far was he from condemning man's longing for happiness, that his whole scheme of life may be said to base itself on an appeal to, and resolve itself into a systematic attempt to cultivate, that instinctive desire, by teaching men to "fix their hearts" "where true joys are to be found."

More important even, and more characteristically Western, than the ultra-Stoicism which dominates Dr. Rhys Davids' own ethical philosophy is the dualism which dominates his metaphysical theory of things. This tendency affects his interpretation of Buddha's ideas in more ways than one, but chiefly in this one way. He insists on things being divided into the existent and the non-existent, which are alternatives, whereas the higher thought of India seems to have divided them into the real and the unreal, which are not alternatives but polar opposites.

Thus Dr. Rhys Davids would say that the Ego exists or does not exist, whereas the Indian thinker would concern himself with the problem of the reality of the Ego, and would see that what is real (or unreal) from one point of view may be unreal (or real) from another. The difference between the two ways of looking at things goes very deep; goes in fact to the root of most of the problems that perplex the student of Buddhism. Existence and non-existence are alternatives; and, if we are to choose between alternatives, we must provide ourselves with a criterion by which we may know the true alternative from the false. But how shall man, who is presumably not omniscient, provide himself with a criterion which will enable him to define the boundaries of the Universe? For it is this, and nothing less, that he attempts to do when he takes upon himself to divide things into the existent and the non-existent. What is the criterion or test of existence?

It is impossible to answer this question except by begging it. In other words, we must say what we mean by existence before we can attempt to distinguish between the existent and the non-existent. But in the very act of defining the word, we provide ourselves, whether we intend to do this or not, with a test of the thing. For example. We ask ourselves: Does a certain thing exist or not? Does a centaur exist or not? Does a mermaid exist or not? It is easy for us to answer these questions, so long as we agree among ourselves that the existent is that which is perceptible by man's bodily senses. In thus defining the word existent, we provide ourselves with a test of existence; and the test is valid just so long and so far as the definition is true.

But the definition is, at best, only hypothetically and provisionally true. In the ordinary affairs of everyday life it is sufficiently true to answer our practical purposes. This is all that we can say about it. To take for granted that it is absolutely true, and that the corresponding test of existence is absolutely valid, is to beg every question which this hypothesis enables us to answer: for, the moment we accept the definition as true without qualification or reserve, we commit ourselves to a vast metaphysical assumption. Does the Ego exist or does it not?

"No," answers the "uninitiated" thinker, "it does not satisfy my criterion of existence.

It is not perceptible by my bodily senses." He fails to see that the question as to the existence of the Ego, which is, ex hypothesi, invisible and otherwise imperceptible, involves the further question as to the validity of his materialistic test of existence. To ask whether the Ego exists or not is to challenge, by implication, the validity of that particular test. Had the test been regarded as absolutely valid, the question as to the Ego would never have been raised. Yet it is only the thinker who has allowed the materialistic conception of existence to dominate his mind and limit his whole speculative outlook; in other words, who has allowed the practical demands of his ordinary everyday life to control the philosophical movement of his thoughts;—it is only the thinker of this crude and commonplace type, who can bring himself to ask whether the Ego exists or not. The teacher who rejects that particular test of existence knows that there is no (final) test, and he therefore abstains from asking a question which is of necessity begged in the act of being asked.

Not only must there be a recognized test of existence, if the controversy as to the existence of the Ego is to have any issue, but there must also be a tacit agreement among the disputants as to the meaning of the word Ego. In the absence of such agreement, the discussion can lead to nothing but loss of temper and confusion of thought. And as in the region of metaphysics such agreement is not to be looked for, since, if it existed, the very raison d'etre of metaphysical inquiry would be gone, one can but conclude that to debate such a question as Does the Ego exist?—a question which takes one in an instant to the ultimate limits of human thought—is not merely a mischievous waste of mental energy, but also a proof of mental blindness on the part of those who allow themselves to indulge in so futile a controversy. Even such questions as Does a centaur exist? or Does a mermaid exist? become unanswerable the moment they become metaphysical. For, though neither a centaur nor a mermaid exists, in the sense of being perceptible by man's bodily senses, each of these fabled beings does exist as a creation of the human mind. Is existence, in that sense of the word, equivalent to non-existence? Perhaps it is: but the question goes to the root of human thought; and it is impossible to answer it offhand without begging all the deeper questions which it involves.

As metaphysical controversy was wholly repugnant to Buddha's type of mind, the antecedent improbability of his having indulged in the most futile of all metaphysical controversies and authoritatively solved the meaningless problem in which that controversy finally centres, is overwhelmingly strong. Moreover, there is, as it happens, positive evidence that, when he was invited to think and teach in the category of the existent and the non-existent, he deliberately refused to do so. The story of the dialogue between Buddha and Vacchagotta will presently be told, and its meaning will be considered. Meanwhile, it is enough for our present purpose to know that, when the wandering monk Vacchagotta challenged the "Exalted One" with the question "Is there the Ego?" and then with the question "Is there not the Ego?" he was in each case answered with silence.

The more carefully one studies the teaching of Buddha, the stronger does one's conviction become that the ultimate category in which he thought was that of the real and the unreal, not that of the existent and the non-existent. The difference between these two categories is that, whereas the existent and the non-existent are (as has been already pointed out) mutually exclusive alternatives, the real and the unreal are polar opposites, and as such always coexist—except of course at the ideal points of infinity and zero—varying together in inverse proportion, or, in other words, being so related to one another that the one falls as the other rises and rises as the other falls. If we are to choose between alternatives, we must be able to apply to each of them from without (so to speak) a recognized criterion or test. When our alternatives are ultimate conceptions, such as the existent and the non-existent, it stands to reason that to apply a test from without is impossible:—

"For God alone sits high enough above

To speculate so largely."

If we are to choose between polar opposites, we must be able to measure them by a standard. This standard is always internal to, and inherent in, the movement of the two opposites from pole to counter pole. It follows that, even when our opposites are ultimate conceptions, such as the real and the unreal, a standard of measurement is available, being inherent in the very movement of our thought. For example, to ask whether the inward and spiritual side of life is existent or non-existent, is to ask a meaningless and therefore an unanswerable question. To ask whether it is real or unreal is to ask a question to which life itself, both in its universal and in its individual movement, is the abiding, though never formulated, answer. That Buddha thought in the category of the real and the unreal is suggested by the whole tenor of his teaching. If there is any one thing which his sayings make quite clear, it is that he regarded outward things and the outward side of life as unreal. But he was not so foolish as to think of them as non-existent. Which is the real pole of existence? is the question which he must have asked himself; and his scheme of life is his answer to that question.

Let us now assume, for argument's sake, that the answer which he gave to life's master question was the opposite of that which the general tenor of his teaching would seem to suggest. Let us go further. Let us assume, with most of the Western exponents of Buddhism, that Buddha was a negative dogmatist, pure and simple,—that he regarded the Ego not merely as unreal but as non-existent. What follows with regard to his scheme of life? That scheme undoubtedly centres in the doctrine of re-incarnation, the very purpose of it being to deliver men from the "whirlpool of rebirth." If there is no re-incarnating Ego, what becomes of the doctrine of re-incarnation? And if this, the keystone of the arch of Buddhist thought, is withdrawn, what becomes of Buddha's scheme of life? Dr. Rhys Davids, and those who think with him, have tried to face this difficulty.

In his first exposition of Buddhism Dr. Rhys Davids saw clearly that denial of the Ego turned the doctrine of re-incarnation into nonsense, and he accepted the consequences of this conclusion. He so expounded the Buddhist belief in re-incarnation as to make nonsense of it, and then boldly affirmed that the belief was in its essence nonsensical. Speaking of those who have trusted themselves to the seemingly stately bridge which Buddhism has tried to build over the river of the mysteries and sorrows of life, he said, "they have failed to see that the very keystone [of the bridge], the link between one life and another, is a mere word—this wonderful hypothesis, this airy nothing, this imaginary cause beyond the reach of reason—the individualized and individualizing force of Karma." But in his American lectures he departs from this logical and intelligible position, and tries to persuade himself that the doctrine of re-incarnation, even if there be no re-incarnating Ego, is sense. "There is a real identity between a man in his present life and in the future. But the identity is not in a conscious soul which shall fly out away from his body after he is dead.

The real identity is that of cause and effect. A man thinks he began to be a few years—twenty, fifty, sixty years ago. There is some truth in that; but in a much larger, deeper, truer sense he has been (in the causes of which he is the result) for countless ages in the past; and those same causes (of which he is the temporary effect) will continue in other like temporary forms through countless ages yet to come. In that sense alone, according to Buddhism, each of us has after death a continuing life." This is an interesting statement of Dr. Rhys Davids' own ideas about human immortality, but as a statement of what Buddha taught it is utterly misleading. It is doubtless true that all the forces of Nature, operating through millions of years, meet in me; and that what I do will produce consequences which will pass on, with an ever widening lateral movement, into the remotest future.

But this is not what Buddhism teaches, in the doctrine of Karma, or has ever taught. "The peculiarity of Buddhism," says Dr. Rhys Davids himself, "lies in this, that the result of what a man is or does is held not to be dissipated, as it were, into many streams, but concentrated together in the formation of one new sentient being." What Buddhism teaches is that I reap the crop which was sowed by some one man who lived before I did, and that in like manner some one man in the future will reap the crop which I am sowing now; and so on, both backwards and forwards. It teaches, in other words, that the current of moral cause and effect flows in the narrow channel of a succession of individual lives (or rather in a number of such channels), whereas modern science, to which Dr. Rhys Davids seems to look for inspiration and guidance, teaches that there is always a dual movement,—from the collective life into the individual, and from the individual life into the collective.

The difference between these two conceptions of moral causation, and between the two derivative conceptions of human immortality, is as wide as it is deep. The question which we have to ask ourselves with regard to the Buddhist conception is a simple one: Is the identity between me and the inheritor of my Karma, or again between me and the man whose Karma I inherit, as real as the identity between the me of today and the me of twenty years hence (if I shall be living then), or again between the me of today and the me of my boyhood? If it is not as real, the doctrine of re-incarnation is pure nonsense from both points of view,—from that of Eastern idealism and of Western science. But if it is as real, the doctrine is sound sense in the eyes of Eastern idealism; and though Western science cannot countenance it, it is equally certain that it cannot reject it, for the matter is one which necessarily eludes its grasp.

Now, strange as it may seem, there is nothing in the Buddhist Scriptures to show that even those thinkers who are supposed to have declared war against the Ego regarded the identity between man and man, in a given line of Karmic succession, as less real than the identity between what a man is today and what he was twenty years ago, or will be twenty years hence. The author of the Milinda dialogues, for example, is supposed to have argued against the Ego. I doubt if he really did. It is quite possible, I think, that his dialogues have a different aim and admit of a different interpretation.

But let us assume that, in theory at least, he denied the Ego, and that in this respect he falls into line with the modern votaries of metaphysical atomism. What then? I cannot find anything in any of his dialogues to show that his belief in individual re-incarnation was other than real. I cannot find anything to show that he regarded the identity between A, who is living now, and B, the future inheritor of his Karma, as in any way different from the identity between the A of today and the A of twenty years ago or twenty years hence. Thoroughgoing denial of the Ego destroys the identity of a man from moment to moment as effectually as from life to life. But—to quote Pascal's words—*"la nature soutient la raison impuissante et l'empeche d'extravaguer jusqu'a ce point."* Even Dr. Paul Carus, whose intense antipathy to the Ego makes him the protagonist of the metaphysical atomists, would probably admit, as a working hypothesis, that he was the same being as Dr. Paul Carus of twenty years ago, just as he would speak of self-culture, self-development, self-control, though all the while he regards the sense of self as entirely delusive. And, in like manner, the author of the Milinda dialogues would have accepted, as a working hypothesis, the identity of himself with the next inheritor of his Karma, even though he regarded (according to our provisional assumption) the sense of self as entirely delusive.

But between these two concessions, which seem to have so much in common, there is a great gulf fixed,—the very gulf which separates Western from Eastern thought. Dr. Paul Carus, who is steeped in the science of the West, would never admit, even as a working hypothesis, that A, who is living now, was the same being as a certain B, who appeared on earth one hundred years ago (or whatever the number of intervening years might be). The idea of one man inheriting all the Karma of another man is one which he could not possibly entertain. The author of the Milinda dialogues might well have said, "I have lived on earth many times already, and shall probably live many times more, but of course there is no I in the case at all." But Dr. Paul Carus could not say this, though he might well say, "I have lived on earth for so many years, and may possibly live for so many more, but of course there is no I in the case at all."

There is nothing, then, to show that the Buddhist of the anti-Ego school is not as sure of his identity from life to life as Dr. Paul Carus is of his identity from year to year, or from day to day. In each case the sense of assurance sinks in theory to zero, but in practice it is strong enough for all the practical purposes of life. In other words, the denial is in each case academic (or "notional") whereas the belief is practical (or "real"). But the difference between the respective ranges of the "real" belief of a Buddhist and the "real" belief of Dr. Paul Carus is immense, and has far-reaching consequences. Within the limits of his own earth life, Dr. Paul Carus combines academic denial with "real" belief; but the moment those limits are passed, the denial ceases to be academic and becomes intensely "real." The Buddhist, who is much more logical, sees no reason for drawing a hard and fast line at either birth or death. Backward and forward, as far as the eye of his thought can reach, his denial of the Ego, however sweeping and uncompromising it may be, is always "notional," whereas his belief in it is always "real." We shall presently learn that the monk Yamaka, who identified Nirvana with annihilation, was persuaded to abandon this "wicked heresy" by a fellow-monk, who reminded him that the arguments against the reality of the Nirvanic life of the "Saint" were not a whit stronger than the arguments against the reality of the true life of the "Saint" whilst on earth. The moral of this story is surely obvious and significant.

I have spoken at some length on this point because I wish to make it clear that, if denial of the Ego is real, if its meaning is fully pressed home, the doctrine of re-incarnation, which is undoubtedly the keystone of the whole arch of Buddhist thought, becomes pure nonsense. The essence of the doctrine is that B inherits the whole of A's Karma, C the whole of B's, and so on. Unless the identity of A with B, of B with C, and so on, is as real as the identity, within the limits of each earth life, of the child with the youth and the youth with the man, the doctrine loses its meaning, and the arch of thought which it holds together becomes a ruinous heap. We must therefore either assume that the arch of Buddhist thought and doctrine had no keystone, or that the Buddhist denial of the "Ego" was "notional" rather than "real." Of these alternative assumptions, reason and common sense alike demand that we should adopt the latter.

Whichever assumption we adopt, we are at liberty to say that the attempts which Dr. Rhys Davids, Dr. Paul Carus and other Western interpreters of Buddhism make to bring the doctrine of re-incarnation into line with the scientific doctrines of heredity, of physical causation, and the like, are sophistical and inconclusive. I have not made an exhaustive study of the eschatology of the modern "religion of science"; but I understand that it recognizes three kinds of immortality. The first is that of living in the lives of our direct descendants,—an immortality which one can enjoy, while still on earth, down to the second or third of the after generations (for a man may live to see his great-grandchildren), but which bachelors, old maids, and other persons who die without issue are not allowed to share. The second is the immortality of fame (or notoriety)—the immortality of a Marcus Aurelius (or a John Lackland)—an immortality which few persons are privileged to enjoy, and which, with very rare exceptions, is of brief duration.

The third is the immortality of living in the consequences of one's actions, so far as these affect for good or for evil the lives of other men. The immortality to which Buddha taught his disciples to look forward has nothing in common with any of these. The immortality of living in the ever-widening consequences of one's conduct is real enough, and the contemplation of it may give satisfaction to certain minds. But the immortality which the law of Karma makes possible is wholly different from this. The Karmic consequences of action are in the main inward and spiritual,—the effect on the doer of what he habitually does. Hence it is that the doctrine of re-incarnation, when divorced from the doctrine of a re-incarnating soul or Ego, loses its meaning and its value, and becomes as wildly fantastic as Western thought too readily assumes it to be. It stands to reason that, if there is no Ego, the inward consequences of a man's conduct will end abruptly at his death. What then? Are we to suppose that the outward consequences of his conduct, which have diffused themselves far and wide during his lifetime, will after his death—perhaps long after his death, for the return to earth may be long delayed—be reunited in the channel of a single human life?

The supposition is not merely incredible, but absolutely unthinkable. The alternative supposition that B, the inheritor of A's Karma, will be rewarded (or punished)—presumably by an omnipotent magician—for A's conduct while on earth is worse than unthinkable. It does violence to one's sense of law on every plane of thought. But when the doctrine of Karma is supported and elucidated by the conception of a re-incarnating soul or Ego, it at once becomes intelligible, even from the point of view of denial of the Ego. To say that conduct always reacts upon character, and that the departing soul will therefore take away with it from earth the inward consequences of its action and bring these back to earth, with all their possible ulterior consequences, at its next incarnation, is to say what is certainly disputable and perhaps untrue but at any rate has the merit of making coherent sense.

The inherent unreasonableness of the doctrine of Karma, as Western orientalists choose to interpret it, will become more apparent when we consider it in its relation to the motives which Buddha set before his followers. The paramount motive was the prospect of escaping from the "whirlpool of rebirth" and attaining to the bliss of Nirvana. That this goal should be won within the limits of a single earth-life, however virtuous, was not—we may rest assured—contemplated by Buddha, or by any of those thinkers who carried on the tradition of his teaching. This is a general statement which admits of isolated exceptions. A man of abnormal spiritual development, like Buddha himself—a man whom a long series of virtuous lives had brought to the threshold of Nirvana—might conceivably cross that threshold before he died, and return to earth no more.

But for the rank and file of mankind the goal of deliverance was a "far-off divine event" to which the journey was in any case long and toilsome, though it might be materially shortened if the Path which Buddha pointed out to mankind—the path of sympathy and self-control—was resolutely entered and faithfully followed. "The Buddhist," says Dr. Rhys Davids, "hopes to enter, even though he will not reach the end of, the Path in this life; and if he once enters therein, he is certain in some future existence, perhaps under less material conditions, to arrive at the goal of salvation, at the calm and rest of Nirvana." "He is certain." But is it he who will arrive at the goal, or someone else? Why does the life of sympathy and self-control tend to shorten the journey to Nirvana? Obviously, because it makes for the spiritual development of the man who leads it; because it strengthens his character, deepens his insight, expands his consciousness, purifies his soul. But what if there is to be no identity between A, who is now walking in the Path, and B, the next inheritor of his Karma? From the point of view of the goal which Buddha set before men, the inward consequences of A's conduct—the reaction of what he does on what he is—are of supreme importance.

But if there is no self, no Ego to return to earth, the inward consequences will, as I have lately pointed out, end abruptly at A's death, and there will be no character—developed, expanded, purified—for A to transmit to B, his new self. We must at any rate assume, if we are to see any meaning in Buddha's appeal to mankind, that the identity between A and B is as real as the identity between the A of this year and the A of next year, however real (or unreal) that identity may be. And this, I think, is what the accredited exponents of Buddhism, including those who may have denied the Ego in theory, have always taken for granted. There is nothing to show that, when Buddhism expounds and enforces the doctrine of natural retribution, it has any doubt as to B inheriting the inward consequences of A's conduct. But the inward consequences of A's conduct are summed up in his character; and if he transmits his character to B, he transmits himself.

It is here that Buddhism parts company with those Western interpreters of it who try, like Dr. Paul Carus, to affiliate it to the (so-called) "religion of science." Whatever theory

Dr. Paul Carus may hold as to the identity (or non-identity) of the man of sixty or seventy years with the same man (as we must call him) at the age of twenty or thirty, he would admit, without hesitation, that it was both reasonable and just that the old man should suffer because the young man had sinned. Similarly, whatever theory the author of the Milinda Dialogues may have held as to the identity (or non-identity) of B with A, he would have admitted, without hesitation, that it was both reasonable and just that B should suffer because A had sinned. But Dr. Paul Carus could never bring himself to admit this: he could never in any way recognize individual re-incarnation.

Let us, however, suppose that Buddha and his followers were in full accord with Dr. Paul Carus. Let us suppose that their denial of the Ego, as an entity which survives death, was not academic, but practical and real. In that case what would become of the paramount motive which they set before their fellow-men? If it were possible for each man, in his own lifetime on earth, to attain to Nirvana, there would be a meaning, even for those who denied the Ego, in the promise of deliverance, though in that case the fulfilment of the Buddhist Law would involve the early extinction of the whole human race. But as, apart from a few isolated cases, the possibility of a man attaining to Nirvana in his own earth-life has never been contemplated by Buddhism, the promise of deliverance, when coupled with an authoritative denial of the Ego, must be regarded as the hollowest of mockeries.

What sense is there in telling me to live virtuously now in order that, if my successors in that line of earth-lives to which I happen to belong are equally virtuous, someone who would otherwise appear on earth 100,000 years hence (let us say) may not be born; and in order that someone else—his immediate predecessor in the given line of lives—may enjoy the evanescent bliss of Nirvana?

To tell A to be virtuous in order that, somewhere in the remote future, Y may be supremely happy for a few years and Z may not be born, is to set him a meaningless task. It is difficult to say which sense is the more deeply outraged by such a doctrine of moral retribution,—one's sense of justice or (for the chain of cause and effect is obviously broken at each successive death) one's sense of natural law. I will now set forth as briefly as possible my reasons for calling the current interpretation of Buddha's ideas a "misreading of Buddha."

The antecedent improbability of a great Teacher breaking away completely from the highest and deepest thought of his nation and his age, is very great. The great Teacher is always a reformer as well as an innovator; and to reform is to go back to an ideal which had been forgotten, or otherwise obscured. The chances are, then, that Buddha, who was unquestionably one of the greatest of all moral teachers, went back from what was corrupt and degenerate in the thought and the consequent practice of his age to what was pure and spiritual. This much we may say before we begin to study his scheme of life.

But when we study that scheme, and find, as we certainly do, that it is the practical application and embodiment of the great ideas of Indian idealism—so much so, indeed, that we may actually deduce from those ideas (given a practical aim on the part of their votary) the leading features of the Buddhist "Law"—we cannot but feel that the probability of the Founder of Buddhism having been an idealist (in the truest sense of the word) at heart—at the heart of his own deep silence—is raised to a very high degree.

And when, having for argument's sake assumed the opposite of this, assumed that the teaching of Buddha was directly and fundamentally subversive of the ideas which found utterance in the Upanishads, we find that the whole system falls to pieces and the wisdom of it becomes unthinkable nonsense, then what has hitherto been probability of a very high degree seems to approach the level of certainty. At any rate, if we may not yet say that the creed which Buddha held but did not openly profess, was the spiritual idealism of ancient India, we may say that the counter-hypothesis—that Buddha's creed was the direct negation of that lofty faith—can easily be disproved. The efforts that are made to bring the teaching of Buddha into line with the negative dogmatism of the "religion of science" would be ludicrous if they were not, in a sense, pathetic. For, in truth, they prove nothing except the depth of the abyss that separates Eastern from Western thought.

BUDDHA'S SILENCE

IT is the silence of Buddha which has misled so many of his commentators. The teacher who, while pointing out to us the ultimate issues of life, keeps silence as to its ultimate realities and ultimate principles, must be prepared for his philosophy—the philosophy that is at the heart of his silence—to be misunderstood. It is not merely that he gives us no clue to the labyrinth of his deeper thoughts, and so leaves each of us free to explore that labyrinth for himself. There is another and a graver danger to which he exposes the faith of his heart. Of those who take a speculative interest in his ideas, few will be content to regard his silence as purely agnostic. The majority will see in it either the negation or the confirmation of their own philosophical prejudices. The positive dogmatist, who has made up his mind that the ultimate realities of existence are such and such, will regard it as a challenge and a defiance, and will apply to it the epithets which he reserves for denial of his own creed. The negative dogmatist will insist that it is a polite concession to the weakness of the "orthodox," and that behind it is a conception of life as fundamentally negative as his own. In either case the silence of the Master will be construed as equivalent to denial and revolt.

This is the fate which has befallen Buddha. Because he said nothing about God he is held—by the "orthodox" as well as by the "unbeliever"—to have "denied the divine." Because he said little about the "Self," and because that little was mainly negative, 1 he is held to have denied the Ego. And he is credited with all the consequences of these tremendous denials. He who on principle kept silence about what is, ultimate is supposed to have elaborated a complete system of negatively ultimate thought.

There is nothing in the history of human thought more dramatic or more significant than the silence of Buddha. Let us try to fathom its depths. That there is a deep spiritual meaning, that there was a deep spiritual conviction, at the heart of it can scarcely be doubted. It was not from indifference that Buddha, of all men, became and remained to the end an apparent agnostic. And, apart from indifference, though there may be silence about "great matters," there can be no agnosticism (in the sense of metaphysical neutrality) in the thinker's inner life. A state of perfect mental equilibrium is incompatible with living interest in the deeper problems of existence. The silence of Buddha seems to have been the deliberate fulfilment of a self-imposed vow. At any rate there was a strong purpose behind it; and that purpose must have been the outcome, not of philosophical indifference, but of some master theory of things.

The more closely I study the stories in which Buddha answers the overcurious with silence and gives his reasons for doing so, and the more freely I surrender myself to the subtle influence of their atmosphere, the stronger does my conviction become that Buddha kept silence, when metaphysical questions were discussed, not because he had nothing to say about great matters, but because he had far too much, because he was overwhelmed by the flood of his own mighty thoughts, and because the channels of expression which the riddle-mongers of his day invited him to use were both too narrow and too shallow to give his soul relief. As it is on the plane of spiritual emotion, so it is on the plane of spiritual thought. "Silence," says one of Shakespeare's characters,

"is the perfectest herald of joy:

I were but little happy if I could say how much."

The babbling river, as another poet reminds us, is overwhelmed and silenced by the flow of the tide-wave from the unfathomed sea. This simile has the beauty of truth. The mind that is visited by world-encompassing waves of thought (or of emotion) has more to say than words can express, or than other minds can receive. There are, indeed, some gifted souls for whom the channel of poetry provides an overflow (rather than an outflow) for their flooding thoughts. For the rest of us (as Buddha saw clearly) there is but one available outlet,—that of action, conduct, life; and life will have a stronger purpose and a larger scope when silence is behind it than when its motive force is a flux of words. So eloquent and so significant is Buddha's own silence, that it seems at last, when one becomes familiar with it, to give a clearer insight into the secrets of his soul than any formulated confession of words could ever have done.

Let us now hear the reasons which Buddha himself (or those who spoke in his name) gave for his silence. Let us study the three stories which Dr. Oldenberg has selected as indicative of his attitude towards the questions with which the thinkers of his day perplexed themselves. The first runs thus:

"Then the wandering monk Vacchagotta went to where the Exalted One was staying. When he had come near him, he saluted him. When saluting him, he had interchanged friendly words with him, he sat down beside him. Sitting beside him the wandering monk Vacchagotta spake to the Exalted One, saying: 'How does the matter stand, venerable Gautama, is there the Ego?'

"When he said this, the Exalted One was silent.

"'How then, venerable Gautama, is there not the Ego?'

"And still the Exalted One maintained silence. Then the wandering monk Vacchagotta rose from his seat and went away.

"But the venerable ananda, when the wandering monk Vacchagotta had gone to a distance, soon said to the Exalted One:

"'Wherefore, sire, has the Exalted One not given an answer to the questions put by the wandering monk Vacchagotta?'

"'If I, ananda, when the wandering monk Vacchagotta asked me: "Is there the Ego?" had answered: "The Ego is," then that, ananda, would have confirmed the doctrine of the Samanas and Brahmanas who believe in permanence. If I, ananda, when the wandering monk Vacchagotta asked me: "Is there not the Ego?" had answered: "The Ego is not," then that, ananda, would have confirmed the doctrine of the Samanas and Brahmanas who believe in annihilation. If I, ananda, when the wandering monk Vacchagotta asked me: "Is there the Ego?" had answered: "The Ego is," would that have served my end, ananda, by producing in him the knowledge: all existences are non-Ego?'

"'That it would not, sire.'

"'But if I, ananda, when the wandering monk Vacchagotta asked me: "Is there not the Ego?" had answered: "The Ego is not," then that, ananda, would only have caused the wandering monk Vacchagotta to be thrown from one bewilderment into another: "My Ego, did it not exist before? but now it exists no longer!""'

In this story Buddha gives two reasons for refusing to answer Vacchagotta's question. He is asked to answer Yes or No. Whichever answer he may give, some school of metaphysicians is sure to claim him as its own. And whichever answer he may give, he is sure to bewilder Vacchagotta.

That Buddha had no patience with the metaphysicians is made clear by this and by other stories. He had many quarrels with them. He objected to them for playing with words, with the result that on the one hand they drew people away from the main business of life and on the other hand profaned by the inadequacy of their symbols the deep mysteries which they professed to explore. He objected to the misconception of knowledge, of truth, of reality, which underlay their shallow dualism, and made it possible for them to assume that all the problems of existence could be brought to the issue of a simple Yes or a simple No. Above all, he deplored the loss of temper which the very futility of their wordy wrangling rendered inevitable,—the loss of charity, the loss of serenity, the loss of self-control, the loss of all the qualities which he had called upon men to cultivate. "The theory that the world is eternal, the theory that the world is infinite, the theory that the soul and the body are identical"—of each of these and of all kindred theories he says the same thing—"this theory is a jungle, a wilderness, a puppet show, a writhing and a fetter, and is coupled with misery, ruin, despair and agony and does not tend to aversion, absence of passion, cessation, quiescence, knowledge, supreme wisdom and Nirvana."

But we shall the better understand his antipathy to the metaphysicians if we consider the second of his reasons for remaining silent,—his fear of either misleading or bewildering Vacchagotta. Dr. Oldenberg thinks that in giving this reason he came very near to saying that there was no Ego, and that it was only regard for Vacchagotta's susceptibilities which kept him silent. This criticism is, I think, based on a misconception of Buddha's mental attitude. Buddha saw clearly enough that the answer to Vacchagotta's question, as to all similar questions, was "Yes and No,"—"Yes" from this point of view, "No" from that. The words that are ascribed to him—words which may well have been his—suggest that some such thoughts as these were passing through his mind: "The Ego is real beyond all reality, but I cannot hope to make Vacchagotta understand this.

If I tell him that the Ego is, he will assume that I mean by the word what he does, and so be led astray. If, foreseeing this, I tell him that the body is not the Ego, the sensations are not the Ego, the consciousness is not the Ego, and so forth,—if, in my desire to bring home to him the transcendent reality of the Ego, I refuse to allow him to identify it with any of those things which he has been accustomed to regard as real,—he will come to the conclusion that there is no Ego, that the word is an empty name.

If, on the other hand, I tell him that, as he understands the word, there is no Ego, that the sense of individuality, of separateness, which seems to him to be of the essence of the sense of self, is delusive (separateness being the very negation of true selfhood), he will be equally bewildered. In either case he will feel that he has been living in a dream. What can I do, then, but keep silent?

Had Buddha shared Dr. Paul Carus' fundamental antipathy to the Ego—to the whole idea of selfhood—he would, I think, without hesitation have answered the monk's question with an uncompromising No; for metaphysical atomism, like every other development of materialism, is very easy to explain, the strength of materialism lying in this, that it is the precise system of thought which the average man, who had forgotten his mother's teaching and silenced the questionings of his heart, would—if he took to thinking—construct for himself. Had Buddha believed in the Ego, as the pious Christian believes in it, as a something (to use Dr. Rhys Davids' words) "which flies out away from the body" and retains its individuality for all time, he would have answered the monk's question with an unqualified "Yes"; for he would have known that the monk's conception of the Ego coincided with, or at any rate approximated to, his own.

That he said neither "Yes" or "No" suggests that he neither believed in the Ego, as the pious Christian believes in it, nor disbelieved in it, as the votary of the "religion of science" disbelieves in it; and leaves us free to conjecture that his conception of the Ego, whatever form it may have taken, transcended the range of ordinary thought and would not suffer itself to be translated into intelligible speech.

The second story has been thus epitomized for us by Dr. Oldenberg:

> *"The venerable Malukya comes to the Master, and expresses his astonishment that the Master's discourse leaves a series of the very most important and deepest questions unanswered. Is the world eternal or is it limited by bounds of time? Does the Perfect Buddha live on beyond death? Does the Perfect One not live on beyond death? It pleases me not, says the monk, that all this shall remain unanswered and I do not think it right; therefore I am come to the Master to interrogate him about these doubts. May it please Buddha to answer them if he can. 'But when anyone does not understand a matter and does not know it, then a straightforward man says: I do not understand that, I do not know that.'*

"We see: the question of the Nirvana is brought before Buddha by that monk as directly and definitely as could ever be possible. And what answers Buddha? He says in his Socratic fashion, not without a touch of irony, 'What have I said to thee before now, Malukyaputta?

Have I said, Come, Malukyaputta, and be my disciple; I shall teach thee whether the world is everlasting or not everlasting, whether the world is finite or infinite, whether the vital faculty is identical with the body or separate from it, whether the Perfect One lives on after death or does not live on, or whether the Perfect One lives on and at the same time does not live on after death, or whether he neither lives on nor does not live on?'

"'That thou hast not said, Sire.'

"'Or hast thou,' Buddha goes on, 'said to me: I shall be thy disciple, declare unto me, whether the world is everlasting or not everlasting, and so on?'

"This also must Malukya answer in the negative.

"'If a man,' Buddha proceeds, 'were struck by a poisoned arrow, and his friends and relatives called in a skilful physician, what if the wounded man said: "I shall not allow my wound to be treated until I know who the man is by whom I have been wounded, whether he is a noble, a Brahman, a Vaicya, a Cudra"—or if he said: "I shall not allow my wound to be treated until I know what they call the man who has wounded me, and of what family he is, whether he is tall or small or of middle stature, and how his weapon was made with which he has struck me." What would the end of the case be? The man would die of his wound.'

"Why has Buddha not taught his disciples, whether the world is finite or infinite, whether the saint lives on beyond death or not?

Because the knowledge of these things does not conduct to progress in holiness, because it does not contribute to peace and enlightenment. What contributes to peace and enlightenment, Buddha has taught his own: the truth of suffering, the truth of the origin of suffering, the truth of the path to the cessation of suffering. 'Therefore, Malukyaputta, whatsoever has not been revealed by me, let that remain unrevealed, and what has been revealed, let it be revealed.'"

In this story Buddha claims to have taught his disciples all that they need to know and can be made to understand. More than this he cannot and will not teach them.

He may know more about the deeper realities of existence than he chooses to reveal. Malukya suggests that he should make open confession of his ignorance, but he makes no response to this. His reason for keeping silent is that, if men are to wait till Malukya's questions have been adequately answered, they will have to wait for ever, and meanwhile the main concerns of life—the pursuit of peace and enlightenment, the practice of self-control, the cultivation of sympathy—will be forgotten and neglected. The average man may either ask the "Doctors" to answer those great questions for him, or he may try to answer them for himself. The result will be the same in either case. The questions will never be answered; the Path will never be entered; and, what is worse, the evil passions which are generated by verbal controversy will poison the springs of spiritual life.

When we read this dialogue we seem to have travelled far from the Indian idea that knowledge of reality is the first condition of "salvation." But, in truth, we have never really quitted it. The metaphysical path to knowledge was one which Buddha looked upon with distrust and aversion; but knowledge itself—the knowledge which has its counterpart in inward enlightenment, the knowledge of reality which makes for peace and deliverance—was the very goal to which the Path was intended to lead.

The truth of things, as Buddha conceived of it, could not be set forth in a series of formulas, for (to go no further) the laws of language would make that impossible; but it could be lived up to and lived in to: and so he bade men control their passions and desires, and cultivate kindness and goodwill, that the consequent growth of their souls might be rewarded by the expansion of their consciousness and the deepening of their insight, till it became possible for them to know (in the truest sense of the word) the fleeting from the abiding, the phantasmal from the real.

The propositions which Malukya challenged Buddha to answer had but little meaning for him. This we may take for granted. But he might conceivably have waived them aside, and tried to disclose to his disciples the inner faith of his own heart.

That he made no attempt to do so does not prove that there was no master theory of things behind his formal teaching. When we read the words "whatsoever has not been revealed by me let that remain unrevealed," we cannot but feel that what "remained unrevealed" was something well worth revealing. What the silence of Buddha does prove, or at least suggest, is that the creed of his heart was too deep for words,—that the realities which it sought to encompass and co-ordinate far transcended the normal range of human thought.

What the first story left us free to conjecture, the second has suggested to us as a plausible hypothesis,—namely, that Buddha's silence was the outcome, not of the hollowness of his creed, but of the very abundance of his spiritual faith. The third story falls into line with the first and second, but brings us nearer to the same conclusion.

"King Pasenadi of Kosala, we are told, on one occasion on a journey between his two chief towns, Saketa and Savatthi, fell in with the nun Khema, a female disciple of Buddha, renowned for her wisdom. The King paid his respects to her, and inquired of her concerning the sacred doctrine.

"'Venerable lady,' asked the King, 'does the Perfect One exist after death?'

"'The Exalted One, O great King, has not declared: the Perfect One exists after death.'

"'Then does the Perfect One not exist after death, venerable lady?'

"'This also, O great King, the Exalted One has not declared: the Perfect One does not exist after death.'

"'Thus, venerable lady, the Perfect One does exist after death, and at the same time does not exist after death?—thus, venerable lady, the Perfect One neither exists after death, nor does he not exist?'

"The answer is still the same: the Exalted One has not revealed it....

"The King is astonished. 'What is the reason, venerable lady, what is the ground, on which the Exalted One has not revealed this?'

"'Permit me,' answers the nun, 'now to ask thee a question, O great King, and do thou answer me as the case seems to thee to stand. How thinks thou, O great King, hast thou an accountant, or a mint-master, or a treasurer, who could count the sands of the Ganges, who could say: there are there so many grains of sand, or so many hundreds, or thousands, or hundreds of thousands of grains of sand?'

"'No, venerable lady, I have not.'

"'Or hast thou an accountant, a mint-master, or a treasurer, who could measure the water in the great ocean, who could say: there are therein so many measures of water, or so many hundreds, or thousands, or hundreds of thousands of measures of water?'

"'No, venerable lady, I have not.'

"'And why not? The great ocean is deep, immeasurable, unfathomable. So also, O great King, if the existence of the Perfect One be measured by the predicates of corporeal form: these predicates of the corporeal form are abolished in the Perfect One, their root is severed, they are hewn away like a palm tree and laid aside, so that they cannot germinate again in the future.

Released, O great King, is the Perfect One from this, that his being should be gauged by the measure of the corporeal world: he is deep, immeasurable, unfathomable as the great ocean. "The Perfect One exists after death," this is not apposite; "the Perfect One does not exist after death," this also is not apposite; "the Perfect One at once exists and does not exist after death," this also is not apposite; "the Perfect One neither does nor does not exist after death," this also is not apposite.'

"But Pasenadi, the King of Kosala, received the nun Khema's discourse with satisfaction and approbation, rose from his seat, bowed reverently before Khema, the nun, turned and went away."

Supreme reality—the ideal object of all high thinking, of all knowledge, of all wisdom—is here symbolized by the Perfect One's existence. And that existence, we are told, is "deep, unfathomable, immeasurable as the great ocean." "When such a reason," says Dr. Oldenberg, "is assigned for the waiving of the question as to whether the Perfect One lives for ever, is not this very giving of a reason itself an answer? And is not this answer a Yes?

No being in the ordinary sense, but still assuredly not a non-being; a sublime positive, of which thought has no idea, for which language has no expression, which beams out to meet the cravings of the thirsty for immortality in that same splendour of which the apostle says: 'Eye hath not seen, nor ear heard, neither have entered into the heart of man, the things which God hath prepared for them that love Him.'"

The nun Khema had caught the spirit of her Master's teaching. The explanation that she gave of his teaching harmonizes so well with those which he himself is reported to have given, when challenged with probing questions by Vacchagotta and Malukya, that we must needs regard it as at least provisionally true. Buddha kept silent because his heart was overfull, because he had too much to say.

What other explanations of his silence can be given?

Three, and three only, suggest themselves to my mind.

The first is that he was a pure and consistent agnostic, an indifferentist not only in the presence of the wrangling dogmatists, but also in the depths of his own soul. Had he been this, had he been what no man is who feels and thinks deeply, he would have told his disciples that he regarded all the statements and all the solutions of the ultimate problems with equal indifference, and in telling them this would have explained and justified his silence.

The second is that his own attitude towards great matters was one of helpless bewilderment. Had it been this, had the light of his clear and authoritative teaching been the reflection of an impenetrable fog of doubt, he would have openly said so, for such a confession would have added force and weight to his contention that men must win deliverance, not by trying to guess metaphysical riddles, but by walking in the Path.

Thus the bare fact of Buddha's silence makes the first and the second explanations of it untenable.

The third is that he was a negative dogmatist, who refrained, for fear of scandalizing his disciples and paralyzing their spiritual energies, from openly formulating his sweeping negations. This is the hypothesis which Dr. Rhys Davids, Dr. Paul Carus, and others are disposed to accept. I have already given my reasons for rejecting the first part of it. I will now consider the second.

Had Buddha been a negative dogmatist, would he have refrained from formulating his nihilistic creed? I think not. So sincere was he and so deeply in earnest, that he would have kept nothing back from his disciples—this we may assume at the outset—which it would have been possible for him to communicate to them.

Now it happens that a creed whose formulæ are all negations is, of all creeds, the easiest to expound; and the fact that Buddha made no attempt to expound his creed is therefore a convincing proof that the faith of his heart was not the "religion of science."

When he expounded his scheme of life, he gave such reasons as he could for inviting men to adopt it. That he kept other reasons in reserve can scarcely be doubted. Had these occult reasons admitted of being stated, he would surely have stated them. That he would have played the opportunist in a matter of more than life and death, that he would have kept silence about the master problems of human thought when it was possible and even easy for him to set forth his solution of them, is to my mind incredible.

The question which confronts us admits of being discussed on other than a priori grounds. There are stories which bear on it. Just before he died Buddha is reported to have said, "I have preached the truth without making any distinction between exoteric and esoteric doctrine; for in respect of the truth, ananda, the Tathagata has no such thing as the closed fist of a teacher who keeps some things back."

The inference which Dr. Rhys Davids draws from these words—that there is nothing esoteric in Buddhism—is not warranted by the premises, and is inconsistent with Dr. Rhys

Davids' own contention that, in his reply to the two young Brahmins who asked him to show them the way to union with God, Buddha "adopted the opportunist position" and gave his sanction to beliefs which in his heart of hearts he disowned. There is always, in the nature of things, something esoteric in the faith of a man who has thought deeply and sincerely.

There are many thoughts which he cannot communicate—the intervening barriers are insuperable—to the rank and file of mankind. There are some thoughts which he cannot communicate even to those who are in close sympathy with his general attitude towards the deepest of all problems.

There are a few thoughts which he is compelled to keep back even from those whose inner life is very near and dear to his own. And, behind and beyond all these, there are movements of his own inner being which will probably some day shape themselves into thoughts, but which meanwhile remain—unformulated and unformulable—below the threshold of his own conscious life.

When Buddha told ananda that he had kept nothing back from his disciples, he was doubtless contrasting in his mind his own methods with those of the Brahmanic teachers of his day,—teachers who kept everything back from their disciples, who sought to regulate the lives of the people down to the minutest details of conduct, yet gave no reason for what they prescribed, and so crushed down the spiritual life of India under the deadly burden of an apparently meaningless ceremonialism. And he doubtless meant that he had told his disciples everything which it was possible for him to disclose to them. More than that he did not mean: or the stories of his silence are all untrue.

But whatever his words to ananda may have meant, it is certain that he who spoke them was not an opportunist: it is certain that, if he had been in possession of a creed as clear, as intelligible, and as easy to formulate as the (so-called) "religion of science," he would have disclosed it to all who came to him for guidance. Dr. Rhys Davids makes no attempt to harmonize the ultra-candour of the man who claimed to have kept nothing back from his disciples, with the shiftiness of the man who kept back from the two young Brahmins, while he responded to their demand for spiritual guidance, his disbelief in the fundamental dogma of their creed.

But the attempt deserves to be made. There is surely a mean between the complacent opportunism which allows a man to simulate complete sympathy with beliefs which he has long outgrown, and the aggressive candour which makes him blurt out, or try to blurt out, whatever is in his mind, with the result that he misleads and deceives his neighbour in the sacred name of Truth.

> *"Ilyades choses," says Joubert, "que l'homme ne peut connaitre que vaguement: les grands esprits se contentent d'en avoir des notions vagues; mais cela ne suffit point aux esprits vulgaires. Il faut, pour leur repos, qu'ils se forgent ou qu'on leur offre des idees fixes et determinees sur les objets meme où toute precision est erreur. Ces esprits communs n'ont point d'ailes; ils ne peuvent se soutenir dans rien de ce qui n'est que de l'espace; il leur faut des points d'appui, des fables, des mensonges, des idoles.*

Mentez leur donc, et ne les trompez pas." It is certainly better to "lie" to men than to "deceive" them. But Buddha did not lie to the "esprits vulgaires" of his day. He kept silence in their presence.

Having rejected as untenable three plausible explanations of Buddha's silence, we are left face to face with the only theory which takes account both of the fact of his silence and of the reasons which he gave for it,—the theory that he had a creed of his own, a creed which went to the root of all great matters, but which, in some sort, bound him to silence. Such a creed was, as it happens, already in existence. The deeply spiritual philosophy which had inspired the authors of the Upanishads was, in its essence, esoteric.

The conception of God—the Supreme Reality—as, on the one hand, the soul or inner life of the Universe, and, on the other hand, the true self of each individual man, is one in the presence of which thought becomes an impertinence and speech a profanation.

The feelings which arise in the soul in response—if there happens to be any response—to an idea which is at once overpoweringly vast and elusively subtle, do not suffer themselves to be systematized or formulated, but pass in an instant, in the first pulsation of their mighty movement, far beyond the limits of any tabulated creed.

This the sages of India instinctively felt, and feeling this they "let their words be few." Even in the Upanishads, which were composed, not for the world at large but for an inner circle of sages and recluses, the language used is that of paradox and negation. That in which all their thinking centred—the Divine in man—was not to them an object of scientific curiosity, a being whose nature could be exhaustively analyzed or whose attributes could be set forth in a series of formulae.

They habitually spoke of him as "That." They shrank from applying any name to him which might suggest either that he was a member of a class, or that he had a distinct individuality of his own. If they predicated anything of him, they at once predicated its opposite. He is swifter than the mind, yet he moves not: he is far and near: he is at once innermost and outermost: and so forth.

The moment of apprehension, as thought strives to grasp him, is also the moment of discomfiture and recoil. Speech, thought, sight, hearing,—each of these in turn is made possible by him, and therefore each in turn fails to reach him. He is beyond sight, beyond speech, beyond mind, beyond the known, beyond the unknown. He is veiled from thought by the excess of his own inward light. Dwelling at the heart of man, as the "unbeholden essence" of all things,—gathering into his infinite inwardness all the outermost boundaries of the Universe,—he is at once too subtle to be grasped by any effort of mental analysis, and too vast to be encompassed by any flight of imaginative thought. "He thinks of it, for whom it passes thought; who thinks of it doth never know it."

Men who had to use such language as this within the narrow limits of an esoteric circle, had no choice but to become silent when those limits were passed. For "those who understand," the language of paradox and negation has a meaning; but paradoxes bewilder the uninitiated, and the language of negation is apt to be mistaken for the language of denial and revolt.

This, then, was the tremendous problem that confronted the sages of the Upanishads. Possessed with a spiritual idea, so deeply, so inexhaustibly true that, if it could but be assimilated by the heart of man, it would in the fullness of time "redeem the world,"—they were debarred, on the one hand by the fundamental laws of thought and language, on the other hand by the very depth and truth of their cherished idea, from revealing it—as an idea—to mankind.

How, then, were they to bring it home to the hearts and lives of their fellow-men? The ceremonial solution of the problem, which they adopted as a counsel of despair, proved to be no solution; and the problem remained unsolved till Buddha himself solved it—whether consciously or unconsciously, is the question that now confronts us—by transferring it to the plane of practical life.

That Buddha's ethical scheme was a practical interpretation, an exposition in terms of human conduct and human life, of the paramount idea of the Upanishads, I have already attempted to show.

Was the coincidence—at every vital point—between the scheme and the idea an accident, or was it deliberately planned? That the latter is by many degrees the more reasonable hypothesis, is too obvious to need demonstration.

If we hesitate to adopt it, the reason is that Buddha, though he worked out the idea, as a principle of action, with consistent thoroughness and consummate skill, not only made no attempt to expound it, but even turned back, on the threshold of their inquiry, all who sought to go behind the scheme to the philosophy that it embodied. But this difficulty will vanish when we remind ourselves that if Buddha, who made it his life's work to preach the gospel of deliverance to all men, had accepted the paramount idea of the Upanishads and made it his own, he would have been bound by the very strength and depth of his faith in it to wall it round with inviolable silence.

Link by link, the chain of proof has been forged which connects the inmost soul of Buddha with the spiritual idealism of ancient India. It is true that, in such a matter as this, demonstration is not to be looked for; but it is also true that each new link adds strength and elasticity to the chain as a whole. The theory that Buddha was at heart a spiritual idealist has received confirmation from many quarters. The last of the arguments that support it—the last and not the least weighty—is that it, and it alone, accounts for and justifies his silence.

7

BUDDHA AND HIS CREED

The creed which I am trying to interpret is that of Buddha himself. With the creed of the Buddhist world, with the creed of this or that Buddhist Church, I have no direct concern. Dr. Paul Carus is gratified because the South Buddhist Church has sent him a certificate of orthodoxy. Would it give him equal pleasure to know that his interpretation of the creed of Christ (let us say) had been officially endorsed by some Presbyterian Synod, or even by the Vatican? I doubt it. Distance may lend enchantment to the "dogmatics" of a Buddhist church; but when one looks nearer home one begins to see things in their true proportions.

It is not in the doctrine of any church or sect that the spirit of the Master's teaching is to be found. For good or for evil, churches and sects are under the control of the average man. On the one hand, they owe their existence to the secret demands of his better nature. On the other hand, they reflect in their theology his secret weaknesses,—his spiritual indolence, his intellectual timidity, his lack of imagination, the essential vulgarity of his thought.

Hence it is that the faith which has been officially formulated is as salt which has lost its savour. If we are to hold intercourse with the soul of a great teacher, and so renew in our own souls the springs of his spiritual life, we must be prepared to go far behind and far beyond the formularies of the religion that calls itself by his name.

It follows—to revert to the case of Buddha and Buddhism—that in considering the meaning of this or that passage in the

Buddhist "Scriptures," one must have recourse to the general impression of Buddha—the man, the thinker, and the teacher—which has been generated by careful study of all the available sources of evidence, including (as perhaps the most important of all) the spiritual atmosphere of the age in which he lived, rather than to the particular interpretation of the passage in question which has conic to be regarded as "orthodox" by the Buddhist world.

Even the fact that there was an apparent agreement with regard to the meaning of the passage between Eastern "dogmatics" and Western scholarship, would count for little in one's eyes, in the event of the given interpretation conflicting with one's general impression of the spirit of Buddha's teaching; for, in the first place, the agreement between Eastern and Western thought would probably prove to be wholly superficial; and, in the second place, scholarship, as such, is debarred by its own aims and interests and by the special preparation which it presupposes, from making that wide survey and that deep and sympathetic study of all the available evidence, which would be needed if the inner meaning of the passage was to be wrested from it.

I have convinced myself that faith in the ideal identity of the individual with the Universal Soul was the hidden fountain head of Buddha's practical teaching. I will now test the worth of this conclusion by applying it, as a provisional hypothesis, to the solution of some of the many problems that perplex the student of Buddhism.

The best way to handle those problems is to consider the grave charges which have been brought against Buddha and Buddhism,—charges which have been so often reiterated that they are now openly endorsed by the "man in the street."

Five of these are of capital importance.

We are told that Buddha denied the Soul or Ego; in other words, that his teaching was materialistic.

We are told that there was no place for God in his system of thought; in other words, that his teaching was atheistic. We are told that he regarded all existence as intrinsically evil; in other words, that his teaching was pessimistic. We are told that he taught men to think only of themselves and their personal welfare; in other words, that his scheme of life was egoistic.

We are told that after Nirvana—the inward state of him who has lifted the last veil of illusion—comes annihilation; in other words (since what is behind the last veil of illusion is ex hypothesi supremely real), that Buddha regarded Nothing as the Supreme Reality, and that therefore his teaching was nihilistic.

Can these charges be substantiated? If they can, we are confronted by the most perplexing of all problems. How comes it that a religion which has such vital defects has had such a successful career? That Buddha won to his will the "deepest heart" of the Far East is undeniable. Was it by preaching the gospel of materialism, of atheism, of pessimism, of egoism, of nihilism, that he achieved this signal triumph? This is the problem into which all the other problems that beset the path of the student of Buddhism must ultimately be resolved."

Let us now consider, by the light of the hypothesis which I am seeking to verify, each of the capital charges that have been brought against Buddha.

THE MATERIALISM OF BUDDHA

Let us assume that, far from denying the Ego, Buddha believed in it, in his heart of hearts,—believed in it with the depth and subtlety of belief which are characteristic of Indian idealism,—believed in it as the "unbeholden essence" of all things, as the all-generating, all-sustaining life which individualizes itself in every human breast, yet is what it really is at the heart of the Universe, and nowhere else. What would be the attitude of one who so conceived of the Ego towards the popular belief—popular, one may safely conjecture, in Buddha's day as in ours—in the intrinsic reality of the individualized Ego, or individual soul? That the Ego is not real, in the fullest sense of the word, till it has become one with the Universal Soul, is the postulate on which all his philosophy, both as a whole and under each of its aspects, would be hinged. On its way to the goal of union with the Divine, the individual soul must needs pass through many stages of unreality. So long as it retains its sense of isolation, its mistaken sense of I-ness, it is, comparatively speaking, unreal. What is real in it is its potential universality. What is unreal is what it regards as of its very essence,—its individuality, its sense of separateness from all other things. Had Buddha looked at the problem of selfhood from the standpoint of Indian idealism, he would have seen that the popular belief in the intrinsic value of the individual Soul is fundamentally false, not on the plane of metaphysical speculation only, but on every plane of human life; and he would have set himself to combat it in each of its many forms.

Of the many forms that it takes I need not speak at length. The materialism of him who identifies his soul (his "self") with his body, or who conceives of it as the "totality" of his own sensations, perceptions, or other states of consciousness; the semi-materialism of him who (like the pious Christian) regards the soul as "something which flies out away from the body at death," or as one of many parts or organs of a complex being; the sentimental clinging to individuality; the metaphysical clinging to individuality;—these may be mentioned as typical forms of that reluctance to regard the Universal Soul as the only true self, which is so characteristic of popular thought in all the stages of its development, and against which Buddha, if I have not misread his philosophy, must have waged a relentless war.

If I am asked why Buddha, who eschewed metaphysical controversy, should have thought it necessary to combat a belief which seems to be primarily metaphysical, my answer is that the belief is not primarily metaphysical, that on the contrary it is the reflection in consciousness of a deep-seated instinct which has vital ethical consequences—the instinct to affirm the ordinary self, to accept it, minister to it, magnify it, rest in it—in a word, the egoistic instinct, the hidden root of every form of spiritual evil, and the first and last of moral defects. As the suppression of egoism was the very end and aim of Buddha's scheme of life, and as in this matter the distinction between theory on the one hand and sentiment, desire, and impulse on the other, is hard to draw and easy to efface, it was but natural that Buddha should wage war against the egoistic instinct even when it disguised itself as a semi-philosophical theory.

But he waged that war, as he did everything else that he took in hand, within the limits prescribed by his own "sweet reasonableness" and exalted common-sense. Leaving it to the metaphysical experts to wrangle over the more abstract aspects of the problem of selfhood, he contented himself with combating on quasi-popular grounds the popular delusion that the individual Ego is real, permanent, self-contained.

Let us assume this much; and we shall see a new meaning in each of the many passages on which Western criticism has based its theory that denial of the Ego was the cardinal article of Buddha's creed. We shall see that, whenever he seems to be denying existence to the Ego as such, what he is really doing is to deny reality to the individual Ego, to the ordinary surface self.

Let us first consider a dialogue in which the principal speaker is the venerable Sariputta, but in which the arguments advanced may well have been devised by Buddha himself, coinciding as they do with arguments which he is reported to have used in one of his early discourses. A monk, named Yamaka, had convinced himself, as many modern interpreters of Buddhism have done, that the "doctrine taught by the Blessed One "amounted to this, "that on the dissolution of the body the monk who has lost all depravity is annihilated, perishes, and does not exist after death." His fellow-monks urged him to abandon what they regarded as a "wicked heresy," but to no purpose. At last they besought the venerable Sariputta to "draw near" to Yamaka and try to convert him to a truer view of the Blessed One's teaching.

"And the venerable Sariputta consented by his silence. Then the venerable Sariputta in the evening of the day arose from meditation, and drew near to where the venerable Yamaka was; and having drawn near he greeted the venerable Yamaka, and having passed the compliments of friendship and civility, he sat down respectfully on one side. And seated respectfully at one side, the venerable Sariputta spoke to the venerable Yamaka as follows: 'Is the report true, brother Yamaka, that the following wicked heresy has sprung up in your mind: Thus do I understand the doctrine taught by the Blessed One, that on the dissolution of the body the monk who has lost all depravity is annihilated, perishes, and does not exist after death?'

"'Even so, brother, do I understand the doctrine taught by the Blessed One, that on the dissolution of the body the monk who has lost all depravity is annihilated, perishes, and does not exist after death.'

"'What think you, brother Yamaka? Is form permanent, or transitory?"

"'It is transitory, brother.'

"'And that which is transitory—is it evil, or is it good?'

"'It is evil, brother.'

"'And that which is transitory, evil, and liable to change—is it possible to say of it: This is mine—this am I—this is my Ego?'

"'Nay, verily, brother.'

"'Is sensation... perception... the predispositions... consciousness, permanent, or transitory?'

"'It is transitory, brother.'

"'And that which is transitory—is it evil, or is it good?'

"'It is evil, brother.'

"'And that which is transitory, evil, and liable to change—is it possible to say of it: This is mine; this am I; this is my Ego?'

"'Nay, verily, brother Yamaka.'

"'Accordingly, brother Yamaka, as respects all form whatsoever—as respects all sensation whatsoever—as respects all perception whatsoever—as respects all predispositions whatsoever—as respects all consciousness whatsoever, past, future or present, be it subjective or existing outside, gross or subtle, mean or exalted, far or near, the correct view in the light of the highest knowledge is as follows: This is not mine;

this am I not; this is not my Ego. "'Perceiving this, brother Yamaka, the learned and noble disciple conceives an aversion for form, conceives an aversion for sensation, conceives an aversion for perception, conceives an aversion for the predispositions, conceives an aversion for consciousness. And in conceiving this aversion he becomes divested of passion, and by the absence of passion he becomes free, and when he is free he becomes aware that he is free; and he knows that rebirth is exhausted, that he has lived the holy life, that he has done what it behaved him to do, and that he is no more for the world.

"'What think you, brother Yamaka? Do you consider form as the Saint?'

"'Nay, verily, brother.'

"'Do you consider sensation... perception... the predispositions... consciousness as the Saint?'

"'Nay, verily, brother.'

"'What think you, brother Yamaka? Do you consider the Saint as comprised in form?'

"'Nay, verily, brother.'

"'Do you consider the Saint as distinct from form?'

"'Nay, verily, brother.'

"'Do you consider the Saint as comprised in sensation?... as distinct from sensation?... as comprised in perception?... as distinct from perception?... as comprised in the predispositions?... as distinct from the predispositions?... as comprised in consciousness?... as distinct from consciousness?'

"'Nay, verily, brother.'

"'What think you, brother Yamaka? Are form, sensation, perception, the predispositions and consciousness united the Saint?'

"'Nay, verily, brother.'

"'What think you, brother Yamaka? Do you consider the Saint as a something having no form, sensation, perception, predispositions or consciousness?'

"'Nay, verily, brother.'

"'Considering now, brother Yamaka, that you fail to make out and establish the existence of the Saint in the present life, is it reasonable for you to say: Thus do I understand the doctrine taught by the Blessed One, that on the dissolution of the body the monk who has lost all depravity is annihilated, perishes, and does not exist after death?'

"'Brother Sariputta, it was because of my ignorance that I held this wicked heresy; but now that I have listened to the doctrinal instruction of the venerable Sariputta, I have abandoned that wicked heresy and acquired the true doctrine.'"

Mr H. C. Warren, from whose translation of the dialogue in his learned work, "Buddhism in Translation," I have made this extract, heads each page in the dialogue with the significant words, "There is no Ego." That is how he interprets the teaching of Sariputta. But surely what Sariputta intended to teach was the exact opposite of this. The monk Yamaka believed that at the death of the "Saint"—at the moment when his cycle of earth-lives had come to an end—he ceased to be. This belief, we are expressly told, was regarded as a "wicked heresy"; and Sariputta disabused Yamaka's mind of it by showing him that it was as difficult for him to "make out and establish" the existence of the "Saint" in the present life as in the life beyond death (and beyond rebirth). He reminds him, in words which, according to tradition, had been used by Buddha himself, that the Ego is not to be identified with form, with sensation, with perception, with the "predispositions," with consciousness, since each of these is transitory and therefore evil, and "of that which is transitory, evil and liable to change it is not possible to say 'This is mine; this am I; this is my Ego.'"

"The ignorant unconverted man... considers form in the light of an Ego, considers sensation... perception... the predispositions... consciousness in the light of an Ego," and therefore clings to those apparent "selves" though they are all transitory and evil. "The learned and noble disciple does not consider form, sensation, etc., in the light of an Ego," and he therefore detaches himself from each of those delusive "selves." Not a word is said, in any part of the discourse, in disproof of the existence of the Ego. The point of the argument is that each of the apparent Egos—the Ego of form, the Ego of sensation, and the rest—is unreal; and that the man who regards the Ego of the "Saint" as non-existent after death, because it will then be finally detached from form, sensation, etc., is bound by the logic of his own delusion to regard the Ego of the "Saint" as non-existent while on earth, since, if the "Saint" has indeed won deliverance, he will have finally detached himself, even while on earth, from each of those phantom Egos, and in doing so will have found his true self.

From this point it is possible to advance to two conclusions. As disbelief in the after-death existence of the "Saint" is a "wicked heresy," it stands to reason that it is also a "wicked heresy" to regard the "Saint"—the true Ego—as non-existent now. This is the first conclusion, which the Western critic who seeks to father upon Buddha his own denial of the Ego will do well to bear in mind.

The second seems to have been tacitly drawn by both Sariputta and Yamaka, and to have carried conviction to the latter's mind. As it is obviously absurd to say that the "Saint" is non-existent now, it stands to reason that it is also absurd to say—as Yamaka had said—that the "Saint" will cease to be after death. The whole discourse is directed nominally against Yamaka's "wicked heresy," but really against the erroneous belief that the individual Ego, the Ego which is associated with form, with sensation, and the rest, is the true Ego,—a belief which had generated in Yamaka's mind the "wicked heresy" that "on the dissolution of the body" the Saint "is annihilated, perishes, and does not exist." Indeed it is no exaggeration to say that in this discourse disbelief in the reality of the Ego—the true Ego which transcends the limits of the transitory, and therefore passes beyond the reach of thought and language—is authoritatively condemned.

Dr. Rhys Davids lays great stress on a discourse in which various attempts to conceive of the existence of the Ego after death are condemned as heresies. Here, as in the dialogue which has just been considered, the Ego is that of the man who has won deliverance while still living on earth, and whose cycle of earth-lives is therefore coming to an end.

The prying attempt to follow the liberated Ego into the life beyond death, into the unimaginable bliss of Nirvana, is repelled as impertinent and delusive, and every form that it takes is condemned as a "heresy." The discourse ends with these words: "Mendicants [Monks], that which binds the Teacher [the Saint, the Perfect One] to existence is cut off; but his body still remains. While his body shall remain he will be seen by gods and men, but after the dissolution of the body, neither gods nor men will see him." "Would it be possible," asks Dr. Rhys Davids, "in a more complete and categorical manner to deny that there is any soul—anything of any kind, which continues to exist, in any manner, after death?"

This criticism (so characteristically Western) is as wide of the mark as is Mr Warren's headline comment on the dialogue between Sariputta and Yamaka. What the preacher is trying to enforce is what Sariputta had impressed upon Yamaka, that the Ego of the "Saint"—the true Ego, for the "Saint" is one who has found his true self does not exist after death in any form or mode which is comprehensible by human thought. Far from denying the existence of the Ego, the preacher is insisting on its transcendent reality. "Neither gods nor men" will see the "Saint" after death, not because he will then be non-existent, but because his being will have out-soared all the categories of human thought.

In these and other such discourses Buddha falls into line with the thinkers of the Upanishads, who described by a series of negations what they regarded as the true Ego,—the Divine in man. The coincidences between his teaching and theirs are so significant that the only way to account for them is to assume that his faith—the deepest faith of his heart—was in its essence identical with theirs.

If the account that he gave of the Ego was purely negative, if he abstained from positive statements (even in that paradoxical form which was dear to the thinkers of the Upanishads), the reason was that he wished men to find out for themselves, by following the Path of soul-expansion, what the Ego really is. He said to them, in thought if not in words: "The Ego is not this thing or that; it is not any of the things with which you are used to identify it. If you wish to know what it is, enter the Path and follow it to the end. Your question will then be answered, for it will have transformed itself into a burning thirst for the ideal and the divine; and in the bliss of Nirvana that thirst will be eternally slaked and eternally renewed."

Dr. Rhys Davids is confirmed in his belief that Buddha denied the Ego, by the fact that the "heresy of individuality" is one of the three "Fetters" which have to be broken on the very threshold of the new life. But here, as elsewhere, Buddha is denying the reality, not of the Ego as such, but of the individual Ego; in other words, he is condemning by implication the blindness of him who regards the limitations which his individuality imposes upon him as the essential conditions of his existence. So, too, when he names among the fetters which have to be broken in the later stages of the Eightfold Path, the desire for life in the worlds of form, and the desire for life in the formless worlds, he is thinking, not of the desire for life as such but of the desire for separate life, for the continuance of individuality,—the hydra-headed desire which is ever tending to counteract the centripetal energy of love.

There is one set of discourses on which those who regard Buddha as a negative dogmatist lay great stress,—the so-called Milinda dialogues, or conversations between the Greek King, Menanda, of Baktria, and Nagasena, the Buddhist teacher. Nagasena seems to have been an acute controversialist who loved argument for its own sake almost as much as Buddha disliked it, and who, had he lived in Europe in the Middle Ages, would probably have nailed theological or metaphysical theses to church-doors. That he had caught the deeper spirit of the Master's teaching is, to say the least, improbable; but that his discourses present to us an interpretation of that teaching, which had gained currency in his day, can scarcely be doubted.

I have elsewhere allowed, for argument's sake, that he may have had an academic antipathy to the Ego. If he had, his discourses do less than justice to their theme. The arguments by which a merely academic belief (or disbelief) is sustained are in the nature of things ineffective. The spiritual atmosphere of his age, the words that he finds himself compelled to use, even his own subconscious convictions—are all against the thinker. In the well known Chariot dialogue, Nagasena is supposed to have proved conclusively that "there is no Ego." I cannot see that he has done this, and I am by no means sure that he has attempted to do it. What he has proved is that, just as the name chariot belongs to the vehicle as a whole and not to any of its parts, so the name Nagasena belongs to the living being as a whole and not to any of his organs or faculties.

If the dialogue is directed against anything, it is directed against the vulgar belief that the Soul is a quasi-material something (like the babe of vapour in mediaeval art) which can be separated from the rest of the man, just as a wheel can be separated from the rest of the chariot; or again that the soul is one among many faculties which go to make up the whole man. The flame simile, which is also supposed to be directed against the soul-theory of the Brahmanic philosophy, is one which that theory, far from rejecting, would accept as singularly apt. For just as fire uses up fuel, and in doing so manifests itself as flame (that is, as burning fuel), so the Soul, in its journey through the earth-life, continually uses up physical matter, and in doing so manifests itself as a living body (that is, as physical matter fused and vitalized by the Soul-fire). When the Soul retires from the physical plane, the body, deprived of its vitalizing influence, disintegrates into dust, just as fuel, when its fire is extinct, turns to ashes; but the Soul itself (if we may follow its progress through the intervening stages of existence) continues to use up matter, though, as the matter used is now impalpable, the Soul-flame becomes invisible till the time comes for it to feed again on the fuel of physical nature,—in other words, to appear again on earth.

Even when Nagasena's hostility to the Ego is unmistakable, his belief in re-incarnation causes his arguments to miscarry. He may flatter himself that he has disproved the identity between A (who is living now) and B (the future inheritor of his Karma); but, as a believer in re-incarnation, he must needs take pains to prove that B will justly be held responsible for what A has done or left undone; and in his attempt to make good this point he has to admit (or rather insist) that the relation between A and B is exactly analogous to that between a "young girl" and the same girl "when grownup and marriageable." Dr. Rhys Davids has truly said that Buddha's "whole training was Brahmanism; and that he probably deemed himself to be the most correct exponent of the spirit as distinct from the letter of the ancient faith." If this is a true statement of Buddha's attitude towards Brahmanism, it surely behoves the student of Buddhism to seek initiation into the deeper mysteries of the "ancient faith," before he attempts to interpret the creed of one who, while breaking with the letter of that faith, "deemed himself to be the most correct exponent of its spirit." This, however, is what the Western critic, with his instinctive contempt for alien modes of thought, is extremely reluctant to do. What he does, in nine cases out of ten, is to carry with him to the study of Buddhism the prejudices and prepossessions of Western thought—foremost among which is the assumption that nothing exists, in the order of nature, except what is perceptible by man's bodily senses—and to insist that the teaching of Buddha shall conform to these, and be measured by their standards. Hence arise misconceptions and misunderstandings which might have been avoided.

If Buddhism seems to our Western minds to abound in errors and anomalies, the reason is that we insist on looking at it through a distorting medium. One who had steeped himself in the spirit of the Brahmanic philosophy before he began his study of Buddhism, would see that wherever Buddha seems to be denying existence to the Ego, what he is really doing is to deny reality to the apparent Ego or superficial Self, so that he may thereby clear the way for the exposition, not in words but in the unwritten language of conduct, character, and life, of the profound conception which is the very quintessence of the "ancient faith,"—the conception "that Brahma and the Self—the true Self—are one."

THE ATHEISM OF BUDDHA

The Christian critics of Buddhism call Buddha an atheist, nominally because he said nothing about God, really because his conception of God differs from their own. I have already attempted to show that the silence of Buddha about God—the Supreme Reality—was quite compatible with a sublimely spiritual conception of God and a deeply spiritual faith in him. I have shown that such a conception and such a faith were in the air that Buddha breathed, and that, if he had accepted them and made them his own, the very reverence which they would have generated would have bound him to silence in the presence of his audience,—the rank and file of mankind. I have shown that his own ethical teaching was the practical exposition of this unformulated theology,—the revelation of it, not as a theology but as a scheme of life, to those who would have been bewildered by it, and who would therefore have misunderstood and misapplied it, had any attempt been made to expound it to them in words, I have inferred from this that Buddha did believe in God, not as the West believes in him, but as the Far East, at the highest level of its imaginative thinking, has ever believed in him,—as the Supreme Reality which is at the heart of the Universe, and which is at once the life and soul of Nature and the true self of Man.

But the fact remains that Buddha, though he preached the gospel of deliverance, said nothing about God. To us, with the Jehovah-virus in our veins, to us who for many centuries have been content to believe that the Universe is under the direct rule of that national deity whose sayings and doings are recorded in the Hebrew Scriptures, it seems the height of impiety to keep silence about God. It is well for us to remind ourselves that in the Far East, in the days of India's spiritual greatness, it was deemed the height of impiety to talk freely about God. We call the silence of the East atheistic.

The sages of India, though they would have thought it discourteous to say so, would have regarded our loquacity as profane. To unveil to the mind of the average man ideas which are in the nature of things so large, so deep, and so subtle that, without mental power of a very high order, it is impossible to grasp their initial—let alone their final—meaning, is to expose the most sacred of all truths to the risk (the certainty, one might almost say) of being misinterpreted and misused. From such a risk the sages of India shrank as from blasphemy against the Divine. It may be difficult for us to enter into this feeling, but it is well that we should know that it did (and does) exist.

The silence of the Far East has another aspect, and one which is equally repugnant to the "orthodox" thought of the West. In itself, in the eloquence of its dumbness, it is an abiding protest, not merely against the profane loquacity of Western dogmatism, but also against its deadly despotism. To tell men that they must, under pain of eternal damnation, believe such and such things about God—or rather accept as divinely true such and such theological formulae, whether they see any meaning in them or not—is to quench in their breasts that spark of spiritual freedom which is also the germ of spiritual life.

It is true that the symbolical presentation of religious truth, which official Brahmanism adopted in preference to the doctrinal, may develop, as it certainly did in India, into a ceremonial despotism as oppressive as any that the creeds of the West have ever exerted. But Buddha's own silence was agnostic, in the deeper sense of the word, to the very core. We could imagine him saying to his disciples: "I have given you my reasons for urging you to enter the Path. If those reasons commend themselves to you, enter the Path and see to what goal it will lead you.

But do not ask me to explain my own explanation. Do not ask me for deeper reasons than those which I have given you. Do not ask me to tell you what I, for one, believe about the greatest of all great matters. The words that make sense to me would ring as nonsense in your ears. The thoughts that bring light to me would dazzle you to the verge of blindness. And I should but deepen your perplexity if I tried to give you the guidance that you seek. But the Path itself will enlighten you if you will trust yourself to it; and when you have followed it far enough you will be wise with a wisdom beyond that of the wisest sage." The idea which underlies the whole of Buddha's teaching—underlying what he said and also what he left unsaid—the idea that knowledge of divine truth must be evolved from within, instead of being imposed from without, is the direct negation of that idea of a supernatural revelation, which underlies all the creeds of the West.

After all, it is not so much the silence of Buddha that the West regards as atheistic, as the creed which that silence hints at and seems, in a sense, to shadow forth,—a creed which seals the lips of those who see deepest into the heart of its hidden truth. The orthodox Christian, who believes that to give assent to a series of formulae is to enter into possession of divine truth, and who therefore regards intolerance as a virtue and self-assertion as a sacred duty, feels instinctively that a creed which will not suffer itself to be formulated, and which therefore makes no attempt to impose its yoke upon human thought, is the hereditary enemy of his faith. His instinct has not misled him. Between the "Higher Pantheism" of India and the Supernaturalism of the Western World there is, in the region of ideas, a truceless war. Had Buddha tried to expound the creed of his heart, it would assuredly have been branded as atheistic by those who now apply that epithet to his silence.

"Such divinity," said the late Canon Liddon, "as Pantheism can ascribe to Christ is, in point of fact, no divinity at all. God is Nature, and Nature is God; everything indeed is Divine, but also nothing is Divine; and Christ shares this phantom divinity with the universe,—nay with the agencies of moral evil itself. In truth, our God does not exist in the apprehension of Pantheistic thinkers; since, when such truths as creation and personality are denied, the very idea of God is fundamentally sapped, and... the broad practical result is in reality neither more nor less than Atheism."

The writer of this passage proves nothing by his arguments but his fundamental inability to understand a creed which belongs to a plane of thought on which his mind has never learned to move: and, having misrepresented that creed beyond recognition, he brands it with a title which he regards as in the highest degree opprobrious and offensive. "Men become personal," says Dr. Newman, "when logic fails; it is their mode of appealing to their own primary elements of thought and their own illative sense, against the principles and the judgment of another." When A calls B an atheist, he does not necessarily mean that B denies the existence of God. What he does mean is that B's conception of God differs fundamentally from his own, and that he cannot by any effort of thought place himself at B's point of view.

On the whole, then, I incline to the opinion that Christianity calls the teaching of Buddha atheistic, chiefly because it suspects that behind his scheme of life and at the heart of his silence dwells a rival conception of God. If this is so, Christianity has misplaced its censure; for if trust is of the essence of faith, there is no conception of God to which the term atheistic is so strangely inappropriate as to that which sealed the lips of Buddha. Curiosity and doubt are the foster-mothers of theology; but he who has once convinced himself, as Buddha must have done, that light and love are at the heart of the Universe, ceases to be curious about God. In the glow of his radiant and all-embracing optimism the petty theories by which man seeks to justify to himself the ways of God and his own timid faith in God, are seen to be worthless and vain. The sceptics who pride themselves on their "orthodoxy" are startled and alarmed by his silence. But out of its depths comes forth, whenever one listens for it, a message, not of atheistic denial but of whole-hearted trust in God,—trust so full, so firmly rooted, and so sure of itself, that silence alone can measure its strength and its serenity.

"And I say to mankind, Be not curious about God,

For I who am curious about each am not curious about God,

(No array of terms can say how much I am at peace about God and about death)."

THE PESSIMISM OF BUDDHA

In each of the charges that it brings against the teaching of Buddha, the West delimits with precision the range of its own thought. When it attempts to prove that Buddha denied the Ego, what it succeeds in proving is that its own conception of the Ego is as narrow and commonplace as that of the materialists and semi-materialists of Buddha's day. For the only reason that it gives for ascribing to Buddha denial of the Ego is that he refused to identify it with any of the things—

form, sensation, and the like—of which the "ignorant, unconverted man" says, "This is mine; this am I."

So, too, when the West accuses Buddha of atheism, it tells us, by implication, how crudely anthropomorphic is its own conception of God. Buddha, who refused to individualize the Ego, would have been false to his deepest convictions had he allowed himself, in any respect or degree, to individualize the Supreme Reality. But because he kept silence about God rather than use words which might seem (however figuratively) to individualize him, he is held to have "denied the Divine." This means that if the West may not worship the Jewish Jehovah or some kindred deity, it will reject as untenable the whole idea of God.

Let us now consider the charge of pessimism which is so often brought against Buddha. In formulating this charge, the West defines with precision the limits of its own conceptions, first of happiness and then of the Universe. The true pessimist—who is also the true atheist—is he who sees darkness, and darkness only, at the heart of the Universe. Was Buddha a pessimist in this sense of the word? That he regarded the earth life as full of sorrow is undeniable. Does this convict him of pessimism? Not unless the earth-life is the only life, and the visible world the "all of being."

The impermanence of everything earthly seems to have impressed itself deeply on Indian thought. In the West we live, and are content to live, from year to year, and even from day to day; and we regard as permanent things that will last unchanged for a few generations, or even for a few years. But the far-sighted Indian mind, looking backward and forward through vast stretches of time, saw that sooner or later everything outward, however secure of life it might seem to be, must change and fade and pass away. To the Brahmanic thinkers the impermanence of things was a proof of their unreality. But Buddha, who made his appeal, first and foremost, to the "general heart of man," saw that impermanence reveals itself to the many, not as unreality but as sorrow. He saw also that the connection between impermanence and sorrow is the outcome of the widespread tendency to mistake the impermanent for the real. Men cling to shadows and lean on reeds. The shadows fail them, and so cause disappointment and disillusionment. The reeds "pierce their bosoms," "and then they bleed." Seeing that this was so and must be so, Buddha did what he could to make men realize that this life, as they conceived it, was full of suffering. But he did this, not because he despaired of Nature, but because he had unbounded trust in her.

Far from teaching men that life was intrinsically evil, he taught them that the evil in it, the suffering which seemed to be of its essence, was in large measure the result of their own ignorance—their "ignorance of the true being and the true value of the Universe"—and that those who could detach themselves from whatever was impermanent and changeable might, even while on earth, enjoy a happiness higher and purer than any that the soul of man could consciously desire. So far was he from being a pessimist, in the deeper and darker sense of the word, that at the heart of Nature he could see nothing but light. If that light dazzled his eyes and blinded him to the lesser light that plays over the surface of life, his blindness was a proof, not of the despair of his soul, but of the very excess of its optimistic faith.

There are passages in the "Imitation of Christ" which might have been written by the Sages of the Upanishads. Such are "Amor ex Deo natus est; nec potest nisi in Deo requiescere." "Fili, ego debeo esse finis tuus supremus et ultimus, si vere desideras esse beatus." "Omnia vanitas præter amare Deum et isti soli servire." If Indian idealism is pessimistic, so is the outlook on earth and on life which finds expression in these inspired aphorisms. But surely it is not pessimism but abounding optimism which makes a man pitch his standard of happiness immeasurably high, and yet believe that the resources of the Universe are more than equal to any demand that the aspiring heart may make upon them.

He who could say to his followers: "What you deem happiness is unworthy of the name. There are better things than this in store for you. There are treasures of happiness in store for you,—pure, perfect, imperishable, real. These will be given to you freely if you will but win them for yourselves":—he who could say this (or the equivalent of this) had reached the highest conceivable level of optimism. To accuse him of pessimism is to make confession of one's own lack of imagination, of insight, and of faith. Those who believe that the surface life is the only life and that its pleasures are the beginning and end of happiness, and who assume that Buddha's faith coincided with their own, may well regard him, when they learn that he saw nothing but sorrow and suffering in the surface life and its pleasures, as the gloomiest and most uncompromising of pessimists. But the charge that they bring against him recoils upon themselves. If the surface life is the only life, and if its pleasures are the beginning and end of happiness, then indeed there is darkness—the darkness of death—at the heart of the Universe. But Buddha's conception of life, if he was true, as he believed himself to be, to "the spirit of the ancient faith," was the exact opposite of this; and what he saw at the heart of the Universe was, not the darkness of death, but the glory of Nirvana.

THE EGOISM OF BUDDHA

On this point the Western critics of Buddhism are divided. Some of them, including Dr. Rhys Davids, Dr. Paul Carus, and other enemies of the Ego, contend that Buddha's teaching was ultra-stoical, in that he bade men do right for right's sake only, the sole reward which the doer was allowed to look forward to being the enjoyment of inward peace during that twilight hour which should precede the final extinction of his life. Others, including the critics who seek to depreciate Buddhism in the supposed interest of Christianity, contend that Buddha was an egoistic hedonist, who taught each man in turn to think of himself and his own welfare only, and whose conception of happiness had so little in it of idealism or aspiration that it scarcely rose above the level of providing for humanity an early escape from sorrow and pain.

The answer to those who regard Buddha as ultra-stoical is that, as a matter of plain historical fact, what he set before men, when he bade them enter the Path, was the prospect, not of doing right for right's sake (he would probably have seen no meaning in those words) but of winning release from suffering—the suffering of those who struggle in the whirlpool of rebirth,—and of entering into bliss—the bliss of those who will return to earth no more.

In giving this answer I may seem to justify the critics who brand Buddha's scheme of life as egoistic. But no. Buddha's scheme of life was as far from being egoistic as from being ultra-stoical. It is the word self that misleads us. With the doubtful exception of the word Nature, there is no word in which there are so many pitfalls. When we ask whether a given scheme of life is egoistic or not, our answer will entirely depend on the range of the self for which the scheme in question makes provision. To get away from self is impossible; but it may be possible to widen self till it loses its individuality and becomes wholly selfless. Long before that ideal point has been reached, long before the individual has become one with the Universal Self, the word egoistic will have lost its accepted meaning.

That Buddha's teaching was entirely free from the cant of altruism may be admitted without hesitation. Accepting as a fact, which can neither be gainsaid nor ignored, that every man naturally and instinctively seeks his own happiness, and that therefore in the last resort the desire for happiness is the only motive to which the moralist can appeal, Buddha took upon himself to teach men to distinguish the semblance of happiness from the reality, to detach themselves from the former and to win their way to the latter. "Tous les hommes," says Pascal, "recherchent d'etre heureux: cela est sans exception. Quelques differents moyens qu'ils y emploient, ils tendent tous a ce but. C'est le motif de toutes les actions de tous les hommes, jusqu'a ceux qui vont se pendre." It is impossible for me to prefer my neighbour's happiness to my own; for if I am asked why I take such pains to make him happy, I can but answer (in the last resort) that it makes me happy to do so.

Buddha's teaching is equally free from the cant of Stoicism. To bid men do right for right's sake "in the scorn of consequence," is as though a doctor should order his patients to eat the right sort of food for the sake of its rightness, and without regard to its effect on the health of the eater. What is it that constitutes rightness in food,—and in conduct? The right food (from a doctor's point of view) is presumably the food that ministers most effectively to the health of the patient; and it is in the interest of his health, and not of any abstract conception of rightness, that the patient is advised to eat it. It is the same, mutatis mutandis, with right conduct. The exhortation to do right for right's sake is saved from being meaningless only by the tacit assumption that right doing makes, on the whole and in the long run, for the happiness of the doer.

Indeed, it is because such and such courses of action make for the true happiness of him who follows them, and for no other reason, that we call them right. In other words, the epithet right, as applied to conduct, withholds its meaning from us until we define it in terms of happiness. That being so, it is surely better that the moralist should make his appeal (as Buddha openly did) to man's unquenchable desire for happiness than to a motive which would be utterly ineffective were it not that its air of sublime disinterestedness is, in the nature of things, a hollow sham.

But, while Buddha steered clear of the quick-sands of altruism and pseudo-stoicism, he took care not to wreck his scheme of life on the less dangerous, because more plainly visible, rock of egoism. It is when we begin to study the details of the scheme, that we see how little it deserves to be called egoistic. Based as it is on the conviction that the Ego—the real self—is not to be identified with "form," with "sensation," with "perception," or with anything else that is impermanent and changeable, it keeps one aim steadily in view,—to detach man, by a course of self-discipline which may last through many lives, from each of his apparent or lower selves, and to help him to find his true self.

As it is attachment to the apparent or lower self—that tendency to identify oneself with what is impermanent and changeable, which makes one say of this thing and of that, "This is mine: this am I: this is my Ego"—as it is this clinging, grasping, self-asserting frame of mind which is the root of all selfishness (to use a homelier word than egoism), it is clear that Buddha's scheme of life, far from, being egoistic or self-regarding, was in its essence a scheme for the extirpation of "self." Buddha did not say to his disciples, what the altruist professes to say, "Thou shalt love thy neighbour better than thyself." He did not even say to them in so many words, "Thou shalt love thy neighbour as thyself." But he bade them enter a path which, if faithfully followed, would lead each man at last to love all men as himself.

For if one is to escape from the impermanent, one must take refuge in the Eternal; and the Eternal and the Universal are the same fundamental reality looked at from different points of view. Every precept that Buddha gave has one positive aim in view,—to help the soul to expand its life or, in a word, to grow. But to the process of soul-growth there are no assignable limits. The soul has not attained to maturity, has not fulfilled its destiny, has not found its true self, until (according to the sublime conception which is at the heart of the "ancient faith") it has become one with the Universal Self, and in becoming one with it has become one with all men and all things. When that stage has been reached, when the Ego has become all-embracing, the last trace of "egoism" will have vanished, and the precept, "Thou shalt love thy neighbour as thyself" (the real meaning of which will not till then have been apprehended) will at last have been fulfilled. So, too, will the desire of the heart for happiness.

It is by the Christian, the professed follower of Christ, that the charge of egoism is most frequently brought against the teaching of Buddha. It is strange that such a charge should come from such a quarter. Will the Christian consent to brand as egoistic the teaching of his own Master? The conception of life which underlies Christ's searching question: "What is a man profited if he shall gain the whole world and lose his own soul?" is, according to the view that we are able to take of it, either ignobly selfish or sublimely self-forgetful. On this point opinions may differ. What is certain is that the gospel of Buddha is neither more nor less "egoistic" than the Gospel of Christ. For at the heart of each gospel is the same overmastering conviction that it is better for a man to find "his own soul"—his own true self—than to "gain the whole world."

In conclusion. The desire for unreal happiness—the Protean desire which Buddha sought to extinguish—leads us into all the highways and byways of selfishness, and into every haunt of error and delusion; and the phantom which is ever flitting before us ends by eluding our grasp. But the desire for real happiness—the desire which Buddha at once appealed to and strove to foster—is the desire (self-justifying and self-fulfilling) for oneness with the All; nor will that "egoistic" desire have found final fulfilment till it has provided an escape for the soul from the prison-house of "self" into the boundless ether of love.

THE NIHILISM OF BUDDHA

The supreme end of Buddhist endeavour, the last term in its ascending "series," is Nirvana. When the Path has been followed to its goal, when the victory over self has been fully won, when the prize of victory has been fully earned, the emancipated soul (if I may use that word "without prejudice") passes away from earth, passes beyond the vision of "Gods and men" and enters the bliss of Nirvana. What does this mean? The "Perfect One" has disappeared from the eye of thought behind the veil of human experience. What is there behind that veil? What is there behind the last of the many veils which life (as we who are living on earth understand the word) hangs before our eyes? The question as to the destiny of the Perfect One and the question as to the real life of those who are now on earth are (as Sariputta saw clearly) one and the same. What is the answer to them?

The answer which the learned criticism of the West ordinarily gives, and which the popular criticism of the West faithfully echoes, is, in a word, Nothing. "Tout se reunit," says Barthelemy Saint-Hilaire, "pour demontrer que le Nirvana n'est au fond que l'aneantissement definitif et absolu de tous les elements qui composent l'existence." According to Eugene Burnouf, "Le Nirvana est l'aneantissement complet, non seulement des elements materials de l'existence, mais de plus et surtout du principe pensant." These statements are typical, and I need not add to them. The word Nirvana means "going out" or "extinction." But, as Dr. Rhys Davids explains with force and clearness, what is extinguished, when Nirvana is won, is not existence but passion and desire. In support of this thesis Dr. Rhys Davids appeals to some verses in one of the Sacred Books of Buddhism, in which "we have an argument based on the logical assumption that if a positive exists its negative must also exist; if there is heat, there must be cold; and so on. In one of these pairs we find existence opposed, not to Nirvana, but to non-existence; whilst in another the three fires [of lust, hatred and delusion] are opposed to Nirvana."

But, though Dr. Rhys Davids is careful to distinguish Nirvana from annihilation, he is bound by his own assumption, that Buddha denied the Ego, denied "that there is anything of any kind which continues to exist, in any manner, after death," to regard Nirvana as the prelude to annihilation.

For him, then, and for those who think with him, Nirvana, on which the Buddhist writings have ever "lavished" "awe-struck and ecstatic praise," is the twilight hour that precedes the night of Nothingness,—an hour in which the "Perfect One," having at last extinguished the fires of lust, hatred and delusion, enjoys the bliss of perfect peace. "Death, utter death, with no new life to follow, is a result of but it is not Nirvana."

It matters little whether Nirvana is itself the night of Nothingness, or the twilight hour which precedes that night. The goal of the Path is, in either case, the premature annihilation of him who walks in it. When the Perfect One has lifted the last veil of illusion and passed behind it into the reality which it hides from thought, he becomes absorbed into Nothing. It follows that the self-existent Reality which underlies all appearances and which is therefore at the very heart of the Universe is, in a word, Nothing.

Did Buddha really believe this? Was it in the strength of this supreme negation that he devoted his life to the enlightenment and emancipation of his fellow-men, and won to his will the hearts of all who listened to his teaching? The hypothesis which we are invited to accept as an established conclusion, is so wildly improbable, that we have a right to ask those who formulate it to bring forward strong documentary evidence in support of it. As it happens, no such evidence is forthcoming. On the one hand, the passages in the Buddhist Scriptures on which the hypothesis has been based all admit of an entirely different interpretation,—namely, that after the death of the body the Perfect One ceases to exist, not absolutely, but only in the sense which "the ignorant, unconverted man" attaches to the word existence.

On the other hand, there are passages in the Buddhist Scriptures in which the hypothesis is directly or indirectly traversed; such as the dialogue between Yamaka and Sariputta, in which the belief that "on the dissolution of the body the monk who has lost all depravity is annihilated" is first condemned as a wicked heresy and then conclusively refuted; or, again, as the dialogue between King Pasenadi and the nun Khema, in which the question as to the existence of the Perfect One after death is shown to be unanswerable, not because the Perfect One will then have ceased to be, but because he will have passed beyond the reach of human thought.

It is worthy of note (though the point seems to have escaped the notice of the Western students of Buddhism) that the question "What becomes of the ordinary, unemancipated man when he dies?" is never asked in any Buddhist dialogue. Why is this? Evidently because the doctrine of re-incarnation is the accepted answer to the question. What interests King Pasenadi, the monk Yamaka, and others is not the general question "What comes after death?" but the particular question, "What becomes of the Perfect One when he finally passes away from earth?" The answer to this question is always the same. "Do not ask. The question is unanswerable. The Perfect One passes, when he dies, beyond the remotest horizon of human thought; and when thought fails, words can do nothing but perplex and mislead."

The truth is that here, as elsewhere, when the West seems to be passing judgment on Buddhism, it is really delimiting the range of its own thought. To the consideration of the problem of the Perfect One's final state, as of all kindred problems, Western thought carries with it the metaphysical assumption which has obsessed it for two thousand years,—the assumption that nothing exists, in the order of Nature, except what is perceptible by man's bodily senses. The religious thought of the West has always taken refuge from the consequences of this assumption in the dream-world of the Supernatural. But the dualism of Nature and the Supernatural was (and is) entirely foreign to Indian thought. Seeing, then, that Buddha transported the Perfect One beyond the vision of Gods and men, and yet provided no asylum for him in any Supernatural heaven, the Western exponents of Buddhism find themselves driven to conclude, with the monk Yamaka, that "on the dissolution of his body" the Perfect One "is annihilated, perishes, and does not exist after death."

But it is Western, not Indian, thought which creates the vacuum that receives the Perfect One's emancipated soul. When Dr. Rhys Davids, after quoting Buddha's words, "While his body shall remain he will be seen by Gods and men, but after the termination of life, upon the dissolution of the body, neither Gods nor men will see him," asks: "Would it be possible in a more complete or categorical manner to deny that there is any soul—anything of any kind which continues to exist, in any manner, after death?" there is an obvious answer to his triumphant challenge.

It is by assuming that Buddha, too, believed in the intrinsic reality of what is perceptible and the non-existence of what is imperceptible, that he proves his point. But has he any right to make that assumption? Is not Buddha's attitude towards the problem of reality the very question which is really (though not ostensibly) in dispute? And inasmuch as Buddha devoted his life to teaching men that the perceptible is the unreal, is it not rash, to say the least, to assume offhand that his mind was ruled by the fundamental postulate of Western thought? Yet, unless his mind was ruled by that postulate, the words on which Dr. Rhys Davids lays so much stress can be shown to have another meaning than that which he ascribes to them, and the conclusion—that Buddha regarded death as the end of life—instead of being obviously true, becomes demonstrably false.

What Buddha meant (if we may argue from the general tenor of his teaching) when he said that, upon the dissolution of the Perfect One's body, neither Gods nor men would see him, was not that the Perfect One would then pass into non-existence, but rather that then at last he would attain to absolute reality. For the perceptible world, as Buddha conceived of it, is the world of dreams and shadows; and it is therefore clear that, until the Perfect One has passed, wholly and irrevocably, beyond the horizon of perception, he has not found rest in the Real.

Let us now attempt, in defiance of Buddha's express prohibition, to penetrate the mystery of Nirvana. The mystery is, in a sense, final. The Path ends—for good and all—in Nirvana. The Western hypothesis that Nirvana is not the final state of the Perfect One, but the prelude to that state, is wholly gratuitous. Not a word is said in any of the passages with which the students of Buddhism have made us familiar, which might seem to suggest that the Nirvanic state ends with the death of the Perfect One's body, or that there is any state of existence (or non-existence) beyond it. That Buddha, who turned the prying mind back on the hither brink of Nirvana, should have looked beyond Nirvana and told men what was awaiting them on its farther shore, is in the highest degree improbable. The progress of the Perfect One is followed till Nirvana begins:

"But there sight fails. No heart may know

The bliss when life is done."

The question, then, which we have to ask ourselves is this: What goal would he be likely to reach who followed the Path to the end? This question suggests a second: What is the Path supposed to do for him who walks in it? The answer to this question is embodied in Buddha's scheme of life. The Path detaches him who walks in it from the impermanent, the changeable, the phenomenal. But it does this, not by the ascetic curtailment of the range of his life, but by the progressive expansion of his consciousness. It will be remembered that Buddha told his disciples in the earliest of his discourses that they were to steer a middle course between the "unworthy and unreal" paths of pleasure on the one side, and mortification on the other. It will also be remembered that the precepts which he gave them aimed, to make a general statement, at the cultivation of two faculties,—self-control and sympathy.

The function of self-control is, on the one hand, to train the will for the task that awaits it,—the task of directing the process of soul-growth; and, on the other hand, to prevent the lower and narrower self from becoming so aggressive as to arrest the outgrowth of the higher and larger self. And the function of sympathy, which carries a man out of himself into the lives of others, is to promote the outgrowth of the higher and larger self, by raising the level and widening the range of one's life. Thus the Path detaches men from the phenomenal, not by cutting it out of their lives or otherwise blinding them to its existence, but by giving them the power (through the expansion of their consciousness) of seeing it in its true proportions and its true light.

It is possible for one who walks in the Path to take an interest and a pleasure in the ephemeral concerns of life, and yet to hold on to them by the very lightest of threads. There is nothing of Puritanical gloom or sourness in the teaching of Buddha. The foreglow of Nirvana falls on the Path and throws its rays on either side of it, till those who walk in it learn at last to take an innocent delight even in the things which they know to be phantasmal.

Now the goal of the Path is the natural consummation of it,—not a reward which will be given by an omnipotent onlooker to those who have kept to the Path and obeyed its commandments, but the end to which the Path naturally and inevitably leads; an end which is not merely pre-figured by the Path, even in its earlier stages, but is also, in some sort, present in promise and potency in those earlier (and all subsequent) stages, just as the full-grown oak is present in promise and potency in the acorn and the sapling, or the ripened peach in the fruit-bud and the blossom.

And inasmuch as the function of the Path is to detach men from the phenomenal by expanding their consciousness, and to expand their consciousness by fostering the growth of their souls, it seems to follow that the goal of the Path will be the ideal perfection of him who walks in it, and that when this ideal state has been reached the consciousness of the Perfect One (as we may now call him) will have become all-embracing, and his detachment from the phenomenal complete. We are now in a position to give this tentative and provisional answer to the question, What is Nirvana? Nirvana is a state of ideal spiritual perfection, in which the soul, having completely detached itself—by the force of its own natural expansion—from what is individual, impermanent, and phenomenal, embraces and becomes one with the Universal, the Eternal, and the Real. In other words, the essence of Nirvana is the finding of the ideal self, in and through the attainment to oneness—living, conscious oneness—with the All and the Divine.

It is true that Buddha spoke of consciousness as one of the five things from which the "learned and noble disciple" must strive to detach himself; but he obviously meant by consciousness what his audience, composed for the most part of ordinary unenlightened men, would have understood the word to mean,—that sense of selfhood which is based on the sense of difference from other things, In the Nirvanic consciousness the sense of selfhood is based on the sense of oneness with other things, or rather of oneness with the vital essence of all things,—with the living Whole. 'When we predicate consciousness of him who has passed into Nirvana, what we mean is that the Nirvanic state of being is on the farther, not on the hither, side of consciousness; that it enormously transcends what we, with our limited range of perception and thought, understand by consciousness, but that it is reached by the continuance of the same process of growth by which consciousness itself has been evolved. The Western mind, which is dominated, even in its seasons of speculative activity, by mathematical and mechanical conceptions, understands by oneness with the Divine a quasi-material absorption into the Whole, which involves the complete extinction of consciousness in him who "Slips into the shining sea."

The Indian conception of oneness with the Divine is the polar opposite of this. If soul is to mingle with soul it must do so as soul, preserving, yet raising to an infinite power, all the characteristics of soul life,—its freedom and self-compulsion (which it now realizes as infinite energy), its thought (which it now realizes as infinite wisdom), its desire (which it now realizes as infinite love). Such, in shadowy outline, is the conception of Nirvana which my study of Buddha's teaching, from the standpoint of Indian idealism, has forced upon my mind. That I carried the conception with me is undeniable, and that I should eventually work round to it was no doubt preordained. But the curve of thought which I have completed has helped me to enrich and deepen the conception, for it has enabled me to trace the steps by which the genius and practical wisdom of one gifted Teacher could transform a philosophical idea into a master principle of action, and so make it available for the daily needs of mankind.

To the Sages of the Upanishads re-union with the Divine was the goal of meditative aspiration,—a goal which few could hope to reach, for the path to it was one which few could find and fewer still could follow. Buddha saw that it was also the goal of spiritual growth, and that as such it could be reached—in the fullness of time—by the lowliest and most ignorant of men. But he saw also that, as the goal of spiritual growth (and therefore of spiritual endeavour), it must be pursued unconsciously; that the path to it must be clearly defined, but that of the goal itself nothing was to be predicated except that it was the home of happiness and peace.

Dr. Oldenberg complains that Buddha's teaching is a "fragment of a circle to complete which and to find the centre of which is forbidden by the Thinker." But if we place at the centre of the circle the sovereign dogma of Indian idealism, if we assume that Nirvana, the admitted end of Buddhist desire and endeavour, is a state of self-realization through union with the Divine or Universal Soul, the circle will complete itself: for we shall see a meaning in every precept that Buddha gave, and in every argument that he used; we shall see a meaning in every discourse and dialogue which Western thought has (on this hypothesis) misunderstood; we shall see a meaning in the Western misunderstanding of Buddha's teaching; we shall see a meaning in Buddha's mysterious silence; and we shall see that his scheme of life was a "perfect round,"—a coherent and consistent whole. Nor are we making a random guess when we fix that particular centre for Buddha's circle of thought. "Of all plane figures the circle alone has the same curvature at every point." If Buddha's ethical teaching was indeed a fragment of a circle, then it is possible for those who care to do so, both to complete the circle and to find its centre. But we must be allowed to assume, before we undertake this task, that the fragment which is before us is part of a circle and not of any less perfect curve.

The conception which Western critics, in their desire to claim Buddha as of their own school of thought, place at the centre of his philosophy, has the grave demerit of turning what is supposed to be the fragment of a circle into a fragment, or series of fragments, of one of the wildest and most lawless of curves. But if we assume that Buddha's scheme of life, as it existed in his mind, was a "perfect round," and that what he chose to formulate was a fragment of that "perfect round," we shall find that there is only one possible centre to it,—the conception which history, psychology, and common-sense unite in suggesting to us as central,—the conception that the Universal Self is the true self of each one of us, and that to realize the true self is the destiny and the duty of man.

THE BANKRUPTCY OF WESTERN THOUGHT

The higher thought of the West is bankrupt, in the sense that it can no longer meet its obligations. When I say this I do not merely mean that its liquid assets are less than its liabilities. It is desirable that the liabilities of thought should at all times far exceed its liquid assets, and it would point to a lamentable lack of speculative enterprise if they did not. What I do mean is that the liabilities which Western thought has incurred are greatly in excess of its resources,—of its realizable as well as its liquid assets.

Let us see how this has come to pass. The function of high thinking is to provide working capital for the speculative enterprises of the soul. The speculative enterprises of the soul take the form of spiritual desires. The working capital which thought provides takes the form of philosophical ideas,—tentative and provisional theories of things. As it seldom happens, in the commercial world, that an enterprise which is thoroughly successful does not ask, from time to time, for fresh capital in order that, without departing from its original aim, it may widen the field of its operations and reach a yet higher level of success,—so in the inner life of man, whenever the desires of the heart receive genuine satisfaction, the proof of this lies in the fact that, in response to a fresh influx of ideas, new desires arise which are really new developments of the old, or, in other words, that the old desires, stimulated and modified by thought, become deepened, widened, purified, and otherwise transformed.

Sometimes, however, it happens that the "ideals" which thought provides, in response to the demands of spiritual desire, become stereotyped into systems of "dogma," and as such are accepted by the heart as fully and finally true. When this happens the development of spiritual desire ceases, or, in the language of commerce, the soul becomes so unenterprising that its liabilities, now brought within a very narrow compass, are fully met by its liquid assets. In this state of ignoble solvency, the soul, having ceased to grow—for its desires are its growing pains—has begun to degenerate and to turn its face towards death. Then comes the inevitable reaction. The expansive energies of Nature, which triumphant dogmatism had long held in check, force at last a new outlet for themselves, and in doing so stimulate the deeper desires of the heart into new activity and direct them into new channels. In such an epoch the need of the soul for fresh capital—for new ideas—is stronger than it has ever been, but the difficulty of finding it is greater. For as the soul has long since closed its capital account, the sources of supply, which are fed by the very demands that are made upon them, will have long since ceased to flow.

The old stereotyped ideas have satisfied the soul for so many years that the organs of spiritual thought, atrophied by disuse, have at last become incapable of supplying new ideas,—the negative dogmas which man formulates in his season of reaction and revolt being, if anything, narrower and more rigid than the positive dogmas of the churches and sects. What happens, then, when the old order changes, is that the soul, carried by its outburst of speculative enterprise far beyond the limits of the ideas which had so long sufficed for its needs, takes upon itself obligations for which its working capital—its spiritual philosophy—is wholly inadequate. The end of this is that it drifts into a state of insolvency, in which it pays the penalty of having so long been ignobly solvent. Or, rather, it is the thought of the age which goes bankrupt, for thought is under a permanent obligation to supply the soul, in its adventurous moods, with the capital which it needs for its enterprises.

This is what has happened in the West. And if we ask ourselves why this has happened, we can but answer that Western thought has, from the beginning of things, allowed itself to be dominated by the ideas of the "average man." The philosophy of the average man is simplicity itself. He begins, as all men necessarily do, with the apparent antithesis of himself and the outward world. While his philosophy is in its sub-conscious stage, he is content to ascribe reality to both the terms of the antithesis. But when he begins to reflect, in his crude way, on "great matters," his standpoint changes. Utterly incapable of subtle thinking, his mind instinctively relapses into the vulgar dualism of the existent and the non-existent. The aphorism, "Seeing is believing," dominates his thought; and the naïvely egoistic assumption that what the Universe seems to be to his bodily senses that it is in itself, and that therefore nothing exists, in the order of Nature, except what is perceptible by the bodily senses, becomes the cardinal article of his faith.

But the consequences of this materialistic assumption are repugnant to his heart. And so, in response to the demands of his heart, his mind devises a supplementary theory of things,—the conception of a world above Nature in which the higher realities of which his bodily senses can take no cognizance, may find an asylum. Foremost among these higher realities are those towards which his religious instincts direct themselves,—supreme, or, as he calls it, divine goodness, divine wisdom, divine power.

Thus instead of one Universe the average man must needs have two,—Nature and the Supernatural World; and between these two a great gulf is fixed in his thought, a gulf of nothingness which makes natural intercourse between the two worlds impossible. But, as always happens in a dualism, the intervening gulf of nothingness drains into itself the reality of both worlds; draining away from Nature her inwardness, her spirituality, and, in the last resort, her life; draining away from the world above Nature its substance, its actuality, and all of it that is convincingly real.

The fatal influence of this dualistic cosmology will make itself felt long after the idea of the Supernatural has lost its hold upon human thought. Meanwhile, the ascendency of the idea is fraught with serious danger to the spiritual development of mankind. It is not enough that a supernatural world should be evolved by thought in response to the demands of the heart. Intercourse with that world must somehow or other be opened up and carried on. And as natural intercourse between the two worlds is impossible, supernatural intercourse must take its place. The gulf cannot be passed by man; but God, who dwells beyond it, can pass it at his own good pleasure and in his own good time.

Hence comes the general idea of supernatural revelation, with all its sub-ideas,—the idea of divinely selected peoples, of divinely commissioned teachers, of divinely inspired scriptures, of divinely guided churches, and the rest. We need not follow the idea into all these details, but we shall do well to follow it into some of its inevitable consequences. What is revealed to man from the supernatural world, by whatever means the intercourse between the two worlds may be carried on, is obviously "the Truth." As such, if it is to be made available for man's needs, it must admit of being formulated and taught. In other words, the dogmatic standpoint and the dogmatic temper are necessary corollaries to the general idea that the truth of things can be revealed to man by the Supernatural God. Between dogmatism and free-thought there is, in the nature of things, a truceless war.

The conception of truth as an un-attainable ideal, the quest of which is "its own exceeding great reward," is wholly incompatible with the dogmatic standpoint. The exercise of speculative thought is indeed permitted by dogmatism, but under conditions which make the concession a mockery. Not only must its enterprises be carried on within narrow and strictly defined limits, but they must also lead it to pre-ordained conclusions. This means that "high thinking," the thought which makes what is defined and accepted the starting-point of its enterprises, is not merely discountenanced by dogmatism, but rigorously repressed.

But the repression (or restriction) of speculative thought means the repression (or restriction) of spiritual desire. For thought both indicates the general direction in which desire is to operate, and provides it with the working capital for its bolder ventures. It follows that, when the working capital which thought is allowed to provide is strictly limited in amount, and when that limited amount is accepted by desire as entirely adequate to its needs, desire itself is bringing its speculative operations to a standstill. In other words, dogmatism limits the scope of desire in the very act of limiting the sphere of thought; and so far as it is successful in imposing those limits, it tends to arrest the growth of the soul.

These are general conceptions. Let us return to the history of Western thought. It is to the genius of one small nation that the West owes, for good or for evil, its spiritual standpoint. Jehovah, the God of Israel, is accepted as the Lord Paramount of the Universe by the greater part of the Western World, those who are in rebellion against his authority being unable to find any rival claimant to his throne. Whatever may be one's own attitude towards the ideas which Israel evolved and formulated, one cannot but admire the strenuousness and force of character which enabled a small, remote, and politically feeble nation to force its conception of God and Man and Nature upon the thought and the conscience of the Græco-Roman world.

But admiration of Israel's character and achievements must not blind us to the fact that his astonishing success as a propagandist was due to his weakness, not less than to his strength. The genius of Israel was essentially practical. In his seasons of spiritual expansion it became poetical; and his poetry, which reflected the intensity as well as the narrowness of his nature, was (at its highest level), in the fullest sense of the word, sublime. But he easily fell, as we all do, below the level of poetic rapture; and when he began to fall, he dropped to ignominious depths. For he had no philosophy, in the deeper sense of the word, to sustain him. Singularly destitute of "ideas," he was incapable of effective self-criticism (though abundantly capable both of self-exaltation and self-depreciation); and he followed his quasi-commercial conception of religious duty into the most meticulous details of legalism, fully believing that in doing so he was working the will of God.

For intellectual meditation, for sustained and concentrated reflection, for the depths and the subtleties of thought, he had no turn whatever. His philosophy was that of the average man, and his triumph has been, in part at least, the triumph of the average man's ideas. Addressing himself to ordinary people—the people who believe that the visible world is the real world, and yet are unwilling to accept the logical consequences of that belief—he won their whole-hearted support by meeting them on their own intellectual level, by speaking to them in their own language, by expounding to them their own theory of things.

His explanation of the Universe, with all its subsidiary conceptions: the conception of a personal and supernatural God, made in the image of Man; of the creation of the visible world by the fiat of God's will; of the disobedience of Man to God's commandments, and his consequent fall from innocence and bliss; of the selection of a certain people as the depository of the truths which God chose to reveal to fallen Man; of the formulation of God's will in a code of law; of the promise of God's favour to those who should obey that law, and of his wrath to those who should disobey it;—all this, as far as it goes, is just such an explanation as the average man, if his curiosity was thoroughly awakened, would, in his attempt to account for the more striking facts of existence and at the same time to give satisfaction to the master desires of his heart, be likely to evolve for himself.

What wonder that when, through the magnetic influence of Christ's gracious and commanding personality and through the self-sacrificing devotion of the high-souled Jews who transmitted that influence to the Gentiles, the Jewish scriptures became known far and wide, the Jewish scheme of things—crowned and completed by the conception of Christ as the mediator between God and Man and the redeemer of fallen Humanity, and so made available for all believers, irrespective of race—should have been accepted as an authoritative explanation of all the mysteries of existence?

It is true that, along with his own philosophy, systematized and dramatized for him by Israel, the average man received some fragments of the spiritual teaching of Christ. But he accepted that teaching, not for its own sake, not for the sake of the philosophy that was behind it—of that he knew nothing, and had it been revealed to him he would have shrunk from it with suspicion and alarm—but for the sake and on the authority of Christ. His own interpretation of it was, as might have been expected, at best one-sided and inadequate, at worst literal and mechanical; and so disquieting were its precepts, owing to his inability to enter into their spirit, that an instinctive regard for his own mental balance and sanity led him in nine cases out of ten to ignore them completely.

But the fact remains that, in a sense and in a manner, he did receive the spiritual teaching of Christ, and that from then till now the ferment of it has been at work in his heart. As, however, it was through the example rather than the words of his Master that the spiritual ideas which have been the leaven of his inner life were transmitted to him, it is not to be wondered at that his reception of them has been in the main a subconscious process, and that they have not materially modified the movement of his conscious thought.

For many centuries, indeed, his acceptance of his own philosophy was complete. Those who offered to shake his faith in it—Gnostics, Arians, Albigenses, and the like—fared ill at his hands. Through his Agent-General, the Pope, and in the Councils which were dominated by his "collective wisdom," he waged relentless war against heretics and schismatics; and at last things came to such a pass that whoever sent even a faint ripple of doubt over the stagnant lagoon of his (so-called) faith, whoever said or did anything which might conceivably give him the trouble of turning over in his orthodox slumber, was liable to be burned at the stake.

This triumph, in the region of speculative thought, of the average over the exceptional man, was a misfortune for the human race. For it involved the suppression of high-thinking, which is in its very essence a departure from the commonplace and the average; and the suppression of high-thinking involves, in the last resort, the suppression of spiritual desire. Not, indeed, that it is possible for spiritual desire to be finally suppressed. The expansive forces of Nature, the expression of which in man's inner life constitutes his spiritual desire, may be dammed back for centuries, but sooner or later they will find a new outlet for themselves. This is what happened in the West.

The revival of classical learning, the invention of printing, the discoveries of distant lands, and other influences which need not here be considered, all working in unison with the secret leaven of Christ's spiritual teaching, combined to generate a new life in the soul of man. Long heralded and long delayed, the day of liberation dawned at last. In the age (or ages) of the Renascence there was a remarkable lateral expansion of desire. In the age (or ages) of the Reformation there was an equally remarkable purification and elevation of desire. The triumph of the average man had been too complete, and its inevitable Nemesis had duly come. The soul of man, which had long lain in a comatose slumber and which had made many abortive efforts to arouse itself, was now at last alive and awake, and ready for new speculative ventures. Full of energy and enterprise, it turned to thought for the working capital that it needed,—for the help and guidance which large ideas alone can supply.

But there was no response to its appeal.

Before the Western mind could begin to think, it had to vindicate its right to think. In other words, it had to fight for freedom. That fight is still in progress, and the end of it is not yet in sight. Meanwhile, the speculative achievements of Western thought have been, in the nature of things, inconsiderable. Of its triumphant success in the sphere of physical science I need not speak. Physical science is not philosophy. Nor need I pause to consider that metaphysical movement which is supposed to have been initiated by Descartes. The successive idealistic ventures which have been one of the distinguishing features of that movement, have all been "apparent failures." The truth is that high-thinking had been so long and so rigorously suppressed that, even in the efforts which the Western mind has made to free itself from bondage to the average man's ideas, it has shown at every turn the baneful effect of his ascendency.

It is a mistake to suppose that the struggle for freedom which has been in progress for five centuries has been wholly, or even in large measure, conducted by men of exceptional mental gifts. It was pre-ordained, one might almost say, that the average man should himself take a leading part in it. Whenever the average man is allowed, as he has been in the West, to control the larger movements of thought, however carefully his philosophy may be formulated by the theologians and guarded by the Churches, the day will surely come when, in his individual capacity, he will rise in revolt against himself in his corporate capacity, and range himself, in his attempt to vindicate the right of private judgment, by the side of the exceptional men whom, in his corporate capacity, he is only too ready to burn.

But, in entering into this anomalous alliance, he illogically claims, and half-unconsciously exercises, the right to impose the fundamental assumption of his philosophy on the minds of his allies. And though he is at one with them in their demand for freedom of conscience, he leaves them, and leaves himself, but little room for the exercise of that sacred right.

This is one among many reasons why the average man's fundamental assumption—that the physical plane is the whole of Nature—still dominates Western thought. In the deadly shade of that assumption his spiritual ideas wither almost as soon as they are born. In his own philosophy materialism is still modified by supernaturalism. But, in rejecting the old theologies which formulated and systematized his belief in the Supernatural, and the old organizations which guarded it from criticism, he has exposed it to the danger of being undermined by speculative thought. Indeed, it is no exaggeration to say that the one solid achievement of critical thought in the West, in recent years, has been to undermine the belief in the Supernatural and to discredit the whole theory of things which was built on that insecure foundation. The immediate consequences of this achievement have been and will long be disastrous. Take away from the philosophy of the average man the conception of the Supernatural,—and materialism, pure and simple, remains.

It is sometimes said that in the present age there is a feud, with regard to "great matters," between the "heart" and the "head." The feud is also, though less correctly, spoken of as one between Religion and Science. Strictly speaking, the parties to the quarrel are two rival theories of things—Supernaturalism, which seems, for the time being, to satisfy the "heart," and Materialism, which seems, for the time being, to satisfy the "head." To identify religion with supernaturalism is as unfair as to hold science responsible for materialism. The religious instinct invented supernaturalism, as an antidote to the materialism of popular thought; and the spread of scientific habits of thought discredited supernaturalism, and so re-habilitated materialism as the philosophy of the average man in his seasons of "free-thought." But the hypothesis of a world above Nature is as little of the essence of religion, as is the materialistic degradation of Nature of the essence of science.

That there is, in the present age, a feud between the "head" and the "heart"—between "reason" and "faith"—is, I think, undeniable. The churches and sects denounce "rationalism" as vehemently as the Free-thinkers and Agnostics (to give them the titles which they have appropriated, but to which they have no claim) denounce "superstition." The very platform on which the head and the heart meet in their controversy, is the tacit assumption that their respective philosophies are the only possible solutions of the problem of the Universe. "Quit the fold of the Church," says the votary of "faith," "and you will sink deeper and deeper into the quagmire of materialism, till you end by denying God, denying the soul, denying the life beyond the grave." "Cease to believe in God," says the "Free-thinker," "cease to believe in the soul, cease to dream of a life beyond the grave, or you will find yourself committed to all the assumptions of supernaturalism, and, sinking deeper and deeper into the quagmire of superstition, you will end by surrendering your conscience to the casuist and your freedom to the priest."

It is a significant fact that in France, where the average man is more logical and clear-headed than in any other country, there are (when all is said and done) two parties and two only,—Catholics and "Free-thinkers." Between these two there is a deep-seated and far-reaching feud. It might almost be said that every Frenchman is bound to range himself on one side or the other in that deadly quarrel, bound to subscribe to all the positive dogmas of Catholic theology or, failing that, to all the negative dogmas of what miscalls itself "Free-thought,"—a creed which centres in the dogmatic denunciation of "the deplorable superstition of a life after death." Between ecclesiastical supernaturalism and secularistic materialism there seems to be no middle term.

But if in France every man is either a Catholic or a "Free-thinker," in other countries, where men are less logical, it not unfrequently happens that the same person passes and re-passes between the two hostile camps.

Again and again one sees the young man who has been nurtured in the ancient faith, reject supernaturalism as an irrational hypothesis, and go forth, exulting in his freedom, in quest of a truer and deeper philosophy; and sometimes one sees the same man, weary of a creed which authoritatively tells him, while the shadows are lengthening on his path, that death is the end of life, creep back in his old age to the fold which he had quitted in his youth, and justify himself for his second apostacy by arguing that, as an interpreter of the deeper mysteries of existence, the heart is, in all probability, more to be trusted than the head.

Assuming that there is a feud between the head and the heart, let us ask ourselves how the feud has originated, what it indicates, and how it is to be healed. We mean by the "heart" the headquarters of desire,—by the "head" the headquarters of thought. The function of the head is to supply the heart with the working-capital that it needs for its speculative enterprises, in other words, with the "ideas" that it needs for the due evolution of its spiritual desires. It sometimes happens that the heart goes to the head for ideas, and is sent empty away. But these are exceptional cases. As a rule, when there is a complete dearth of ideas, the reason is that there has been no demand for them, the soul having become so un-enterprising that the unexpended balance of its original capital proves to be more than sufficient for its needs.

But Nemesis waits, as we have seen, on this ignoble solvency. Sooner or later the soul will awake from its orthodox slumber, and make itself ready for new speculative ventures. Then there will be an immense expansion of desire, and a corresponding need for new ideas. For a time, indeed, that need will not be acutely felt. A sustained attempt will be made to pour the new wine into the old bottles, to finance the new enterprises with the old capital. But after a time the inadequacy of the old ideas will be realized; and the heart will go to the head for the new ideas that its expanding desires imperatively demand. But the head, having had no call made upon it, will have long since ceased to enlarge its own capital; and when the heart goes to it, it must either confess itself insolvent, or try to dissuade the heart from committing itself to enterprises which it (the head) is unable to finance.

In self-defence it will take the latter course. It will say to the heart: "These enterprises for which you ask financial help are mad and impossible, and will end in your utter ruin. Abandon them, one and all, and limit your desires to what is measurable and attainable. For that I will provide you with the limited amount of capital that you will need, but on one condition,—that I am allowed to become a partner in your business."

How will the heart receive this advice? The new desires for which it needs working capital are not revolutionary ventures, but natural and necessary developments of its old desires. To tell it that these new desires are mad and impossible enterprises is to tell it, by implication, that the whole of its business is unsound. Both the head and the heart will feel instinctively that the former's response to the latter's demand for ideas amounts to this. Were it possible for the head to say, in response to the heart's appeal: "Your business has contracted and otherwise deteriorated owing to your having, through indolence and timidity, neglected to expand it: but the business itself—the fundamental desires which you seek to exploit—is sound enough; all that is needed is that you should enlarge your capital and develop your business in new directions and on a bolder scale":—were it possible for this stimulating answer to be given to the expectant heart, the inner life of man would be quickened into new activity, and a new season of soul-growth would be begun.

But it is not possible. Were the head to tell the heart that what the latter needs, above all things, is fresh capital, it would thereby make open confession of the emptiness of its own coffers. What it will find itself driven to do is to discountenance the enterprises of the heart,—not its new ventures only, but the spirit of enterprise which is and has ever been the breath of its life; to tell the heart that spiritual desire—the desire which directs itself towards the far-off and mysterious—is in the nature of things a vanity and a delusion; in fine, to invite it to wind up the business which it lives to transact, and to embark on a new career which bears the same relation to the old that the till of a village grocer bears to the counting-house of a merchant prince.

What will happen when the heart, in its hour of expansive energy, receives this chilling rebuff? Who shall blame it if it resolves hence-forth to forswear its alliance with the head; if it abandons its dream of finding new ideas to match the new desires that had begun to renew its life; if it recoils from the new desires, as from phantoms which are luring it to destruction; if it goes back at last to the old discredited ideas and the old devitalized desires, determined at whatever cost to patch up its dwindling business and carry it on as best it may?

That I may make my meaning clear, let me trace in outline the history of one of the master desires of the heart,—the desire for immortality. I select this desire for consideration because, of all spiritual desires, it is at once the most popular and the most profound; and I call it a spiritual desire because it unquestionably directs itself towards the far-off and the mysterious. When it was still in its infancy, the crude conceptions of supernaturalism were sufficient for its needs. The pious Christian was content to believe that on a certain day in a not very distant future his body, which he found it difficult to distinguish from his real self, would rise again from the dead; that he would then appear before the judgment-seat of Christ; that if he had lived well while on earth he would be rewarded with eternal happiness; that if he had lived ill he would be punished with eternal misery.

This theory of things was provided by the head in response to the demands of the heart; but when once the theory had been accepted and formulated by the Christian Church, the head was forbidden to criticize it, forbidden to modify it except in unessential details, forbidden even to think about it except within the clearly defined limits which Catholic theology had marked out.

The consequence was that thought (in the deeper sense of the word) got out of touch with the idea of survival, lost all interest in it, held entirely aloof from it. For a time the desire for immortality was satisfied with the doctrines of a bodily resurrection and a future judgment; but satisfaction is the grave of desire; and as the heart, like the head, was forbidden to speculate (in its own way) about the destiny of the departed spirit, it too lost interest in the problem, and instead of moving onward, as desire should always do, it began to oscillate between two ignoble feelings,—callous indifference and superstitious fear. When the tyranny of dogmatism was relaxed, and some measure of freedom was restored both to the head and to the heart, the former began to criticize the current eschatology and to turn away from it as irrational, while the latter began to turn away from it as ignoble and inadequate.

So far, so good. Had it then been possible for the head to supply the heart with larger and deeper conceptions of what is vulgarly called "the future life," the heart would have begun to discover new depths and new developments in its desire for immortality; and, in its attempt to interpret these, the head would have begun to discover new depths and new developments in its theory of immortality; and in this way man's whole conception of Nature would have been expanded and enriched. But 1,000 years of forced inaction had atrophied the constructive energies of thought, and its critical power alone remained. Even the critical power of thought, which cannot be dissociated from the constructive, had suffered from the despotism which confined it, so far as any freedom was allowed it, to the study of physical phenomena, and forbade it to meddle with "spiritual things." For criticism, in the truer and deeper sense of the word, it had no capacity.

Its growing power of analytical criticism enabled it to undermine the foundations of supernaturalism. But when it had done this work, it had gone as far as it was possible for it to go. The dreamland of the Supernatural had vanished, and "Nature" remained. But it was the Nature of the average man. The philosophy of the average man, with its central assumption that the outward and visible world is the whole of Nature, was still in the ascendant; and now that the corrective influence of supernaturalism had been withdrawn, the latent materialism of that commonplace philosophy began to resume its sway. To free itself from that sway was beyond the power of thought. Incapable of constructive criticism, it could do nothing but bow its neck to the yoke of the very assumption which the heart had instinctively rejected as intolerable, and in its effort to free itself from which it had, in conjunction with the head, devised the theory of the Supernatural. To expose the unsoundness of that provisional theory was (and is) within the power of thought. To devise a better theory was (and is) beyond its power and, for the time being, beyond its aim.

What will happen, then, when the heart, no longer able to rest in the old doctrines of Resurrection and Judgment, of Heaven and Hell, but still cherishing the desire for immortality, goes to the head for light and guidance? It will be told that not only are the old ideas about immortality false and hollow, but that there are no ideas which can take their place. It will be told that the desire for immortality is itself a delusion—the primary delusion, of which the fables of the theologians are a fitting interpretation,—and that it must be surrendered if the heart is to find peace. And if the head is asked to justify these sweeping negations, it will give reasons for them which strike at the root, not of this desire only but of spiritual desire as such.

That it may the better prove how entirely it is under the control of the average man, it will appeal to his primary assumption—that the visible world is the only world—as to a self-evident truth; and if the authority of its favourite axiom is questioned, it will support it with many arguments, each of which is a mere re-statement of the axiom under a more or less transparent disguise; and, having thus established its authority, it will draw inferences from it which prove, as it contends, that not the idea of immortality only, but the idea of spiritual life, the idea of spiritual freedom, the whole "soul-theory" (as it contemptuously calls it), is baseless as a dream. And that it may the better prove how incapable it is of interpreting a genuinely spiritual desire, such as the longing for immortality, it will take upon itself to scold the heart for cherishing a desire which, besides being demonstrably delusive, is base, selfish, and unmanly,—a "lust for positive happiness," which poisons morality at its fountain-head.

The desire for immortality may or may not be delusive—demonstrably delusive it certainly is not—hut it is the very cant of pseudo-stoicism to say that it is base and selfish. For, after all, what is the desire for immortality? Is it not the desire, which man shares with all other living things, to grow—to continue to grow—to ripen—to move towards the goal of natural perfection?

"We feel that we are greater than we know."

We feel that the scale of our life and the scope of our work are great beyond measure, and that it would be as reasonable to expect an oak tree to make the full measure of its possible growth in a single season as for the soul to make the full measure of its possible growth in a single life. It is the soul's belief in itself which makes it desire immortality, just as it is the oak tree's belief in itself which makes it wait expectantly for the warmth and moisture of another spring; but the soul's desire for continued growth is entirely redeemed from selfishness by the fact that, in the higher stages of its development, the soul can continue to grow only by becoming selfless. It is true that in the quasi-concrete forms which the desire takes, in the pictures which man makes for himself of the "future life," he shows the limitations of his undeveloped nature,—the materialism of his unimaginative mind, the selfishness of his unexpanded heart. But the desire itself is unselfish, with all the unselfishness of a cosmic force.

Rebuffed and rebuked by the head, the heart recoils upon itself; and as the head cannot provide it with the illuminating ideas about immortality for which it asks, and as it cannot surrender a desire which is a part of its very life, it has no choice but to revert to the old ideas, to accept these as of Divine authority, and to confine the desire (which had struggled in vain for freedom and expansion) within the narrow channel which they provide. This means that, owing to lack of working capital, its speculative enterprise has failed; and this again means that thought, which is bound by its charter to supply the heart with "ideas," is unable to meet its obligations, and is therefore, in a word, bankrupt..

Neither the head nor the heart is to be blamed for this fiasco. The scale of the catastrophe is so large, and the forces which have combined to produce it are so complex and have been so long in operation, that it is impossible to say where the responsibility for it is to be laid. Also, it may be admitted that for the heart to be at open feud with the head is better than for the two to work together, as they have sometimes done, in chains. To that extent one may regard the quarrel between them with something of fatalistic complacency. But it is a mistake to say, as is sometimes said, that the quarrel is a necessity of. Nature, and to suggest that there are two kinds of truth—truth for the head and truth for the heart—and that these have nothing in common. Truth, like Nature, is in the last resort one and indivisible. So is the soul. The division of the soul into the head and the heart may be a necessity of thought, so far as thought comes under the control of its instrument, language; but it is not a necessity of Nature. If the distinction between the two is to be maintained, it must be on the understanding that one of the most vital functions of each is to co-operate with the other, and that neither can do its own special work effectively except in alliance with the other.

The heart is like a woman. Its intuitions are sound, but its attempts to justify them are fallacious and inconclusive. "Le caur," says Pascal, "a ses raisons que le raison ne connait pas: on le sait en mille choses." This is quite true; but the heart, left to itself, will not only fail to discover its hidden reasons, but will insist on giving other reasons—quite wrong reasons—for its fundamentally right conclusions. For if the heart takes upon itself to interpret some strong and true desire which possesses it, the chances are that it will fall a victim, in its search for an explanation, to the first commonplace theory that comes in its way, or, failing this, will revert to some old worn-out theory which in its own secret recesses it has already discarded; with the result, in either case, that the evolution of the desire will be arrested, and its pent-up energies put to some baser use. In other words, the right conclusions of the heart, being obscured by wrong reasons, will recede into the background; and the heart will end by substituting for these its own misinterpretations of them,—misinterpretations which are wholly due to its perverse attempt to understand and explain what it sees and feels.

It is true that in the medium of poetry—which never argues, never apologizes, never explains itself—the conclusions which the heart reaches by the divination of instinctive desire, may find a safe retreat. But to sustain life in that fluid medium, in which no problem is ever solved but all reasons and all conclusions are held in solution, is to the full as difficult as to breathe the rarefied air of abstract thought. Reasons for its intuitive conclusions, ideas to justify and direct its spiritual desires, the heart must have: but to discover those reasons, even if they be locked up in the heart itself, to discover the meaning, the function, and the purpose of the heart's desire is, after all, the business of thought; and the home of thought is what we call the head.

Here we come to a paradox from which there seems to be no escape. If we ask in what court the case between the head and the heart is to be tried, we can but answer: In the court of reason, the court which is presided over by the head. This shows how fundamentally fallacious—how unreal and unnatural—is the dispute in question. When the heart takes upon itself to anticipate or reverse the ruling of the head, it violently usurps the function of the latter, and gives a verdict in its own favour in a court whose authority it has refused to recognize. The heart should go into the court of reason, not as a suitor against the head—that feud is, I repeat, fundamentally fallacious—still less as a judge, but as a witness who is deeply interested in a case which is ever on trial, and whose evidence deserves to be received and weighed.

When the head refuses to accept the depositions of the heart, and then makes light of the heart's protest, it is, in its judicial capacity, deliberately ignoring evidence which bears directly on the matter in dispute. In thus ceasing to be impartial, it abdicates its judicial functions, and takes a side in the very case which it has undertaken to try. This is equivalent to closing its court; and when the court of reason is closed, a state of chaos ensues, in which there is not even the semblance of order, until might becomes right and cuts the knots which cannot otherwise be loosed.

In the West, then, we have the strange spectacle of the head, which ought to be judicial and impartial, playing in its own court the role of a partisan and an advocate; while the heart, which is and ought to be an interested witness, finding that the Presiding Judge refuses to accept its evidence, takes forcible possession of the judicial bench and gives judgment on the case in dispute, using arguments the insufficiency of which it had fully recognized in the very act of entering the court. For it is this, and nothing less than this, which happens when reason gives judgment against "faith," having from the outset refused to listen to its evidence; and when "faith," in revenge, claims, on rational grounds, the right to reverse the rulings of reason.

The feud between the head and the heart is at once an abiding proof of the ascendency of dualism in Western thought, and a practical example of the working of that fatal fallacy.

Spirit or matter, life or machinery, inward or outward, faith or reason, the heart or the head,—again and again we are invited to make our choice between what are supposed to be mutually exclusive alternatives, though they are really aspects—at once antithetical and correlative—of the same fundamental reality. In the order of Nature there is no abiding feud between the head and the heart. When we say that there is such a feud, what we mean is that for the time being the head and the heart—thought and desire—are unable to co-operate, the result of this being that neither is fulfilling its true function, and that the whole machinery of the inner life is deranged. The readiness of the Western mind to accept this state of things as normal, shows how deep-seated is the evil and how urgent is the need for a remedy. It is also equivalent to an admission that the title of this chapter is justified, and that Western thought is no longer solvent. When thought is solvent, when it is able to supply the ideas that desire needs, not for its ignoble satisfaction but for its expansion and development, the head and the heart cease to be enemies, and become what Nature intends them to be,—fellow-workers and friends.

LIGHT FROM THE EAST

Unable to meet its obligations, unable to supply the soul with the ideas that it needs for the due interpretation and evolution of its desires, Western thought can save itself from hopeless insolvency only by borrowing ideas from some other source. If it will condescend to do this, and if, having enriched its treasury with these new ideas, it will put them to a profitable use, by bringing them into harmony with what is true and of lasting value in its own theory of things, it will not only extricate itself from its embarrassments, but will be able in due course to pay back its debt with more than compound interest.

But the ideas that are borrowed must be those which the soul really needs. Now the soul needs, above all things, to be allowed to believe in itself. Belief in oneself is the supreme motive force in Nature, the power which is behind every desire, every enterprise, every effort, to grow, every "instinct to live." What we call the feud between the heart and the head is really the soul's indignant protest, on the plane of instinct and desire, against a theory which satisfies it, for the time being, on the plane of conscious thought,—the theory that the material world is the whole world, that all phenomena, up to and including the spiritual life of man, admit of being stated and explained in terms of physical force and physical law, and that therefore the soul itself is not a reality but an empty name. In other words, the heart's revolt against the head is the soul's protest against its own disparagement of itself. The first, and in a sense the last, desire of the soul is to be allowed to believe in itself; for all faith, all hope, all joy, all that makes life worth living, is present in embryo in that one belief.

The soul, then, must be allowed to believe in itself; and if this, its fundamental act of faith, is to be really effective, if it is to give the soul the stimulus and the guidance that it needs, if it is to make an end of the intestine strife that tears the soul asunder, it must be free from any suspicion of doubt. This means that no attempt should be made to prove the reality of the soul. For if its reality were provable, it would obviously not be final or complete. Proof implies the unprovable. To prove reality is to build, in the last resort, on the rock of what is unprovably real. How do I know, for example, that the outward and visible world is real, in any sense or degree? Because my senses and my reason assure me (provisionally and within limits) of its reality.

But what is the value of this assurance if I, whose reality is unprovable, am other than real? And because my reality is unprovable, it stands to reason that, just so far as the reality of the outward world is provable, it is to that extent provisional and incomplete. It is my secret doubt as to the intrinsic reality of the outward world, which makes me attempt to prove it; and when the process of proof has reached its conclusion, its very conclusiveness becomes the measure of its failure; for it is only by postulating a higher and more intrinsic reality (in myself) that I am able to prove that the outward world is real in any sense or degree. For most men, indeed, the proof of the reality of the outward world is a process which gives satisfaction long before it has reached its final term,—in other words, long before the appeal to the soul's guarantee has become necessary. From this we may infer, if we please, that the average man's instinctive and sub-conscious belief in the solvency of the guarantor is complete, though he is incapable of the sustained effort of thought which might enable him to realize the significance of this belief, or even to become conscious of its existence. But what distinguishes the soul from all other objects of speculative thought, is that any attempt which may be made to prove its reality is, in the nature of things, foredoomed to miscarry at the very outset. This fact is deeply significant; but it is on its vital rather than its metaphysical significance that I wish to dwell. Belief in its own reality is the very root of the soul's life: to prove or attempt to prove its reality is to undermine and otherwise weaken its roothold; and to weaken its roothold is to retard the process of its growth.

But to allow the soul to believe in itself is to make faith, instead of reason, the basis of one's philosophy of life. The answer to this possible protest is that the highest function of reason (as the word is understood by those who oppose it to faith) is to prove; and that, inasmuch as proof implies the unprovable, the philosophy that is based on reason hangs in mid-air instead of resting on the solid earth. This means that no philosophy is or can be based on reason, and that every philosophy, including materialism itself, is based on an act of faith. But as every act of faith resolves itself into faith in the source of all faith, the soul (even the materialist's belief in the intrinsic reality of the outward world being resolvable, in the last resort, into belief in his own self as the guarantor of its reality), it seems to follow that the soul's belief in itself is the only belief which is self-sanctioned, and therefore the only philosophical postulate which allows the thinker to proceed at once on his way.

If the soul is to believe in itself, it must break away, finally and completely, from Western standards of reality, or rather—for the Western mind does not think in the category of the real and the unreal 1—from Western criteria of existence. While it is engaged in freeing itself from these fetters, its conception of Nature will undergo a profound and far-reaching change. Vast possibilities will begin to dawn upon its vision. No longer bound by the crude assumption that the palpable is the real and the impalpable the non-existent, it will begin to use its long-pinioned wings; and as it ascends from height to height, and discovers horizon beyond horizon, it will begin to suspect that, after all, the normal limits of human vision may not be the limits of the Universe.

It will begin to wonder whether there may not, after all, be other worlds than that which the bodily senses reveal to us; other planes of being than the physical; other senses in man than those which he shares with the lower animals; other forces than those of material Nature. In the light of this dawning conception, the postulate of a supernatural order of things, which has done so much to narrow and debase man's conception of Nature, will become finally discredited by being justified and explained.

The idea of the Supernatural cannot be wholly illusory. However erroneous, however mischievous may be its mode of expressing itself, we must needs believe that at the bottom of an idea which has ruled the lives and swayed the hearts of men in many lands and many ages, there is a real experience and a real desire.

The supernatural world is the impalpable side of Nature, including all that is "inward and spiritual," expressed in a semi-materialistic notation. It follows that, when the soul is allowed to believe in itself, the supernatural world will be re-absorbed into Nature by a quasi-spontaneous process, for the inward side of Nature will then be seen to be the real side,—the substance of which the outward world is the shadow, the vital essence of which the outward world is the expression and the form. Nor is it only the soul's conception of Nature which will expand indefinitely when the conventional criterion of existence becomes discredited.

It is also the soul's conception of itself. Allow the soul to believe in itself, and it will try to discover what its self really is. This means that it will wander far and wide, wander to the uttermost ends of the world, in quest of its own boundaries; and as these will never be discovered, it will not rest till it has absorbed all things into itself. In other words, it will not rest till it has spiritualized Nature,—spiritualized her so completely that the very things which it once regarded as the only substantial realities will begin to pass before it as moving shadows, and the material world, which it once regarded as the Alpha and Omega of Nature, will begin to melt into a dream.

Two things, then, will happen when the soul has learned to believe in itself. Its conception of Nature, freed from the limits which the popular criterion of existence imposed upon it, will be raised to an infinite power. So will its conception of itself. And these two parallel conceptions, meeting at last "at infinity," will become one.

Thus the first idea that the soul needs, if it is to be restored to a state of spiritual solvency—the idea that the soul itself is real—will give an immense stimulus to its flagging vitality, will rekindle the flame and widen beyond measure the range of its desire, will revive its dormant spirit of enterprise, will dispose it for new and daring adventures. But if these adventures are to be properly equipped and directed, further ideas will be needed; and these, too, must be provided by thought. The general idea of the soul's intrinsic reality must be supplemented by speculative ideas of large import,—ideas as to the law of the soul's life, as to its inward standard of reality, as to its origin and its destiny, as to the relation between its individual and its universal self. In evolving these ideas, thought will half lead and half follow desire, and will thus both guide and stimulate it.

But if the ideas are to be effective, they must remain ideas, and not be allowed to degenerate into formulae. To go far into detail, to map out a complete chart for the soul on the eve of its voyage of discovery, would stultify its spirit of enterprise; and to stultify its spirit of enterprise is to damp down the very flame of its life.

If the chart which thought provides is both complete and correct in all its details, it must needs be that the far-off world of mystery which draws to itself the soul's desires has already been fully explored and surveyed, and that there is nothing left in it to discover. It is by desire, even more than by thought, that the blighting influence of dogmatism makes itself felt; and desire is the soul's instinctive effort to grow.

The very basis of dogmatism is the false assumption that ultimate truth is communicable from without—as "theological information"—instead of being the inmost life of the soul, a life which the soul must win—or rather, evolve—in and for itself. When the soul realizes that it is real—and, if real at all, then supremely real—it will also realize that truth, which is the subjective counterpart of reality, is intimately its own; and it will instinctively reject all teaching which does, or pretends to do, for it what it ought to do and must do for itself. Thus the primary idea that the soul is real will automatically protect the soul from the cramping and warping pressure of dogmatism, and, while disposing it to welcome all sub-ideas which give it stimulus and guidance, will strengthen it to reject the teaching that is merely formal, and that does not reveal to it what is and has ever been its own.

This leads me to say again that, whatever spiritual ideas the thought of the West may borrow from whatever quarter, it must be able to assimilate these, if they are to rescue it from its present state of insolvency, and make them its own. I mean by this, first, that it must learn at last to recognize them as belonging to that inner life of the soul which it is the function of thought to interpret; and, next, that as they come to it—nominally from without, but really from within—it must meet them along its own line of approach, and give them the particular expression which is in keeping with its own criticism of life. For just as the individual soul, in the course of its development, should prove its individuality by universalizing itself in its own particular way, so if the soul of the West is to make the ideas which it borrows really productive, it must transform them by processes of its own till it has made them available, first for the special needs of the West, and then for the more general needs of Humanity. In this, and in no other way, will it be able to pay them back in due season, enriched and expanded by the use that it has made of them.

Four things, then, are needed if the bankruptcy of Western thought is to come to an end. In the first place, the idea that the soul is ultimately real—an idea which the heart imperatively needs, but which the head is unable to supply—must be borrowed from some other source. In the second place, the idea must be accepted on its own evidence, and therefore without any shadow of reserve or doubt. This means that the source from which the idea is borrowed must be one in which, having always been regarded as demonstrably indemonstrable, it has the force and authority of an axiom,—not of a mere assumption, still less of a logical conclusion. In the third place, with this master idea the soul must borrow the subsidiary ideas by which it has been interpreted and otherwise supported in the land of its origin; but it must take care that these subsidiary ideas, while giving it stimulus and guidance, do not in any way cramp or deaden its life, or impede the free play of its thought and its desire. In the fourth place, it must make the ideas that it borrows its very own; for until it has done this it will not be able to trade with them to advantage; and it is only by trading with them to advantage that it can hope to pay them back, with the generous interest which is due for so timely a loan.

In asking the West to adopt this heroic remedy, I can appeal to a precedent which Christendom at least will regard as authoritative,—to the example of Christ. Nearly 2000 years ago, when the ideals of Paganism had exhausted their influence, and when, as a consequence of this, the soul of the West was sinking deep into the mire of materialism—a materialism of thought as well as of desire—Christ renewed its failing strength, and drew it back to firm ground, by borrowing from the Far East the master idea of the soul's intrinsic reality and the derivative ideas that revolve round this central orb, and by making these his own. As regards the source to which he went, the ideas that he borrowed, and the use that he made of them, we who revere Christ as our Lord and Master, shall do well to follow his lead.

To the pious Christian, who believes that Christ brought his ideas—or shall I say, his store of "theological information"?—down to earth from the supernatural Heaven, the suggestion that he borrowed ideas from India, or any other terrestrial land, may possibly seem profane. Yet Theology itself admits, or rather insists, that Christ was (and is) "very man" as well as "very God"; and if he was "very man," if he was open to all human influences, we may surely take for granted that his pure and exalted nature was peculiarly sensitive to the spiritual ideas of his age. That Christ had come under the influence of the spiritual ideas of the Far East is a hypothesis which explains many things, and for which therefore there are many things to be said. To attempt to prove in detail the indebtedness of the "Gospel" to the "Ancient Wisdom" would carry me far beyond the limits which the aim of this work has imposed upon me.

But I would ask anyone who can approach the question with a genuinely open mind to make the following simple experiment. Let him first saturate himself with the spiritual thought of India,—with the speculative philosophy, half metaphysical, half poetical, of the Upanishads, and with the ethical philosophy of Buddha. Let him then study the sayings of Christ, making due allowance for the distorting medium (of Jewish prejudice and Messianic expectation) through which his teaching has been transmitted to us. He will probably end by convincing himself, as I have done, that the spiritual standpoints of the Sages of the Upanishads, of Buddha, and of Christ were, in the very last resort, identical.

With this hypothesis to guide us, let us study some of the more characteristic sayings of Christ. What is the "Sermon on the Mount" but a systematic and strenuous attempt to revolutionize human life by giving men a new ideal and a new standpoint,—by substituting, in accordance with the central trend of Indian thought, an entirely inward for an entirely outward standard of moral worth? The sayings in it which seem to be violent and paradoxical, when we interpret them literally, disclose their meaning and their purpose directly the light of this conception is turned upon them.

To say that "every one that looks upon a woman to lust after her hath committed adultery with her already in his heart" is, one would think, to disparage by implication the self-control which arrests lawless desire on the threshold of lawless action; but the words had to be spoken in order that the reality of the inward standard might be emphasized, and the hollowness of formal rules, when divorced from the spiritual principles that are behind them, might be brought home to his hearers. The words, "if thy right eye cause thee to stumble pluck it out and cast it from thee" are, as they stand, a hard saying. But when he spoke them, Christ was but expressing in his own language the profound truth which Indian thought had long insisted upon,—that the outward self (form, sensation, perception and the rest) is unreal and valueless, in comparison with the overwhelming reality and incalculable value of the inward life. His stern and terrible command is in its essence the echo of what Buddha had said, centuries before, in quite other words: "The material form is not the self: the sensations are not the self: the perceptions are not the self: the conformations [predispositions] are not the self: the consciousness is not the self."

The "Kingdom of Heaven," which figures so prominently in Christ's discourses, is obviously the kingdom of soul-life;—a kingdom which is ever at hand, ever in the midst of us; which immingles itself with "the world," or kingdom of the surface life, as the eternal immingles itself with the transitory, the real with the phantasmal, truth with illusion, light with darkness; or, again, which waits with divine patience at the heart of "the world," as "perfect peace" waits at the heart of fever and strife. To enter this inward Kingdom is to enter "the Path" into which Buddha led his disciples. To become (in the fullest sense of the words) a naturalized citizen of the Kingdom is to pass into Nirvana.

When Christ says, "Lay not up for yourselves treasures upon the earth, where moth and rust doth consume, and where thieves break through and steal; but lay up for yourselves treasures in heaven, where neither moth nor rust doth consume and where thieves do not break through nor steal; for where thy treasure is there will thy heart be also," he is but harping on the theme, so familiar to Indian thought, of the impermanence of outward things and the permanence of the inward life. When he likens the kingdom of heaven to the "hidden treasure" or the "pearl of great price," to win which a man will sell all that he has, he is but echoing the teaching of the Indian sages that the Self within the self is alone real, and that all the things which we prize must be surrendered in order that He may be won.

Even the words which Christ is reported to have used about his own kinship to and oneness with "the Father"—words on which all the fantastic structures of Christian theology have been based—are but the expression, in a new notation, of the sublime Indian doctrine that "He is the true self of every creature,"—that "Brahma and the self are one." Lastly, the great question in which the whole of Christ's spiritual teaching is summed up and typified—"What shall it profit a man if he gain the whole world and lose his own soul; or what shall a man give in exchange for his soul? with its implicit assumption that the soul is greater and more precious than "the whole world," is the very question which India had again and again asked herself, and in which all her meditations on great matters had centred.

The ideas which dominated Christ's teaching, and which, according to my hypothesis, had come to him from the Far East, were not wholly new to the Græco-Roman world of his day. Xenophanes, Parmenides, Pythagoras and (above all) Plato had expounded them, each from his own point of view and in his own language, to esoteric circles of disciples. But no popular exposition of them had been attempted in the West till Christ came ender their influence and was captivated by their truth and beauty. Whether they were consciously or unconsciously adopted by Christ matters little. The broad fact confronts us that the ideas which he expounded coincide, at every vital point, with ideas which were current in India many centuries before the Christian era. Had India, through all those centuries, been entirely walled off from Western Asia and Southeastern Europe, the coincidences between the teaching of Christ and the teaching of Buddha and his forerunners might conceivably be regarded as purely fortuitous.

But never, before the establishment of British rule in India, had the opportunities for intercourse between East and West been so numerous or so favourable as in the centuries which immediately preceded the birth of Christ. For during a part, at least, of that period a chain of partially Hellenized kingdoms stretched from India to the Mediterranean, forming a broad highway along which the spiritual ideas of India travelled, slowly but surely; Westward. We need not lay much stress on the inscription which records the intention of the Buddhist Emperor, Ashoka, to send missionaries from India to Syria, Egypt, and other Hellenized lands, in order to preach the gospel of deliverance; for we have no evidence that those missionaries were ever sent. But the migration of a spiritual idea is not dependent, wholly or even mainly, on the labours of its accredited agents. The decadence of religion and philosophy in the Greeco-Roman world during the centuries which intervened between the death of Alexander and the birth of Christ, had created a spiritual vacuum which was waiting to be filled; and the westward set of the current of Indian ideas was as natural a movement as that of the Trade Winds or the Gulf Stream.

But if we may not say that Christ originated the ideas which he expounded, we may—and must—say that he was grandly original in the use that he made of them. The inspired teacher is not he who invents new ideas—for great ideas are never invented—but he who having received them, from whatever quarter, is able to assimilate them and make them his own. It is because he did this to the largest and most luminous ideas that have yet dawned upon the human spirit, that Christ must take rank with Buddha as one of the foremost teachers of mankind. What Buddha had done to the ideas of the Upanishads, Christ did to the same ideas when they had come to him, as they probably did, through the medium of Buddha's ethical teaching, he made them available for the daily needs of ordinary men.

But the method by which Christ worked was entirely his own. To graft the spiritual idealism of India on the stem of Hebrew poetry, and so to bring it home to the heart, rather than to the mind or the conscience, was the work of his life. Leaving it to thinkers, like Plato, to develop the idea of soul-growth through the medium of abstract thought,—leaving it to moralists, like Buddha, to develop it through the medium of a scheme of life,—Christ was content to develop it through the medium of poetic emotion. Out of the rival conceptions of God which were symbolized by Brahma and Jehovah respectively, he devised a third—the "resultant" of their respective forces—the idea of the All-Father who loves and is loved by his children, men. Setting before men, as Plato and Buddha had done, the finding of the soul or true self as the goal of their life's endeavour, he neither gave them reasons for pursuing that goal (as Plato had done) nor directions for pursuing it (as Buddha had done), but he gave them instead of these a motive for pursuing it—of all motives the strongest and the purest—the quasi-personal love of the All-loving God.

Where Plato and where Buddha were strong, each in his own way, Christ was by comparison weak; but he had a strength which was all his own. Plato reasoned about God. Buddha kept silence about God. Christ made him the theme of his poetry. Each of these modes of dealing with the idea of the Divine has its own merits and its own defects. The defects of Christ's treatment of the idea are obvious. The teacher who tries to popularize spiritual truth by formulating it in terms of poetry, may almost be said to invite men to literalize and despiritualize his teaching. Christ took this risk and paid the penalty of his daring. But though the penalty was a heavy one, yet when he had paid it in full there was a substantial balance in his favour. As a speculative thinker he does not compete with Plato. As a systematic teacher he does not compete with Buddha. But as a source of spiritual inspiration he has no rival.

With Christ's example before us, we need not hesitate to go for spiritual ideas to the only land in which they have ever (as far as we know) been indigenous,—to Ancient India. In the India which gave birth to the Upanishads, belief in the soul grew on its own stock and sprang from its own roots. No attempt was made to prove the reality of the soul, or to apologize for the belief in it. So far as any reason was given for the "soul-theory," it was a reason which proved—if I may be allowed the paradox—that the reality of the soul is unprovable.

"Only by soul itself

Ts soul perceived.—when the Soul wills it so!

There shines no light save its own light to show
Itself unto itself."

The idealistic ventures of the West have all suffered shipwreck on the rock of the average man's "common-sense,"— an euphemistic title for his spiritual indolence, his lack of imagination, and his inability to think clearly or coherently. But the spiritual thought of India, in the days when her soul was awake and active, was, at its highest level, strictly esoteric. In the teaching of Buddha we have the nearest approach to popularizing it that was ever made; but what Buddha submitted to the average man were, not the conclusions of Indian idealism, not the reasons for those conclusions, but their practical consequences.

That the average man was deeply interested in the soundness of Buddha's scheme of life, was no reason (so its author seems to have thought) for allowing him to examine the philosophical conceptions that underlay it. The average man is deeply interested in the stability of the Forth Bridge; but had the engineers of that structure invited him to handle the profound mathematical problems which had to be solved before their designs could be completed, they would justly have been deemed insane. Not less insane would it have seemed to the Master Thinkers of India to allow the average man to handle the problem of reality, or any kindred problem.

It is true that to ignore the average man in the region of high thinking is a loss to the life of a nation as well as a gain; and that India has paid heavily for having ignored him. But the gain to her thought, while her spiritual life was at or near its zenith, was immense. Serenely indifferent to the verdict of the market place, Indian idealism never explains itself, never gives account of itself, never even for a moment distrusts itself. This means that under its aegis the soul's belief in itself is complete. And this again means that the soul is not curious about itself, or about the worlds of which it is at once the centre and the circumference; that it is content with ideas and impatient of formulae; that high thinking is neither the master nor the servant of spiritual desire, but its peer and its other self; that the head is ready to give the heart the guidance that it really needs,—the guidance that stimulates to fresh endeavour, not the guidance that blinds the vision and paralyzes the will.

It is to India then—the India of the Upanishads and of Buddha—that the West must go for the ideas, both central and subordinate, which shall rescue it from its embarrassments and restore it to a state of spiritual solvency. The central idea for which it is waiting is that of the reality of the soul. Of the sub-ideas to which this idea is central it must select those which it will find most easy to assimilate. For if it is to put the ideas that it borrows to a profitable use, it must make them its own; it must, in a manner, recreate them by bringing them into harmony with the highest achievements of its own thought. Now the highest achievements of the Western mind are and have long been scientific.

It is in the sphere of physical science that its most successful work has been done, and that its most characteristic qualities have been developed. There are obvious reasons—in the West, where for centuries men have been authoritatively taught to identify the impalpable with the supernatural, there are special reasons—why the physical or palpable side of Nature should have been the first for Science to explore. But there is no reason why Science should confine her operations to that particular sphere. To be immersed in physical matter is not of the essence of Science. What is of her essence is the secret faith which is the mainspring of all her energies,—the faith of the soul of man in the intrinsic unity of Nature, its latent belief that the Universe is "not an aggregate but a whole." The aim of science—an aim which is not the less real because it is seldom consciously realized—is to discover one all-pervading substance, one all-controlling force, one all-regulating law. Subordinate to, but vitally connected with, the belief in the unity of Nature is the belief in law,—the belief of the soul in the veracity of Nature, in the stability and self-identity of the Universe.

These two beliefs (if we are to call them two) constitute the true creed of Science. They are beliefs, be it observed, not disbeliefs. Each of them has its counterpart in what I may call a cosmic desire,—in the instinctive response of the soul to a message from the heart of the Universe. What passes in certain quarters for the creed of Science is a series of dogmatic negations or disbeliefs. But the true creed is a faith, a hope, and an aspiration; and, sooner or later, it will find expression for itself in action, in conduct, in life.

Such being, in its essence, the creed or secret faith of Science, it is a shock to the scientific thought of the West, when it asks philosophy to give it the ground plan of the Universe, to find itself face to face with the dualism of popular thought. The very raison d'etre of Science is to prove that the Universe is an organic whole; and it is therefore an insult and a mockery to the mind which has long been living in an atmosphere of scientific effort and achievement, to be told that there are two worlds or spheres of being in the Universe, not one; that these two worlds are parted by an unfathomable abyss of nothingness which makes natural intercourse between them impossible; and that the Supreme Power which is supposed to have fashioned the world of Nature, and which now dwells apart from it in the supernatural Heaven, reveals itself at its own good pleasure to the dwellers in Nature by suspending the laws which are (one must believe) the expression of its own being,—in other words, by stultifying its own work and thwarting its own will.

What wonder that the Western mind, in the violence of its reaction from so irrational a philosophy, should surrender itself to a theory of things which it regards as the only possible alternative for dualism,—to a materialistic monism in which unity is achieved by suppressing the impalpable, and therefore by despiritualizing and devitalizing the Universe? And what wonder that it should be unable to realize, owing to the poison of dualism being still in its veins, that a monism which is based on a comprehensive negation is not an alternative for dualism, but a new version of it;—the attempt to escape from dualism, by suppressing one of the terms of a given antithesis, leading one of logical necessity into the toils of a deadlier fallacy,—the fundamental dualism of the existent and the non-existent? If the "advanced" thought of the West desires, in general, to convince itself of the unity of the Universe, it desires, more particularly, to bring the life of the soul—to bring the moral and spiritual worlds in which the life of the soul expresses itself—under the reign of natural law. This desire, which is 'both legitimate and salutary, is systematically thwarted by the dogmatic teaching of those who pose as the champions of the soul. For twenty centuries the "soul-theory" has been presented to the consciousness of the West in the notation of the Supernatural. As so presented, it outrages at every turn man's sense of law and his cognate (and virtually identical) sense of justice.

To teach man that sin entered the world because his "first parents" violated an arbitrary command of the supernatural God; that because of this one original act of disobedience the whole human race stands condemned to eternal death; that the death of Christ on the cross has made it possible for men to escape from the terrible consequences of Adam's sin; that this one brief earth-life decides for all time the destiny of each individual soul; that either eternal salvation or eternal damnation awaits the departed spirit; that grace (the higher life of the soul) is a supernaturally communicated gift, a water of healing which (as some contend) is "laid on" at every priest-served altar, or (as others contend) takes possession of the "elect" in a sudden and irresistible stream,—to teach man such things as these is to make open mockery of his sense of law and order and justice, and to warn him at the outset that there can be no science of the inner life. To this mockery and this warning the scientific thought of the West has begun to reply with open defiance.

Forbidden by supernaturalism to bring the life of the soul under the sway of natural law, it is being led by the secret logic of its faith (for it cannot but cling to its intuitive conviction that the realm of natural law is co-terminous with the Universe) to disbelieve in the life of the soul, to ask for proofs of its existence, and at last to relegate the whole "soul-theory" to the limbo of exploded superstitions. In thus abandoning the "soul-theory," the advanced thinkers of the West imagine that they are undoing the demoralizing work of supernaturalism. But in this matter, as in their treatment of the general problem of dualism, the remedy that they offer is worse than the disease.

The West has never realized—so faulty has been its ethical training—that the inward consequences of moral action are regulated by one of Nature's most just and most inexorable laws; and the normal attitude of the average man towards the problem of moral responsibility is that, apart from legal and social considerations, it matters little how one acts. He still feels, however, that it matters something; for the general idea that moral goodness makes for the well-being of the soul has always been formally countenanced by supernaturalism, and is still, in some degree, a restraining, if not an inspiring, influence in his life. But let him be fully convinced that he has no inward life, and that therefore his conduct can have no inward consequences,—and it will not be long before he feels his way to the logical conclusion that (again apart from legal and social considerations) it matters nothing how one acts.

We see, then, that the advanced thought of the West has, unknown to itself, a true and deep philosophy of its own,—a philosophy which centres in recognition of the essential unity of Nature and of the all-pervading supremacy of natural law. In virtue of this unformulated philosophy, it is the sworn enemy of dualism in general and of supernaturalism in particular; but it cannot yet realize what its hostility to dualism means, or where it is to find the remedy for the evil which it dimly discerns. The remedy for dualism is not the monism (if one must call it so) which suppresses one of the terms of a world-embracing antithesis, but the higher monism which recognizes that each term is the complement and correlate of the other; nay, that there is a reciprocal relation between the two in virtue of which each in turn owes to the other its meaning, its purpose, and (in the last resort) its very right to exist;—which recognizes, for example, that silence "implies sound," that failure is "a triumph's evidence," that the supernatural world is at the heart of Nature, that form is as truly the expression of spirit, as spirit is the soul and life of form.

Such a monism was once taught in the Far East. The Indian doctrine of the fundamental identity of the individual and the universal life, and, more especially, of the ideal identity of the individual with the Universal Soul, makes an end, once and for all, of the false dualism of the human and the Divine, [1] and provides for the return of the Lord and Giver of Life from his exile in the supernatural dreamland to his home at the heart of Nature. If Western thought will accept this doctrine as a provisional theory of things, and try to master its meaning, it will be able to extend the conception of natural law to the inner life of man and to all the worlds—moral, aesthetic, poetic, religious, and the rest—which the ferment of that life has generated; it will be able, in due course, to take in hand the task for which its special bent and special training are even now equipping it, the task of building up the science of the soul.

When it takes that task in hand, it will find that Buddha has anticipated it, to the extent of indicating the main lines on which it will have to work. An attempt has been made by some of the Western exponents of Buddhism to show that the teaching of Buddha falls into line with the anti-idealistic theories of the dominant school of Western thought. The attempt has not been successful; for it can be shown, I think, that Buddha based his scheme of life, not on rejection of the "soul-theory," but on wholehearted acceptance of it. But those who contend that Buddha's philosophy is modern and Western, have come within a little of stumbling upon an important truth. Though he belonged to a far-off age and a far-off land, the founder of Buddhism was akin to us in the scientific bent of his mind, in his grasp of the idea of law. His teaching does not fall into line with our thought, for in truth he was far more "advanced" than we are; but it is possible that our thought, as it develops, will come into line with his teaching.

The scientific achievements of the West, so far as they have any philosophical significance, fall under two main heads, the discovery (if I may use the word), on the physical plane, that the Kingdom of Nature is under the reign of law (a conception of Nature which Science must have unconsciously brought with her to her work of investigation, and which has made that work possible); and the further discovery that all laws of Nature are subordinate to the master law of development or growth. [1] Both these discoveries were anticipated by Buddha; but they were made by him—or by the thinkers who sowed what he reaped—not on the physical plane, but on the spiritual, on the plane of man's inner life. Buddha realized, as no man before (or since) had ever done, that the soul is a living thing, and that, as such, it comes under the all-pervading, all-controlling law of growth. And he realized the practical bearing of this conception. Physical science says to the husbandman, "Do such and such things, and your crops (taking one season with another) will be abundant: neglect to do them, and your crops will be poor;" or, in other words, "Bring your husbandry into harmony with certain laws of physical Nature, and you will fare well. Disregard those laws, and you will fare ill."

What the science of the West is doing for the growth (and the development) of wheat and barley, Buddha did for the growth of the soul. He taught men that, if they would bring their lives into harmony with certain fundamental laws of Nature, their souls would grow—as well-tended crops grow—vigorously and healthily; and that the sense of well-being which accompanies successful growth, and which, when consciously realized, is true happiness, would be theirs. He taught them this; and, in teaching it, he made that appeal to their will-power which is his chief contribution to the edification, as distinguished from the instruction, of the soul.

The husbandman must take thought for his plants if their lives are to be brought into harmony with the appropriate laws of Nature; but the plant which we call the soul must take thought for itself. Penetrated with the conviction that what a man does reacts, naturally and necessarily, on what he is, and so affects for all time the growth of the soul and its consequent well-being; penetrated with the conviction that conduct moulds character, and that character is destiny,—Buddha called upon each man in turn to take his life into his own hands, and himself to direct the process of his growth.

This message was his legacy to the ages. It is for Western thought to take it up and repeat it, developing in its own way the mighty ideas that are behind it. Dr. Rhys Davids seems to think that it is "unmanly" 1 to take thought for one's soul; and it is possible that care for the soul has at times taken forms which are open to this reproach. But when the idea of soul-growth is interpreted in the light of the idea of inexorable law, it loses the sickly savour which clings, in some slight measure, to the ideal of saintliness, and one begins to realize that to take oneself in hand and to make one's soul grow, by the constant exercise of initiative and self-control, is to rise to an even loftier level than that of manliness (which, after all, is but the virtue of a sex), to the level of true manhood.

The scheme of life in which Buddha embodied his science of the soul is in the highest degree bracing and stimulating; and one of the chief sources of its tonic influence is the sternness with which it insists on the merciless majesty of Nature's laws. Just as physical science warns us that, if we drink polluted water (let us say), our health will suffer, and the elimination of the poison from our bodies will be a long and painful process, so Buddha warns men that wrong-doing is not less certain to work itself out of the soul as sorrow and suffering than is right-doing to work itself into the soul as health, and therefore as happiness and peace.

That nothing can come between conduct and its inward consequences—between what we do and what we are and shall be—is the conviction on which the whole of his teaching is hinged. The ideas about God and Man and the Universe which have made possible the Christian belief in the forgiveness of sins, belong to a quarter of thought in which his mind never moved. Unlike Jehovah, who is angry and then repents and forgives, the power which is at the heart of Nature:

"Knows not wrath nor pardon."

If we sow the seed of wheat we shall reap wheat, and reap it, if we have been wise husbandmen, in abundant measure. But if we sow the seed of thistles, we must know for certain that our crop will be thistles, not wheat.

These ideas are eminently congenial to the scientific tone of Western thought; and the day will come (I venture to predict) when the conception of life which they embody will be accepted in the West as the sanest and truest conception that the mind of man has yet devised, and as the only stable foundation on which to build—what will surely be the fittest monument to

Buddha's greatness—the science of the soul. The task of building that monument, of interpreting in the light of modern experiences and adapting to modern needs the spiritual ideas of ancient India, will probably devolve upon the West (which is unconsciously preparing itself for the task by its arduous work in the field of physical science), rather than upon the East.

Should that be so, and should the West rise to the level of its opportunity, it would at last find itself in a position to pay back the loan that had saved its credit; for it would have traded with its borrowed ideas to the best advantage, and would have duly enriched them with its own thought, its own labour, and its own life.

Before these things can come to pass one practical difficulty will have to be overcome. It is possible that the sentimental thought of the West will offer as strong an opposition to the idea of the life and destiny of the soul being regulated by inexorable law, as is now offered by the intellectual thought of the West to the root-idea of soul-life. But the advanced thinker of that distant day will be able to re-assure his weaker brethren.

For he will remind them that the Universal Soul, which is the true self of each of us, and which the process of soul-growth will therefore enable each of us to realize, is the same for all men; and he will ask them to infer from this that the most inexorable of all Nature's laws is the law to which even the master law of growth is in a sense subordinate,—the law which makes the Universe one living whole, the law of centripetal tendency, the law of Love.

BIBLIOGRAPHY

Batchelor, Martine and Kerry Brown: *Buddhism and Ecology,* London, Cassell, 1992.

Bell, Sir Charles: *Portrait of a Dalai Lama: The Life and Times of the Great Thirteenth,* Boston, Wisdom Publications, 1987.

Cook, Elizabeth: *Holy Places of the Buddha,* Berkeley, Dharma Publishing, 1994.

Dargyay, Eva M.: *The Rise of Esoteric Buddhism in Tibet,* Delhi, Motilal Banarsidass, 1977.

Dayal, Har: *The Bodhisattva Doctrine in Buddhist Sanskrit Literature,* London, Kegan Paul, 1932.

Eppsteiner, Fred: *The Path of Compassion: Writings on Socially Engaged Buddhism,* Berkeley, Parallax Press, 1988.

Eppsteiner, Fred: *The Path of Compassion: Writings on Socially Engaged Buddhism,* Berkeley, Parallax Press, 1988.

Gombrich, Richard F.: *Buddhist Precept and Practice,* Delhi, Motilal Banarsidass, 1991.

Gonda, Jan: *Vedic Literature: Samhitas and Brahmanas,* Wiesbaden, 1975.

Hakeda, Yoshito S.: *Kukai, Major Works,* New York, Columbia University Press, 1972.

Haldar, J. R.: *Early Buddhist Mythology,* New Delhi, Manohar, 1977.

Jones, Ken: *Beyond Optimism: A Buddhist Political Ecology,* Oxford, Jon Carpenter, 1993.

Keown, Damien: *The Nature of Buddhist Ethics,* New York, St. Martin's Press, 1992.

Khoroche, Peter: *Once the Buddha Was a Monkey: Arya Sura's Jatakamala,* Chicago, University of Chicago Press, 1989.

Lalwani. K.C.: *Kalpa Sutra of Badrabahu Svami*, Delhi, Motilal Banarsidass. 1979.

Lamotte, Etienne: *The Suramgamasamadhi Sutra*, London, Curzon, 1998.

Mookerjee, Satkari: *Buddhist Philosophy of Universal Flux*, Delhi, Motilal Banarsidass, 1980.

Morrell, Robert: *Early Kamakura Buddhism: A Minority Report*, Berkeley, Asian Humanities Press, 1987.

Nyanatiloka, *A.: Guide through the Abhidhamma Pitaka,* Kandy, Buddhist Publication Society, 1971.

Payutto, Prayudh: *Buddhist Economics: A Middle Way for the Marketplace*, Bangkok, Buddhadhamma Foundation, 1994.

Poppe, Nicholas: *The Twelve Deeds of Buddha*, Seattle, University of Washington Press, 1967.

Powers, John: *Wisdom of Buddha: The Samdhinirmocana Sutra*, Berkeley, Dharma Publishing, 1994.

Sarkisyanz, E.: *Buddhist Backgrounds of the Burmese Revolution*, The Hague, Martinus Nijhoff, 1965.

Sotoshu Shumucho: *International Symposium: The Future of the Earth and Zen Buddhism*, Tokyo, Sotoshu Shumucho, 1991.

Sprung, Mervyn: *The Problem of Two Truths in Buddhism and Vedanta*, Boston, Reidel, 1973.

Strong, John: *The Legend of King Asoka*, Princeton, Princeton University Press, 1983.

Thomas, E. J.: *The Life of the Buddha as Legend and History*, London, Routledge & Kegan Paul, 1927.

Titmuss, Christopher: *The Green Buddha*, Devon, Insights, 1995.

Wells, Kenneth E.: *Thai Buddhism, Its Rites and Activities*, Bangkok, Christian Bookstore, 1960.

INDEX

❑❑❑